Women, Work, and Representation

Lynn M. Alexander

Women, Work, and Representation

NEEDLEWOMEN IN VICTORIAN ART AND LITERATURE

OHIO UNIVERSITY PRESS

ATHENS

Ohio University Press, Athens, Ohio 45701
© 2003 by Ohio University Press
Printed in the United States of America
All rights reserved

Ohio University Press books are printed on acid-free paper ∞ ™

12 11 10 09 08 07 06 05 04 03   5 4 3 2 1

Library of Congress Cataloging-in-Publication Data

Alexander, Lynn Mae.
Women, work, and representation : needlewomen in Victorian art and
literature / Lynn M. Alexander.
p. cm.
Includes bibliographical references (p.) and index.
ISBN 0-8214-1493-3 (alk. paper)
1. English literature—19th century—History and criticism.
2. Needlework in literature. 3. Working poor—England—History—19th
century. 4. Poor women—England—History—19th century. 5. Art,
English—19th century. 6. Needleworkers in literature. 7. Sewing in
literature. 8. Women in literature. 9. Poor in literature. 10. Sewing
in art. 11. Poor in art. I. Title.
PR468.N4 A44 2003
820.9'926464—dc21

2002192663

Contents

Illustrations

Acknowledgments

This book could not have been written without the cooperation of many individuals, libraries, and institutions.

I want to thank the following for their invaluable assistance: in the United States, the libraries of the University of Tennessee at Martin, the University of Tulsa, Vanderbilt University, and the Yale Center for the Study of British Art, and the Forbes Magazine Collection; in Great Britain, the collections of the University of Keele, the British Library, the Manchester Central Library, the John Rylands Library of the University of Manchester, the Whitt Library of the Courtauld Institute of Art, and the Museum of London; and in South Africa, the Johannesburg City Art Gallery.

Some of the ideas presented in this book appeared in articles published in the *Victorian Newsletter* (1991) and in *Tulsa Studies in Women's Literature* (1999). Excerpts were read at meetings of the South Atlantic Modern Language Association (1996) and the Research Society in Victorian Periodicals (1994), and at the University of Tulsa Comparative Literature Symposium (1997) and the Locating the Victorians Conference (2001).

The legend for each plate includes artist, title, date, and provenance (if known). Where the provenance is unknown or private, the source of the plate is identified; the abbreviation *RA* indicates the Cassell series *Royal Academy Pictures*.

I am indebted to Joseph Kestner, Kay Meyers, Daniel Pigg, and Andrew Schopp for their friendship and their insights during the writing of this work.

The Victorian Seamstress

FACT AND FICTION

The condition of woman, has in all ages of the world, been an unerring criterion of the existence or extent of civilization.

— R. B. Grindrod, *Slaves of the Needle*

If there be one mechanical art of more universal application than all others, and therefore of more universal interest, it is that which is practiced with the NEEDLE. From the stateliest denizen of the proudest palace, to the humblest dweller in the poorest cottage, all more or less ply the busy needle.

— [Elizabeth Stone], *Art of Needlework*

When I first began looking at Condition-of-England literature I quickly became aware of two things: most of the protagonists are women and much of the fiction was written by women. After a little thought, both facts are not as unlikely as they might appear. By choosing a woman to represent the suffering of the working classes, an author was more likely to strike a sympathetic note with the audience. Further, many reformers would have agreed with R. B. Grindrod's assessment that the treatment of women within a society is a measure of the culture's attitude toward humanity generally. And fiction was one of the few public forums open to women.[1] My further reading revealed that one occupation received much more attention than any other — needlework. From the early 1840s through the close of the century novels, essays, and poetry focused on women earning their living by sewing. Perhaps part of the appeal was the universality of the occupation; as Elizabeth Stone notes, virtually all women, regardless of class, sewed. Thus a protagonist earning her living by sewing would sound a common note with readers. And although the portrayals and the apparent underlying purpose of the presentations varied, from demonstrating the exploitation of young, impoverished, middle-class women to exposing the sufferings of the working poor generally, the occupation remained constant. Many of these works were illustrated, and I soon realized that the verbal and the visual were strongly connected, often building on each other to make the desired point. My final realization dealt less with the occupation than with the presentation. As I continued to document the longevity of the seamstress in Victorian literature and art I came to realize that such a study presented the unique opportunity to study the evolution of a symbol, from its beginning as a literal presentation, to its symbolic manifestation, to its acceptance as a cultural commonplace. But in order to understand the semiotic life cycle, we must focus on the symbol itself, how it first appeared and then how it developed and changed. First we need to investigate the occupation of seamstress and its representation in Victorian periodicals, literature and art; then we need to examine how the portrayal changed and what such changes indicate about occasion, audience, and purpose.

A comparison of the actual with the illustrated shows how writers emphasized certain aspects of the condition of the seamstress to make her representative of the poor, while ignoring many of those which would set her apart. Many writers, such as Thomas Hood, tied her to images of family; novelists often blurred class distinctions and created a rural background. Painters, beginning with Richard Redgrave in 1844 (*The Sempstress*), usually portrayed the seamstress working alone in an attic room with a few sticks of furniture and a spindly plant, often a primrose, in the window. The image runs contrary to most parliamentary accounts of the time and to most early fictional narratives, but it served to further isolate the seamstress from the stigma of industrialization. In fact most needlewomen, whether slopworkers gathered in someone's room for company or dressmakers attached to a respectable millinery house, worked in groups. Yet the pathos evoked by Redgrave's picture was so great that it became the dominant image of the seamstress; other artists imitated it and later fiction writers modified their portrayals to match it.

I

Upper- and middle-class Victorian women were usually educated and trained to think of their future solely in terms of matrimony, but for many women this ideal state was not possible. The census report of 1851 recorded 8,155,000 females age ten and above, as compared to 7,600,000 males

(Pike, 156). The report also showed that 24.86 percent of the women in England and Wales were unmarried at age thirty, 17.89 percent at age thirty-five, and 11.88 percent at age fifty (Neff, 12). However, as Wanda Neff points out in *Victorian Working Women*, "When the census figures are subjected to the cold eye of a later age, it is not the proportion of 100 women of all ages to 96 men which is disturbing, but rather the proportion of mature men who remain bachelors. Out of every 100 men in 1851 in England and Wales, 25.89 were unmarried at the age of 30; 18 at the age of 35; 10.74 at the age of 50. Women were 'redundant,' then, not because there were too many of them, but because the men did not marry" (12). Since women proportionally outnumbered men, and allowing for the norm of an older man marrying a younger woman, with almost 20 percent of men unmarried at age thirty-five and over 10 percent at age fifty, statistically a Victorian woman socialized for a life as a wife and a mother was very likely to find her expectations were unfulfilled.

One reason some men postponed or avoided matrimony was the uncertain economic climate of the age. The costs of establishing a home, maintaining a household that included servants, and supporting a family were prohibitive when compared with those of maintaining a bachelor's flat, especially in uncertain economic times. But potential suitors were not the only ones affected by the fluctuating economy; many families found themselves fallen economically, often forcing children, raised to expect a life of leisure, to find employment. Even experienced businessmen went under. For many young women a decline in family fortunes meant a decline in matrimonial prospects.[2] Thus an economic crisis often created an untenable situation, since the expenses of the young woman would continue to be the responsibility of the eldest male family member until she married, which she was unlikely to do because of the family's economic situation.

The decline of finances, usually attributed to "the accidents of commercial and professional life," was not the only circumstance forcing women to remain single and/or consider employment. The emigration of single men to the colonies, the tendency for middle-class men to marry later, and a mortality rate that favored women also contributed to an increasing need for middle-class women to find some means of support outside of matrimony.[3] In "Why Are Women Redundant?" W. R. Greg sums up the situation for many Victorians:

There is an enormous and increasing number of single women in the nation, a number quite disproportionate and quite abnormal;

a number which, positively and relatively, is indicative of an unwholesome social state, and is both productive and prognostic of much wretchedness and wrong.

There are hundreds of thousands of women—not to speak more largely still—scattered through all ranks, but proportionally most numerous in the middle and upper classes,—who have to earn their own living, instead of spending and husbanding the earnings of men; who, not having the natural duties and labours of wives and mothers, have to carve out artificial and painfully-sought occupations for themselves; who, in place of completing, sweetening, and embellishing the existence of others, are compelled to lead an independent and incomplete existence of their own. (282)

According to Greg, England's "unnatural" gender imbalance had three causes: a desire for luxuries, male emigration, and profligate male behavior. As a solution, Greg advocates "the removal of 500,000 women from the mother-country, where they are redundant, to the colonies, where they are sorely needed." As a result, he believed, "all who remain at home will rise in value, will be more sought, will be better rewarded" (315). Whatever the cause, for many middle-class Victorian women, matrimony, their expected path in life, did not materialize. And while many women remained dependent on their fathers, brothers, or other male relatives, a far larger number were forced by economic decline to search for another respectable source of support. Regardless of the circumstances surrounding a woman's decision to work, in the mid-nineteenth century only two acceptable employment options were available to middle-class women: governess or seamstress.

The position of governess was more socially genteel, but many women were unable to meet the high qualifications. A governess was expected to be able to paint, do fancy needlework, play a musical instrument, dance, and speak at least one—often two—foreign languages. If a woman was unable or unwilling to work as a governess, she sought a position as a dressmaker or a milliner, employment that was thought to be a way for a woman to maintain herself without having to "sacrifice [her] gentility or [come] to terms with a coarse and vulgar way of life" (Pike, 169).[4] As Christina Walkley explains, "it was work to which they were accustomed and may have enjoyed, which had nothing intrinsically ungenteel about it" (2). The association of needlework with domesticity and the daily tasks of middle- and upper-class women made it an acceptable employment for young women who had "fallen on hard times."

II

Conditions in the dress trade were not as favorable as they appeared, however. In *Women Workers and the Industrial Revolution*, Ivy Pinchbeck notes that as early as 1747 the *London Tradesman* published an article cautioning parents not to place their daughters in dressmaking unless they were able to set them up after their apprenticeship. The article further states that in spite of "'vast profits' the milliners 'yet give but poor, mean Wages to every Person they employ under them: Though a young Woman can work neatly in all manner of Needle-Work, yet she cannot earn more than Five or Six Shillings a Week, out of which she is to find herself in Board and Lodging'" (289). In the 1833 parliamentary discussions concerning factory legislation, it was pointed out that cotton millers were found to be healthier than milliners and laborers in other branches of industry (102, 189). Mary Anne Walker, a lecturer at an 1842 Chartist meeting,[5] compared slopworkers' wages with the Queen's pension.[6] "[I]t was shameful that while Englishwomen were receiving but 5d. the pair for the making of policemen's trousers, a German woman was receiving 100*l.* a year; wrung in taxes from the earnings of the hard-working men of England" ("Chartist Meeting," 6). And in his 1864 report to parliamentary investigators, "The Sanitary Circumstances of London Dressmakers and Other Needlewomen in London," Dr. William Ord testified:

> But without attaching too much importance to statements of extreme protraction of work hours, it may safely be said that the hours of work are generally too long, and so arranged as to give few opportunities for bodily exercise.... [T]he ordinary hours of work are from ten to twelve hours, exclusive of meal times.
>
> But, as stated before, the hours of work are much lengthened during the season. The London spring season commences in the end of March or the beginning of April, and lasts till about the middle of July; but there is also a shorter and less important season in ... November and December. In a large number of houses the earliest time of quitting work during the season, is 10 or 11 o'clock, and under the pressure of court ceremonials, the work is often carried on far into the night ... in the commoner work-rooms ventilation is certainly disregarded, and it is not uncommonly found that ventilators, even when provided, are obstructed

either willfully or of neglect.... The proper ventilation of bed-
rooms is even less regarded than that of workrooms. (Pike,
171–73)

Although records indicate needlewomen had been underpaid and over-
worked since the late seventeenth century, and a few newspaper articles
during the eighteenth century indicate some awareness of the problems
associated with the trade, it was not until the 1843 publication of *The Second Report of the Children's Employment Commission* that public interest
was caught. The suffering and acceptance of the female workers and the
outrage of the male physicians who testified created a sense of pathos and
sacrifice that appealed to Victorian sensibilities.

However, for Victorians it was an anonymous tract entitled *The Perils
of the Nation: An Appeal to the Legislature, the Clergy, and the Higher and
Middle Classes,* published in 1842, that sounded the first warnings about
the abuses of the dress trade. In this work, Charlotte Elizabeth Tonna presents a terse, heavily documented argument for government intervention
in factories, mines, small workshops, and distressed agricultural areas. As
the subtitle indicates, Tonna addresses her appeals to distinct groups of
readers—virtually all male—and yet one of the longest sections discusses
"female influence." In this section Tonna brings forth the plight of the
seamstress and suggests methods of relieving her suffering. After detailing
the long hours, extremes in temperature, lack of ventilation, and the poi-
sonous effect of some dyes, she declares:

> The remedy for this, the liberation of thousands of slaves from a
> bondage which no English female ought to connive at, or to toler-
> ate for one moment, lies in the hands of those whom we at pres-
> ent address through their male friends; and their line of duty is
> so easy that we should be sorry to think it required more than a
> simple direction of their notice to the point. Announcing their
> determination to deal with such employers only as will give a
> pledge not to impose on their work-women tasks beyond their
> natural strength, or such as can encroach on the appointed day
> of rest,—they must also be prepared to give a fair price for what
> they require, enabling the dress-maker or milliner to employ more
> hands, and with adequate remuneration for their toil. Care must
> also be taken to allow a sufficient time for the completion of the
> work. (362)

Although Tonna's tract is nonfictional and directed to a limited audience, its impact on later fictional representations of the seamstress must be noted. In this study, for the first time, the feminine employments of dressmaking and millinery were yoked to mining and factory employment, a device frequently employed by fiction writers who followed during the 1840s and 1850s. But Tonna's treatise was unique both in her call for government intervention and in the metaphorical terms she used. Tonna is the first writer to borrow the analogy of industrial worker as slave, established in the 1830s by spokesmen for the radical cause such as Richard Oastler, and to apply the term with all its connotations directly to needlewomen.

Victorians were forced to acknowledge the conditions faced by seamstresses in 1843 with the publication of *The Second Report of the Children's Employment Commission*, containing the testimony of over one hundred dressmakers and physicians. R. D. Grainger's deposition to parliamentary investigators concerning dressmakers and milliners revealed that there were fifteen thousand women employed in London millinery houses, many of them under age eighteen.[7] The testimony Grainger recorded told of "inordinately long" hours, unsanitary working conditions, insufficient food, and the reneging of contracts. According to Grainger:

> The evidence of all parties establishes the fact that there is no class of persons in this country, living by their labour, whose happiness, health and lives, are so unscrupulously sacrificed as those of the young dress-makers. They are, in a particular degree, unprotected and helpless, and I should fail in my duty if I did not distinctly state that, as a body, their employers have hitherto taken no steps to remedy the evils and misery which results from the existing system. . . . there are no occupations [other than exceptionally dangerous ones such as needle grinding] in which so much disease is produced as in dressmaking, or which present so fearful a catalogue of distressing and frequently fatal maladies. (14:30–33)

Many journals published lengthy excerpts from the *Second Report*, and some began to publish independent articles concerning the seamstress. Others presented editorial arguments, such as those found in "The Workwomen of London" from the *Lady's Newspaper*:

> We do not believe that such a thing is possible as to find fifteen thousand men fagged and worn to death in this way. If the attempt

were made to reduce them to such slavery, before a week was over we should have them rioting in our streets, breaking windows to get into prison, or doing, perhaps, worse. Women cannot make their grievances heard in this way, and especially such women as the class we speak of; which, for the most part is composed of persons reduced to their present necessity by misfortune; and because they are patient and orderly, dying rather than make the only demonstration of their sufferings which could avail them, they are left to suffer. So much for the chivalry of Parliament and humanity of the nation. (qtd. in Walkley, 9)

Such editorials separated needlewomen from the violence associated with Chartism and with much of the working-class reform movement in general. They also laid the foundation for the image of suffering martyrdom that would dominate much of the later seamstress fiction.

A few journals used poetry to show the needlewoman's situation, the best-known example being Thomas Hood's "The Song of the Shirt," published in the 1843 Christmas issue of *Punch*. Illustrations were used by many journals to indicate the harsh existence of seamstresses. For example *Punch*'s 1844 cartoon "Exhibition of the English in China—Case IV—A Sempstress" shows a woman bent over with her face in her hands, one shirt in her lap and another on a table, and the ironic caption provides the moral: "nothing shows the humanity of the barbarians in a more favourable light than the great attention which is paid by the rich and high to the comforts of their milliners, dress-makers, and sempstresses…" (220). By far the great majority of periodicals, however, relied on fiction to present the conditions of needlewomen through a representative example.

III

For Victorians the move from fact to fiction was a natural one, for they were convinced of "both the epistemological validity and the transformative possibilities of art … [and] refused to bracket aesthetic creation from the broader ethical and political claims they wished to make on their readers" (Born, 2). During the period from 1840 through 1850 the seamstress became a popular literary figure, appearing as the heroine in more than twenty popular English works and as a supporting character in many more, and from 1840 until 1900 she was the focus of more than fifty illustrations in widely read English periodicals and exhibited paintings. The seamstress was popular for a variety of reasons. First, she was a product of the industrial revolution. The industrialization of the textile industry lowered the price of fabric and made it possible for middle-class women, as well as those in the aristocracy, to follow the whims of fashion. Therefore, the dressmaker or milliner was a familiar figure to readers and viewers, a person whom they frequently encountered in their everyday routine. And the seamstress escaped the stigma of being a factory worker. Because of class issues and the low moral standards associated with factory work, this was an important distinction, even for writers addressing the problems of the working classes. The seamstress was someone to whom readers could respond without prejudice.

The seamstress was also a popular aesthetic figure because of her universality. Regardless of their social class, all women in Victorian England were taught to sew.[8] Thus people encountering a woman sewing in literature or in art could identify with the character—either as women who sewed or as men whose mothers, wives, and sisters sewed. It is not surprising, then, that an important aspect of the seamstress for reformers was the ease with which she could be tied to traditional images of the home. One of the major concerns expressed about industrialization and the subsequent employment of women in the factories was the effect they would have on the family unit. To many, the employment of women signaled a breakdown of the traditional family structure, in which the male wage earner supported and protected his family and the woman fulfilled the role of wife and mother. Such fears were often invoked in agitating for labor reform involving women and children. For example, in advocating a reduction in the number of hours women were allowed to work, Lord Ashley first cites medical experts as to the detrimental effects of long hours, especially on women of child-bearing age. But then he turns from images evoking sympathy to those evoking fear—fear of the destruction of the traditional family, and thus of traditional gender roles:

> But listen to another fact, and one deserving of serious attention; that the females not only perform the labour, but occupy the places of men; they are forming various clubs and associations, and gradually acquiring all those privileges which are held to be the proper portion of the male sex. These female clubs are thus described:—
> "fifty or sixty females, married and single, form themselves into clubs, ostensibly for protection; but, in fact, they meet together to drink, sing, and smoke; they use, it is stated, the lowest, most

brutal, and most disgusting language imaginable." Here is a dialogue which occurred in one of these clubs, from an ear-witness:—
"A man came into one of these club-rooms, with a child in his arms; 'come lass,' said he, addressing one of the women, 'come home, for I cannot keep this bairn quiet, and the other I have left crying at home.' 'I won't go home, idle devil,' she replied, 'I have thee to keep, and the bairns too, and if I can't get a pint of ale quietly, it is tiresome. This is only the second pint that Bess and me have had between us; thou may sup if thou likes, and sit thee down, but I won't go home yet.'"

Whence is it that this singular and unnatural change is taking place? Because that on women are imposed the duty and burden of supporting their husbands and families, a perversion as it were of nature, which has the inevitable effect of introducing into families disorder, insubordination and conflict. (24–25)

Ashley voices a frequently heard fear, that the work outside the home would lead to women's no longer possessing the knowledge and skills necessary to keep a home. Or it could produce women without any need to rely on male support—and thus be subservient to male authority figures—because they were financially independent. The seamstress, however, provided a feminine worker who could easily be tied to more traditional symbols of hearth and home, often heightened by ties to a past rural environment, and, indirectly, reinforced a sense of paternalism in the calls for reform.[9]

It is also likely that for many feminine readers and viewers the seamstress would spark the realization that, because of the uncertain economy, they could easily be placed in a similar situation. In fact, many reform-oriented works of literature highlighted this theme by presenting detailed introductory material establishing the young seamstress's background and the economic situation that has necessitated her decision to work, or by creating complex secondary plots concerning the young woman's parentage. For example, Elizabeth Stone opens *The Young Milliner* by detailing Ellen Cardan's life before she is forced to enter the millinery trade. Ellen's mother has died and there are no other relatives who can support the young woman. In their discussion of Ellen's future, both the local curate and the landlady, Mrs. Baring, apply the term *lady* to Ellen and her mother. Mrs. Baring comments, "'This lady [Ellen's mother] has evidently seen better days; and what with people, when reduced, not liking to push themselves on their friends, and what with friends seldom being over-anxious to look after their poor relations, such things come to pass every day'" (5). For women readers, there would be the suggestion that Ellen and her mother could be the readers' friends, acquaintances, or even themselves. In *Fanny, the Little Milliner* Charles Rowcroft creates an elaborate subplot wherein the orphaned Fanny is the daughter of a viscount, legitimate though unacknowledged, spirited away by circumstances.

And, finally, the plight of the seamstress was an issue that could be taken up equally by interventionists and those advocating a laissez-faire approach to the issues of industrial reform and workers' rights, thus receiving twice the attention, as activists tried to persuade readers of the merit of one approach or the other. For women it also presented a unique opportunity to participate in enacting reform: either through discussing the issue and influencing male relatives who were enfranchised or, even more directly, by boycotting millinery establishments known to abuse workers. The seamstress was a familiar figure to all levels of society, from the reader of the *Times* and the viewer at the Royal Academy to the reader of *Reynolds's Miscellany*.

Many of the fictional presentations of the seamstress, regardless of the political stance taken by the author, were based on known facts. For example, Charlotte Elizabeth Tonna based much of the first section of *The Wrongs of Woman* on the 1843 *Second Report*. Even details from the novel such as Frances King's frustration at matching silks rather than learning the millinery trade parallel testimony recorded in the *Report*: in testimony number 548, Penelope Ducmanton complains that although she paid a premium and has been an apprentice for three years, she has been principally employed matching silks and therefore has not learned the business. She estimates that if she had been properly taught, she would be receiving a salary of eighteen to twenty pounds at the time of the interview; but she was obliged to serve two more years receiving only her board and lodging (14:213). Later works, such as Charles Kingsley's *Alton Locke* and George W. M. Reynolds's *The Seamstress*, used sources such as Henry Mayhew's *London Labour and the London Poor,* as well as parliamentary reports, for details of living and working conditions faced by slopworkers. In contrast, most paintings of needlewomen create a romanticized image, an isolated figure of sorrow and suffering, with only background details—the late hour as indicated by a clock and guttering candles, the ill health indicated by the medicine bottles with hospital labels, or the lack of food indicated by empty cupboards and dirty teacups but no plates—linking the artistic symbol to the worldly referent.

Authors, for the most part, were initially concerned with the working and living conditions faced by dressmakers and milliners. The testimony presented before Parliament showed that long hours, bad ventilation, close quarters, and poor food contributed to health problems leading to blindness and death. And while death from consumption was common among Victorians in general, during the 1840s and 1850s approximately 8 percent more women than men died from it. In fact, in mid-Victorian England approximately half, sometimes more, of all women fifteen to thirty-five years of age who died were killed by some form of consumption. These figures are particularly relevant because the Victorian age-specific death rates for the general population are very nearly equivalent to rates for the working classes of the period. During the entire era no more than 5 to 15 percent of the total population of England and Wales was of the middle or upper classes (Johansson, 169, 174), and once a woman was forced to earn a living she was placed statistically in the working class.

One might assume, however, that, since these women did not move into the working classes until their teens, they would have a lower mortality rate because they were healthier generally. Such an assumption would probably be in error. While no statistics concerning the mortality patterns of middle-class Victorian women were ever published, Joseph Fox presented some data on comparative death rates among Quaker men and women.

Mortality Rates of Male and Female Quakers in the 1850s

Age	Males	Females
0–1	148.2	107.3
[2]–4	56.0	47.3
5–9	5.6	6.8*
10–14	3.4	4.9*
15–19	7.8	8.4*
20–29	8.8	9.1*
30–39	7.8	11.4*
40–49	9.9	11.4*
50–59	14.0	16.8*
60–69	44.7	33.8
70–79	85.8	74.6
80–89	178.3	216.2*

*Rates for females are higher than those for males.
SOURCE: Sheila Ryan Johansson. "Sex and Death in Victorian England: An Examination of Age- and Sex-Specific Death Rates, 1840–1910." In A Widening Sphere: Changing Roles of Victorian Women, ed. Martha Vicinus (Bloomington: Indiana University Press, 1977), 173.

The Quakers were eminently middle class, and Fox argued that his data could be extended to represent most middle-class women (Johansson, 173). The common assumption has been that the higher mortality rate among women was due to complications in childbirth. However, according to the general statistics of the period, the increase in female mortality actually occurs between ages ten and thirty-four, a span beginning too early to attribute simply to childbirth. Furthermore, young girls aged five to nineteen were the last to achieve consistently lower death rates, rather than their male counterparts. Sheila Johansson suggests in "Sex and Death in Victorian England" that because of the lesser value placed on women by Victorian society, girls received poorer nourishment than boys, leaving them weaker, less able to survive harsh conditions, and more susceptible to illness. It is logical then that young women, age approximately fourteen to nineteen, who were working long hours without sleep, nourishment, or fresh air, would become ill.

Whatever the cause, consumption was so common among women in general and seamstresses in particular that in 1845 *Punch* cautioned its readers: "The question has been mooted, whether consumption is contagious. We do not mean to assert that it is; and we would not frighten anybody, especially a sensitive young lady, or her anxious mamma, unnecessarily; but we do declare that we should not, were it consistent with our sex, at all like to be in the frocks of those whose dresses have been wrought by consumptive fingers" ("Punch on the Silkworm," 92). Although not specific in its call to action "in behalf of the over-worked silkworms," the article is typical in suggesting that the women who frequented millinery shops needed to address the issue of abuse. Illustrations were used by some journals to indicate the harsh existence of seamstresses, while others relied on fiction to present the conditions of needlewomen through a representative example. The periodicals of the 1840s and 1850s portray both the harsh conditions faced by needlewomen and the almost inevitable outcome—with the heroine usually succumbing to consumption—while addressing the question of the middle- and upper-class patron's responsibility.

IV

Also of concern to reformers generally were the terms of employment faced by young women entering the profession. Women who wished to become dressmakers or milliners first had to serve an apprenticeship period. The length of apprenticeship varied from two to seven years, and usually required the payment of a premium. In her study of working women, Ivy Pinchbeck notes that "poor children were frequently apprenticed by the parish, there being plenty of small mistresses glad to take them for the sake of the premium and their labour" (289). Harriet Baker testified to Grainger that a two-year apprenticeship cost between thirty and forty pounds a year (1843 *Second Report*, no. 525). Many of the apprenticeships discussed in the 1843 *Second Report* varied in duration from two to five years; however, according to Pinchbeck, "a five to seven year apprenticeship was required and a milliner in good business demanded a fee of at least £40–£50. The capital required to set up in business afterwards varied from £100 to £1,000 according to the scale of business, but at least £400 to £500 was considered necessary 'to set up genteelly'" (287). During the apprenticeship, the woman was usually given her room and board but received no wages. In *Mary Barton*, Elizabeth Gaskell presents a shorter period of apprenticeship, but one without benefit of room and board:

> Mary was to work for two years without any remuneration, on consideration of being taught the business; and where afterwards she was to dine and have tea, with a small quarterly salary (paid quarterly because so much more genteel than by week), a *very* small one, divisible into a minute weekly pittance. In summer she was to be there by six, bringing her day's meals during the first two years; in winter she was not to come till after breakfast. Her time for returning home at night must always depend upon the quantity of work Miss Simmonds had to do. (63)

Although apprenticeships as brief as two years were mentioned in the testimony taken for the 1843 *Second Report*, none of the young women were allowed to live at home and all paid premiums. Mary Barton's employment would not have been out of the realm of possibility, however, if one considers that for two years she works at no expense to her employer (no cost for meals or for laundry or the other aspects of boarding workers) while she learns the business.

In keeping with Victorian standards, dressmakers and milliners were to have Sunday off as a day of rest and to attend church services. For many women, however, free Sundays were a problem, and for some the day became a source of tension with their employers. Some of the seamstresses interviewed for the 1843 *Second Report* told investigators about working long hours Saturday night "because there was Sunday to rest." Others stated that they received no meals on Sunday, and they were expected to occupy themselves elsewhere during the day. A few said that they received meals, but had "black looks for dining at the house on Sunday." In Tonna's *The Wrongs of Woman*, Frances King's father pays Mrs. B., the owner of the shop where his daughter is apprenticed, an extra two pounds and twelve shillings for Sunday meals after learning that the premium he paid for her apprenticeship does not cover Sunday expenses. In *Ruth*, Elizabeth Gaskell illustrates the common attitude of shop owners toward Sundays, and the recourse taken by many seamstresses:

> On Sundays [Mrs. Mason] chose to conclude that all her apprentices had friends who would be glad to see them to dinner and give them a welcome reception for the remainder of the day; while she . . . went to spend the day at her father's house . . . Accordingly, no dinner was cooked on Sundays for the young workwomen; no fires were lighted in any rooms to which they had access. On this morning they breakfasted in Mrs. Mason's own parlour, after which the room was closed against them through the day by some understood, though unspoken prohibition.
>
> What became of such as Ruth, who had no home and no friends in that large, populous, desolate town? She . . . commissioned the servant, who went to market on Saturdays for the family, to buy her a bun or biscuit, whereon she made her fasting dinner in the deserted workroom, sitting in her walking-dress to keep off the cold, which clung to her in spite of shawl and bonnet. (33–34)

For women who earned no salary during their apprenticeship, the lack of food and fire on Sundays presented a severe hardship. But Victorian readers were equally appalled by testimony concerning the late hours milliners were forced to work on Saturdays "because there was Sunday to rest," causing many women to sleep on Sunday rather than attend church services. Discussed in virtually every novel, the issue was one that was particularly perplexing in an age already troubled by the seemingly paradoxical combination of overt Christian morality and increasing religious doubt. Ann King's explanation to her doctor in *The Wrongs of Woman* is typical of the way novelists presented the issue:

> "For some time I went to church on Sundays, and that did me good, body and mind; but after a while, I was forced to lie in bed

all the Sunday morning, and when it was fine in the afternoon I
had a bit of a stroll in the nearest park."

"And left off going to church?"

"None of them would go with me, sir; and I had fainting fits so
often I didn't like to be by myself." (406)

For Victorian readers this account, and others like it, would be especially
troubling because the young woman described has unknowingly entered a
high-risk profession, is still morally strong, and desires to attend religious
services—but is prevented by the crippling effects, both physical and moral,
of her profession.

After serving her period of apprenticeship, a woman became an "improver." If she moved to a new house at this point, she would have to pay
another premium, although lower than that of an apprentice. From this
level a woman would move to third, second, or first hand. With each step
there was increased responsibility and increased wages. Nevertheless, the
wages were still considerably lower than those of men in comparable trades:
in 1864, a second hand could earn between fifteen and twenty-five pounds
a year (Lord, 70), less than half the one pound two shillings earned weekly
by a "fair-average tailor" in 1849 (Mayhew, 17 December 1849, 226–29).
The duties of a seamstress moved from simple seaming to cutting and
fitting, and finally to superintending and instructing. As revealed in the
1843 *Second Report* and reiterated by writers such as Tonna, many women
were kept in ignorance to prevent their progression in the field. Some shop
owners deliberately withheld information and the teaching of skills because
they were afraid that women would leave to set up rival establishments.
But for most owners keeping their apprentices ignorant was a matter of
economics—a third hand earned between twelve and sixteen pounds, while
a second hand was paid between twenty and twenty-five pounds, and a
first hand earned anywhere from thirty to eighty pounds, depending on the
quality of the shop.

Women who could not afford to pay the premiums necessary for apprenticeship usually became slopworkers—they worked out of their homes,
having obtained work through a middlewoman. Such women usually made
shirts or trousers, occasionally obtaining piecework from millinery houses
during the season. Some large dressmaking establishments seasonally employed as many as fourteen hundred pieceworkers.[10] And in 1852, T.
Hughes claimed in *A Lecture on the Slop-System* that three out of every
four garments sold in England were made by slopworkers in London or in

one of the other large towns; in London alone, in 1849, there were estimated to be 14,000 female slopworkers, 11,440 of whom were under the age of twenty (4–5, 8). The wages paid to slopworkers were notoriously low. It is little wonder, then, that during the later 1840s and the 1850s the slopworker served as a paradigm of suffering among the urban poor in the works of writers as varied as Charles Dickens, Elizabeth Gaskell, and George W. M. Reynolds, as well as in visual representations as diverse as Richard Redgrave's *The Sempstress,* John Everett Millais's *Stitch! Stitch! Stitch!* and numerous *Punch* cartoons.

While preparing his series for the *Morning Chronicle* in 1849, Mayhew interviewed several slopworkers. One woman of "excellent character" gave the following testimony:

> Upon the average, at all kinds of work, excepting the shirts, that I make, I cannot earn more than 4s. 6d. to 5s. per week—let me sit from eight in the morning till ten every night: and out of that I shall have to pay 1s. 6d. for trimmings, and 6d. candles every week; so that altogether I earn about 3s. in the six days. But I don't earn that, for there's the firing that you must have to press the work, and that will be 9d. a week. . . . So that my clear earnings are . . . say 2s. 3d. to 2s. 6d. every week. (*Unknown Mayhew,* 120–21)

Ord's 1864 parliamentary report on sanitary conditions presents similar statistics for day workers and slopworkers who found seasonal work in millinery houses and generally supports the testimonies found in Mayhew's series. According to Ord, although the out-door (non-residential) milliners usually worked twelve to thirteen hours a day, generally 8:00 or 9:00 A.M. until 9:00 or 10:00 P.M., in most shops the only meal supplied to the day workers was tea. The report continues:

> The amount of wage, comparatively unimportant in the in-door hands, becomes therefore in the case of day workers a question of the greatest importance. As far as I can learn, the general minimum wage for day workers is 9s. a week with their tea.
>
> With these nine shillings they have to find dress, lodging, fire, and food. Girls who live with their parents or friends, casting their earnings into a common stock, and girls who club together, can manage fairly upon this wage; but for those who live alone the

amount is not sufficient to provide proper food after dress and lodging are paid for. They must pay 2s. 6d. or 3s. a week for lodging, and out of the remaining 6s. or 6s. 6d. find dress and food. (Pike, 173–74)

Some women chose to work as out-door seamstresses or slopworkers in order to stay at home, perhaps trying to remain as close as they could to the ideal of not having to work outside the house. But many women worked in their homes because they or their families could not pay the premium required for an apprenticeship. Elizabeth Stone presents such a case in *The Young Milliner* with the character of Bessie Lambert. Because neither Bessie nor her mother has enough money to pay an apprentice's premium, they must both work out of their home, where the most either can earn for ten hours of work is fourpence half-penny (137). Although Stone's emphasis, like Tonna's, is on the women working in millinery houses, the writers who followed shifted their attention to slopworkers.

Early novelists had concentrated on women employed in millinery houses because their social class, although made unstable by their working, was sufficient to warrant interest and concern from the middle- and upper-class reading public. Later novelists used the already accepted figure of the seamstress to address a new concern, the condition of the working classes generally. And even though the literature and art concerning slopworkers was aimed at spurring the middle and upper classes into some kind of reform, some aspects of the representations were misleading: virtually all portrayed slopworkers as young women, often displaced from the middle class, struggling alone, often in an attic room. This romanticized vision of a struggling heroine may have occasionally been found in reality, but frequently the women involved were married with children, sewing to provide a second income or to replace one lost to the illness or injuring of the male head of household. And rather than living in a dry, romantic garret, all too often these women and their families lived in damp, often polluted, cellar dwellings.

Thus, whether spurred by paintings such as Richard Redgrave's *The Sempstress* or merely recognizing the opportunity to enlarge public interest, writers after 1843 shift the portrayal of the seamstress from a realistic accounting of a particular group of workers to a stylized symbol of the suffering caused by urban industrialism among the working poor generally. Although the change in focus necessitated a shift from dressmakers and milliners to slopworkers, transitional writers blurred the differences in order to transfer established reactions to the new context. For example, Frances Trollope's *Jessie Phillips* has a rural setting, allowing a mix of upper and working classes unattainable in an urban setting. And while Elizabeth Gaskell's *Mary Barton* has the daughter of factory workers obtaining a job in a millinery shop, the emphasis remains on the working-class community in which she lives—and the only time we see her working is when she is assisting a friend who is a slopworker.

The shift from dressmaker to slopworker also marks a change in issues. The works published before 1844 focus on the seamstress and the hardships she faced. Literature published between 1844 and 1849 uses the needleworker as a vehicle to focus on the hardships of the working classes, often not dealing with the conditions specific to seamstresses at all. With the publication of Mayhew's *London Labour and the London Poor,* attention returned to the seamstress herself. Contributing to the renewal of interest in the seamstress was also the possibility of a solution to her plight—emigration. Although an unprecedented number of literary works dealing with needlewomen were published during 1850, the attention was short-lived: fewer than a dozen novels dealing with seamstresses were published between 1851 and 1859. And despite the abuses recorded in the 1864 *Report to the Children's Employment Commission,* the literary interest remained slight. In contrast, most seamstress paintings appear after 1850, with the majority being exhibited after the 1864 *Report.* Yet the later report does not seem to serve as a source; the majority of the visual images build on the iconographic vocabulary established by the earlier literature and by Redgrave's *The Sempstress.*

Fiction writers emphasized the fact that many of the young women employed in dressmaking establishments were farmers' daughters or daughters of impoverished middle-class households. In these cases the young women were employing a skill learned at home, often with the intention of returning there after learning the trade. Not only were these girls seen as more respectable, and thus more deserving of sympathy, than the offspring of the working classes, but for many middle-class readers there would be a kind of fearful recognition that the young woman portrayed could easily, under slightly different circumstances, be their daughter. For this reader, the sufferings of the young girl would be more harrowing because they take place outside of normal class confines, and her inevitable death or, even worse, fall into prostitution would be seen as a tragedy. Artists later built on the iconography with a flower serving as a visual reminder of a rural past.

Some writers took the crossing of class boundaries allowed by the use of the seamstress a step further, creating a character who is a member of the aristocracy, although she is unaware of it. Usually her mother has, for some reason, been disowned before the child's birth, so that the daughter grows up unaware of her heritage. Usually she has been raised in a middle-class home, and when she must earn her living she is accepted as a member of the impoverished middle class but inevitably revered by fellow workers for her nobility of character. Usually extremely beautiful, she is often pursued by debauched gentlemen but possesses the inner strength necessary to resist such temptations. At first such a portrayal would seem a denial of the seamstress as a representative of the working poor. But the portrayal was actually very effective—it exaggerated her sufferings while creating a bridge between the classes. The seamstress was simultaneously a child of the upper, ruling classes and a part of the poor, exploited classes.

V

The seamstress first appeared in Victorian fiction in 1833, when *Tait's Edinburgh Magazine* published John Galt's "The Seamstress." The story centers around Miss Peggy Pingle, a victim of "pinched gentility," forced to earn her living following the death of her father. And it is Miss Pingle's character, as an example of Scottish "eydency," that is the focus of the story: "the English have but the word 'industry', to denote that constant patience of labour which belongs equally to rough and moderate tasks; but the Scots have also 'eydency', with its derivatives, descriptive of the same constancy and patience, in employments of a feminine and sedentary kind. We never say a ditcher or a drudger is eydent; but the spinster at her wheel, or the seamstress at her sewing, are eydent. . . ." Galt's interest in the seamstress as an illustration of "a genuine case of industry free from labour" (21) apparently results from ignorance concerning the hardships encountered by seamstresses—despite the concerns about working conditions already being voiced in some women's magazines—rather than intentional oversight. Galt informs readers: "We make this important distinction between the wheel and the needle, because, although we have often overheard malcontent murmurings against the former, yet we do not recollect, in any one instance, the latter spoken of either with complaint or disparagement" (23). Yet he may have been aware of some of the problems seamstresses faced, since following her mother's death he has Miss Pingle rising to work earlier and being forced to work with a smaller candle. And while the other women note the "new stinting in her narrow means," it is with "a kind-hearted hypocrisy" that they invite her to tea (21). Nevertheless, it is clear that for Galt the occupation is one associated with a particularly feminine diligence—work that can be demanding or tedious, but not associated with suffering, danger, or death.

Although Miss Pingle is forced to practice "the frugalest economy of pinched gentility" (23), her greatest hardship is the sameness of her days: "Day after day was with Miss Pingle as the to-day is like the yesterday—twins could not more resemble each other" (21). The patient acceptance of this existence is the character trait that Galt wished to portray. His story salutes a trait he considers typical of Scottish women, and to be venerated for its femininity. It is interesting to note that while one of the late narratives concerning seamstresses, Julia Kavanagh's *Rachel Gray*, published in 1856, is also a character study illuminating the same kind of patience with a repetitious existence, it was primarily the visual artists who chose to extol this perception of needlewomen. And, like *Rachel Gray*, the majority of these works, such as George Edgar Hicks's *Snowdrops* (1858), Frank Holl's *The Song of the Shirt* (1875), or Thomas B. Kennington's *Widowed and Fatherless* (1888), appeared after much of the fictive interest in the seamstress had abated. Usually shown in a bare but clean room, indicating that any respite comes from simple things such as family or a flower, the seamstresses in these paintings are working or are pausing only for a moment.

Three years after the appearance of Galt's short story, Charles Dickens published *Sketches by Boz,* which includes a study of a seamstress in the section entitled "Characters"— "The Mistaken Milliner: A Tale of Ambition."[11] In this story Dickens creates a character seeking both monetary and social gain. Miss Martin is a working-class woman who is never content with what she has, and who attempts to gain wealth and status by becoming a singing star. Even though Galt's and Dickens's stories are similar in the choice of the heroine's profession, the works differ both in characterization and in effect. Although Dickens's milliner owns her own shop, she is of the working classes rather than the impoverished gentility of Galt's character. Further, rather than exhibiting patience with the repetitious nature of her employment and finding contentment with her life, Miss Martin is ambitious, hoping to become a singing star. And finally, where Galt's story is an attempt to educate English readers about the Scottish temperament, Dickens's story is a moral about misdirected ambition.

Dickens's story reflects several beliefs about dressmakers commonly held in the first half of the nineteenth century: that they were well paid but never satisfied, and always looking for a way of moving up socially, usually by taking advantage of someone else. Many of these prejudices were reflected in the popular magazines until the publication of the Children's Employment Commission's 1843 *Second Report*. For example, the 1842 opening issue of *Punch* ran a series of "Young Lovers to Sell" and included "The Milliner"—along with a politician, a pet parson, a speculative mama, a man about town, and other stereotypical social climbers—portrayed as a foolish young woman who spurns a draper in the hopes of marrying Lord Vapour. But when she "entreat[s] him to cause [her] fine dream to come true," she is rejected with "words frigid and few." The verse ends with a warning delivered by the poet:

> Then mark me, sweet satin-stitch! *I* am the *beau*
> Whose knot must be tied up by thee:
> Refuse not—lest forced to the Borough to go,
> With "plain work done here" in thy window to show,
> If thou'lt not my VALENTINE be. (10)

Much as in Dickens's story, the moral seems to be that a seamstress should not, but will, try to rise above her station, and the consequences can be dire—as suggested by the references to having to seek relief and to take in piecework. Prefacing the poem is a half-page illustration with a dejected, weary milliner as the focal center, surrounded by small, comic sketches of Lord Vapour proposing in her dream and of the rejected draper. The effect is comic, but the combination of poem and picture reflects the early stereotype of needlewomen as being prepared to take advantage of every possible opportunity. Some of this prejudice may have arisen from the seamstress's ambiguous social position: to say that a woman had fallen economically indirectly cast doubts on her moral integrity through the strong connotations *fallen* had for Victorians. Such aspersions would have been furthered by the fact that an economic fall, much like a sexual one, could make a woman unsuitable for marriage, and that for many women there was a direct correlation between economic need and sexual ruin.

Dickens's sense of timing and his awareness of Victorian society's fascination with the suffering of the helpless and the meek had him frequently incorporating the seamstress in his work. He returned to the seamstress in 1839 with the publication of *Nicholas Nickleby*. Early in the novel economic circumstance forces Nicholas and Kate Nickleby to find employment, and their uncle secures Kate a position with a London milliner. Ralph

Nickleby informs Kate's mother, "Dressmakers in London, as I need not remind you, ma'am, who are so well acquainted with all matters in the ordinary routine of life, make large fortunes, keep equipages, and become persons of great wealth and fortune" (121). His statement reflects the attitude of most upper-class Victorians that for young women of the upper and middle classes who had suffered economic reversals and were forced to find employment, a position in a millinery house was ideal. Even after the publication of the 1843 *Second Report* and of Henry Mayhew's series *London Labour and the London Poor*—which appeared in the *Morning Chronicle* during 1849 and 1850 and contained scandalous tales of abuse and suffering—a well-read man such as Thomas Carlyle could write: "no needlewoman, 'distressed' or other, can be procured in London by any housewife to give, for fair wages, fair help in sewing. Ask any thrifty house-mother. No *real* needlewoman, 'distressed' or other, has been found attain-able in any of the houses I frequent. Imaginary needlewomen, who demand considerable wages, and have a deepish appetite for beef and viands, I hear of everywhere." It is not surprising then that, in 1839, Dickens would show Ralph Nickleby making such fulsome pronouncements about Kate's future, and her mother believing them.

Despite the assurances given by Kate's uncle, a conversation he has with Kate gave Victorian audiences their first glimpse of the reality of the dress-maker's existence: "'You will live, to all intents and purposes, here [at the dress shop], . . . for here you will take your meals, and here you will be from morning till night—occasionally perhaps till morning again'" (124). This initial suggestion of adverse working conditions, specifically drudgery and long hours, is reinforced when Kate notes the physical effects of the occu-pation on the young women she sees as she walks to work her first morn-ing at the shop. Dickens's choice of modifiers—"sickly girls," "patient toil," "monotonous existence," "painful occupation," "feeble gait"—cap-tures many of the aspects of needlewomen and their clients—"thoughtless" and "luxurious"—that were to become motifs in the works that followed. Also notable is the analogy to the silkworm and the connotation that, like prisoners, the young women must somehow steal small breaths of fresh air and glimpses of sunlight:

> At this early hour many sickly girls, whose business, like that of poor worm, is to produce, with patient toil, the finery that bedecks the thoughtless and luxurious, traverse our streets, making towards the scene of their daily labour, and catching, as if by stealth, in

their hurried walk, the only gasp of the wholesome air and glimpse of sunlight which cheers their monotonous existence during the long train of hours that make a working day. As she drew nigh to the more fashionable quarter of town, Kate marked many of this class as they passed by, hurrying like herself to their painful occupation, and saw, in their unhealthy looks and feeble gait, but too clear evidence that her misgivings were not wholly groundless. (208)

Although Kate observes the effects of dressmaking on women, she does not experience them herself, since the shop where she works soon closes. Such closings were not uncommon, but unlike real needlewomen, Kate has no trouble obtaining another, more secure position as a lady's companion. Thus while Dickens presented Victorians with the first indications of the harsh conditions faced by dressmakers and milliners, it was not until the publication of *A London Dressmaker's Diary* in 1842 that these circumstances were dealt with in detail.

VI

Although studies of social protest fiction have long acknowledged female authorship, investigation of female protagonists has lagged behind. For example, in *The Working Classes in Victorian Fiction*, P. J. Keating distinguishes among six kinds of working-class characters (26), but does not refer to a single female character, despite the fact that working-class women and girls play important roles in many of the works he examines, and are very representative figures. One of the most common working-class female protagonists is the seamstress. Indeed, she appeared so often in both the literature and the artwork of the later nineteenth century that she came to be viewed as "an exclusively Victorian institution" (Casteras, *Images*, 110). That the people of an age should find a figure to identify as their own is not remarkable; there exists in each age "a shared code, a set of interlocking tropes and similitudes" by which the people of that age identify themselves (Greenblatt, 86). It is interesting that an age that prided itself on innovation and technological progress would choose as one of its signifiers a female figure whose work goes back to earliest records and who benefited little from industrialization.

The seamstress, however, was an effective symbol for Victorian reformers because as a woman she was seen as powerless, one easily taken advantage of. She appeared so lacking in power that she presented no threat to the status quo, nor would the granting of protection be seen as threatening. There were no images of mob scenes or riots surrounding her—indeed the isolation of her occupation, especially as depicted by later visual artists, increased the perception of her as helpless. But because of the instant recognition she inspired, the seamstress was a powerful symbol.

Over time, the portrayal of the seamstress changed. Not all depictions used, let alone stressed, the early analogy between seamstress and slave. Early presentations focused on the dressmaking trade, while later presentations focused on shirtmakers; seamstress reform gave way to labor reform; pictures of women starving to death in garrets gave way to portraits of introspective women meditating over their work. Despite the changes in presentation, intent, and characterization, certain elements tie together the images of the seamstress found in the art and fiction of the mid- and late nineteenth century: setting, character, social status. For even as the intent behind her usage changed, succeeding artists and writers built on the image previously created, shaping it to fit their purposes rather than discarding it. The result is the semiotic evolution of a character from the literal to the representative to the sentimental disintegration through acculturation. The study that follows is a chronological exploration of the representations of this Victorian institution, the suffering seamstress, from the anonymous publication of *A London Dressmaker's Diary*, in *Tait's Edinburgh Magazine* during November 1842, through the exhibition of Thomas Benjamin Kennington's *Adversity* in 1890.

In this chapter I have primarily focused on nonfictional materials, both Victorian and modern, to investigate how the Victorians' understanding of labor, particularly that of needlewomen, developed. The literature published during the 1830s, including texts by writers such as John Galt and Charles Dickens, represents a transition from idealized portraits of domesticity to documented realism. In the second chapter I argue that, beginning with *A London Dressmaker's Diary* (1842), the portrayal of the seamstress began to emphasize realism, and the publication of *The Second Report of the Children's Employment Commission* (1843) accelerated that transformation, which culminated with the publication of Thomas Hood's "The Song of the Shirt" (1843). And as a result of public response to Hood's poem, a variety of illustrations began appearing in publications such as *Punch*.

During the late 1840s the image of the seamstress moved from factual representation to symbol. In chapter 3 I look at a variety of works from periodicals (stories, poems, and accompanying illustrations) as well as paintings, concentrating on narrative and aesthetic devices in order to analyze the development of the seamstress as a class symbol. Chapter 4 focuses on one year, 1850, when as many literary works featuring seamstresses were published as in all the preceding years. Although there were a number of illustrations published, mainly accompanying the fiction, there was not a particularly impressive increase in the number of paintings of needlewomen. I examine the difference between the underlying realism of the fiction and the romanticism of the art, which leads to questions such as why the visual medium did not follow the same trend as the fiction.

As I discuss in chapter 5, the number of publications involving seamstresses during the remainder of the decade seems scant after the flurry of literature in 1850. Yet interest in reform continued, with parliamentary studies and journalistic reports of abuse being published. It was also during this period that the number of paintings featuring needlewomen began to increase. A distinct shift in the portrayals of the women began to occur, with the emphasis moving from realism to sentimentalism. The image of the seamstress appeared in illustrations, galleries, and art shows.

In chapter 6, I argue that reformists' needs ran counter to aesthetics, and that the lack of reform undercut the power of the symbol for the majority of writers; however, the romanticized portrayal of needlewomen in Victorian art allowed the symbol to continue to affect Victorians on an emotional and sentimental plane. The majority of images by the artists of the period are not the haunting, gray shadows of Redgrave and Watts, but sentimentalized pictures of young women whose possible suffering is implied only through symbolic elements earlier associated with needlewomen. Such portraits undercut the urge for reform by evoking pathos rather then empathy or anger. And the artists who strove to maintain a hard, realistic edge opted to create narrative pictures, which move the viewer from specific issues of reform to individual stories of suffering, or focus on larger issues such as the treatment of the elderly in workhouses. Thus in this book I argue that, rather than remaining static, the image of the seamstress moved from being focused on her suffering, recognizable through an established iconography, to being a symbol for the working poor, and then, through acculturation and changes in aesthetic taste, to being familiar and sentimental.

Establishing the Image

Oh! men with sisters dear!
Oh! men with mothers and wives!
It is not linen you're wearing out,
But human creatures' lives.

—Thomas Hood, "The Song of the Shirt"

Although Dickens's *Nicholas Nickleby* first called attention to the condition of Victorian needlewomen in 1839, it was not until the 1842 publication of *A London Dressmaker's Diary* that the figure of the seamstress again appeared, this time as the center focus of the narrative. Published anonymously in *Tait's Edinburgh Magazine,* the "diary" is a fictional narrative portraying the day-to-day physical and mental conditions of London needlewomen.[1] Purporting to run from 9 October through 1 December 1841, the diary deals with many of the issues and findings that were to be presented a few months later with the publication of *The Second Report of the Children's Employment Commission* on 30 January 1843. Other fictional works dealing with the plight of needlewomen soon followed: *The Young Milliner* and *The Pageant* in 1843, *The Wrongs of Woman* during 1843 and 1844, and *The Orphan Milliners* in April 1844.

Many Victorians, however, would have first read about the harsh working conditions milliners and dressmakers encountered through the multitude of articles, published in virtually every newspaper and journal during 1843, that quoted extensively from the Blue book reports. The wide coverage of the testimony concerning needlewomen is significant, since, as Richard Altick notes, the blue-covered published results of parliamentary investigations were "the most unimpeachable source on living and working conditions among the urban and rural poor" (89). Equally significant is the place of their appearance before the Victorian public, the periodical press. For, as Lyn Pykett explains, "far from being a mirror of Victorian culture, the periodicals have come to be seen as a central component of that culture— an 'active and integral part'" (7). As such they shaped Victorian perceptions as well as being shaped by the perceptions. Further, not only are periodicals and newspapers "cultural products," but they allow for the construction of a communal identity through the text.[2] Thus through periodicals readers come to identify themselves "as a solid community moving steadily down (or up) history" when, in fact, nation and class are "imagined communities": concepts rather than discrete physical entities (Anderson, 26). On Saturday, 20 May 1843, the *Pictorial Times* featured the plight of the seamstress in an article entitled "Slaves of the Needle." Although the first two paragraphs provide some general background information, the rest of the five-column spread consists of excerpts from the 1843 *Second Report*. As the lead story in an illustrated Saturday paper, the article also has a dramatic illustration: a diptych contrasting the sufferings of the needlewomen with the leisured lives of their clients (figure 2.1). On the left is a crowded workroom full of young women bent over their sewing. The clock, centered on the back wall, shows a few minutes after 3:00 A.M.; the lights indicate that it is late at night; and a used tea tray is set aside on the floor. The viewer's eye is first caught by the figures on the left side of the section: slightly left of center two young women in plain, dark dresses are seated at a right angle sewing on a large piece of light fabric. Further to the left one young woman, also in a dark dress, with her lap covered by her work, is holding her head and pressing her eyes in despair, while behind her another is standing as if startled. As the eye travels along the horizontal line created by the pool of light and the bent heads of the young women, their sorrow and exhaustion become evident, with the last woman in the picture wearily holding a hand to her forehead. The scene on the right has been set parallel for a deliberate contrast: it, too, is of a crowded room, but it is an elegant reception with both men and women. There is the same dark vertical line to the left of the drawing, this time created by the dark gown of an elegant woman and her two male escorts. The horizontal line is created by the light of a chandelier, which falls evenly over the crowd and on two seated female figures, all richly dressed and apparently pleasantly engaged. The implications are clear: the seamstresses are single, defenseless, impoverished women, "slaving" to create what others take for granted. Thus "Slaves of the Needle" presents one of the first of several synchronic portrayals of needlewomen and their clients.

I

The material being presented concerning the physical, mental, and moral situations faced by women in the needlework industry was shocking, and the writers bringing these issues before the public for the first time felt they would not be believed. Compounding the issue for women writers was the assumption of separate spheres, which held that women would not expose themselves unnecessarily to unpleasantness that was outside their sphere—the home—and that dealt with public issues such as politics or business. Thus verisimilitude was particularly important to the female authors of the early novels concerning seamstresses. Works published after the report

THE MILLINERS.　　　　　　　THE DUCHESSES.

FIGURE 2.1　"The Milliners and the Duchesses," *Pictorial Times* (20 May 1843): 145.

of the Second Commission often cite the report or actually lift passages from it. However, in *A London Dressmaker's Diary,* published before any citable documentation was available, verisimilitude is created through form: the diary. The diary format allows for a mixture of specificity and generalization virtually unattainable through any other genre. The detailed recounting of events creates a sense of reality while the anonymity of the narrator creates a sense of universality. Added to these responses was a strong combination of empathy and sympathy, since the protagonist is of some social standing, although impoverished and therefore forced to earn her living. Though written before the publication of the parliamentary findings, the diary recounts typical experiences and thus leads the way for later writers.

Because of the sensitive nature of the topic, the writers who followed did not feel secure about their novels' audience reception. They therefore felt the need to actually document their narratives. In the introduction to *The Young Milliner,* Elizabeth Stone assures her readers of the truth of her portrait: "The Narrative itself is, of course, fictitious; but the circumstances adduced are unexaggerated and strictly true. The Authoress has availed herself of facts which she drew from private authentic sources; but her statements are fully borne out by parliamentary documents which have been published since her story was written" (ii). Stone again refers her reader to parliamentary documents as a source of confirmation and further information when she footnotes a passage that she felt might be viewed as extreme: "On Sunday morning, about ten o'clock she retired to bed, after being (for it had been a dreadfully busy week) at work for upwards of seventy hours consecutively." The note reads: "This circumstance will no doubt appear to many readers as a gross exaggeration. I beg merely to refer them to the 'Report and Appendices of the Children's Employment Commission,' lately presented to parliament, and published since these pages were written" (289). The presentation of fiction and fact as distinct quantities create a particular effect: the fiction involves the reader in the lives of the young women, while the references to the 1843 *Second Report* imply that the actual conditions are even more distressing.

Stone's open acknowledgment of government documents is by no means the exception to the rule. In the preface to *The Pageant,* Francis Paget refers to the "Inquiries of the Children's Employment Commission" and quotes briefly from a minister who testified to the overall horror of working conditions but doubts that few of his audience, "the upper ranks of London society" (80), will read the parliamentary reports in their entirety:

But there are few of the young, and happy, and light-hearted, who care to pore over the ponderous folios of a Parliamentary Report, and fewer still, probably who have fathomed the deep abyss of sin, and suffering, of which our Metropolis is the vortex. . . .

. . . It has been conceived, therefore, that a short tale in which these subjects are brought before the reader, may be not altogether without its use. It may reveal facts, of which, many perhaps were previously in ignorance; it may awaken in others, a sense of their responsibilities; it *ought* to induce those who read it, to reflect deeply upon the probable *end* of such a state of things. (viii–ix)

Paget further supplements his fiction with documented evidence, following up the novel with two appendices: the first from the testimony collected by R. D. Grainger for the 1843 *Second Report*; the second from testimony gathered by a subcommissioner from milliners who were prevented by their employer from testifying at the hearings, but who were willing to speak else-where.[3] In a similar approach, at the end of "Milliners and Dressmakers," part 1 of *The Wrongs of Woman*, Charlotte Elizabeth Tonna includes a chapter entitled "Consequences" in which she also acknowledges her use of government documents and directly quotes from parliamentary reports:

All this appears in evidence, taken before the authorised commis-sioners; and it also appears, on the testimony of a highly respect-able and experienced surgeon, who for twenty years has had much practice among this branch of labourers [seamstresses], that "in no trade or manufactory whatever is the labour to be compared to that of the young dressmakers: no men work so long. This is corroborated by official authority. *It would be impossible for any animal to work so continuously with so little rest.*" (415)

The direct quotation is from the testimony of Mr. Devonald. His statement is taken from volume 14 (number 625) of the *Parliamentary Papers,* as are most of the four pages of documentation Tonna uses to conclude the section concerning seamstresses.

Even with parliamentary documentation, Tonna was worried about dis-belief and accusations of exaggeration from her readers. Twice she states that she has purposely moderated the picture she is presenting. Before beginning her narrative, Tonna identifies her intended audience and her purpose, then writes: "we will, as much as possible, spare the feelings of our readers, and leave them to draw inferences where description would be scarcely tolerable" (399). The second reference to moderation occurs at the end of "Milliners and Dressmakers." After citing her parliamentary sources, Tonna informs her readers that she has "not tinted the picture so darkly as a strict adherence to truth would have warranted [her] doing, because such a course was not requisite: [she] only wished to show the natural results of the system" (417). Thus, even with proof of validity, early writers were worried about strong reactions that would turn readers away rather than induce sympathy, and thereby reform, for needlewomen.

Unlike her predecessors, Camilla Toulmin does not use documentation or refer to possible sources of confirmation in *The Orphan Milliners*, but instead creates a sense of validity through her presentation of setting, through verb tenses, and through limited narrator omniscience. For example, the opening of Toulmin's story sets a scene that is seemingly verifiable: "There is a certain spot in one of the midland counties, which, for the sake of preserving its incognito, I will call Willow-dale. It is really but three or four miles from a market town, yet lying away from the high road, and still further removed from any railroad ..." (279). This first section, establishing the scene, is told in present tense, as is the final section of the tale. The story itself, however, is in the past tense. The present-tense frame creates the feeling that the towns of the opening and closing and the people inhabiting them are contemporary, and therefore real. The narrator furthers the sense of reality by declaring her inability to relate the thoughts of characters, such as the customer who thoughtlessly places orders at the last minute, and the occasional "unrecorded" detail, as when the narrator admits "there is no exact record of what 'hot and nice' thing it was one shilling purchased" (282). This sense of incomplete knowledge, coupled with a lack of involvement on the part of the narrator, leads to a sense of objectivity and therefore verisimilitude, despite the lack of supporting evidence or confirmation.

For Toulmin's readers who had been following the issue over the sixteen months since the publication of the original 1843 *Second Report*, visual memory may have supplied further support: her novel's opening illustration (figure 2.2) is strikingly similar to the left half of the diptych published eleven months earlier in the *Pictorial Times*. Although the angle is slightly different, the clock is on the left wall, and it is not quite as late—a few minutes before 1:00 A.M.—the positioning of the young women in the crowded room is very similar. Here, too, we have a figure to the left covering her eyes and holding her head in despair. Centered in the picture is a light gown with two women in modest, dark dresses, facing one another, working on it. Another young woman wearily holds her head. There is, however, no contrasting picture. Toulmin focuses on the working women and on the shop owners, rather than on the clients.

Another means of developing credibility was by using, or creating, personal testimony. Echoing the depositions gathered for parliamentary reports, such presentations are found primarily in reformist tracts (such as *Confessions of a Needlewoman!*) or in supplementary material (such as the introduction to Paget's *The Pageant*), where a brief, detailed account of one woman's story is sufficient either to make the point or lend credibility to the narrative to follow. *Confessions of a Needlewoman!* purports to "reveal the remarkable trials, sufferings, and temptations of Susan Fry," a London slopworker, including "her heartless seduction, cruel desertion, and untimely end." Supporting the sensational rhetoric is a cover sketch of a casket covered with a drape reading "fashion's slave," topped by a milliner's dummy formed from a skull and wearing a bonnet. Ironically, the need for a character to whom Susan Fry can reveal her experiences, and who can thus save her from a similar fate, means that the reader's initial interest and sympathy are captured by someone other than the suffering needlewoman. Indeed, the penny tract begins more as a temperance pamphlet, with the young protagonist suffering at the hands of an alcoholic stepmother. It

FIGURE 2.2   "The Orphan Milliners,"
Illuminated Magazine 2 (April 1844): 279.

is not until the reader is halfway through that Susan Fry appears, offering the orphaned young woman a place to stay when she ventures to London—and it is only in the final eighth that Fry tells her story. Interestingly, even in a document that professes to be a true confession, the need for further documentation exists: before Fry reveals her own history, she tries to convince the young woman that one cannot survive on the wages made by sewing, stating that "some of the needle-girls, dear, don't earn four shillings a week, work as they will" (10). An asterisk follows the statement, and the note at the bottom "confirms" the statement using an excerpt from a court proceeding that details the earnings of a woman accused of theft (pawning some of her materials).

II

A close examination of the portraits of the seamstress presented in early literary works shows the development of patterns of characterization and plot that run throughout the two decades of literature concerning needle-women. Foremost among these are background, working and living conditions, and final ramifications. Although no presentation is an exact copy of the one preceding it, the similarities are unmistakable: the typical fictional seamstress is young, often around sixteen years of age; of the middle-class, but impoverished; from the country; and with no feminine role model (her mother is either dead or ineffective). The young woman usually boards at the millinery establishment, but occasionally lives with her family and walks to and from work, inevitably unescorted. She usually works with women who have been worn down morally by the job—as evidenced by drinking, innuendo, and the reading of "immoral" books—and is often held up to ridicule because she clings to her high moral standards. The needle-woman is subjected to long hours; at least once is she shown working several days without sleep, in an unpleasant room, with little or no break for meals. Often she has a friend who, unable or unwilling to continue under such conditions, falls into prostitution in the hopes of a better life—although it is occasionally the protagonist, rather than a friend, who becomes a prostitute. In the end, weakened by the long hours, poor ventilation, and poor food, the young woman usually dies. A good example, almost synoptic in its brevity, is "The Dressmaker's Apprentices; A Tale of Woman's Oppression," a short story (less than two pages) that appeared in Lloyd's Penny Weekly Miscellany in 1844. In the course of the story every common element can be found, almost as if the author had a list.

Many of the similarities in presentation arise from the affinity of purpose: the desire to bring the plight of the seamstress before the public and to incite some type of reform. In the early works it was especially important to gain the attention and the sympathy of the readers. In later works the background of the seamstress is often ambiguous, even occasionally working class, but the earliest works are very clear concerning the background of the young women. In *A London Dressmaker's Diary,* the young woman's mother has died some years earlier; her family has a servant at home, but no money to send a younger brother to school. Ellen Cardan in *The Young Milliner* is sixteen years old, an orphan from an impoverished family of good social class. She is educated, but not sufficiently to be a governess. In *The Pageant,* Lucy Brooke is encountered only once, and then only briefly, as she is already dying of consumption. But it is made clear that she is of good social standing and a personal acquaintance of Walter Blunt, a wealthy landholder in Nottingham and brother of Lady Blondeville, around whose daughters and their gradual social awakening the story focuses. In *The Wrongs of Woman,* the two sisters—Ann, age seventeen, and Frances, age fifteen—are the daughters of a small farmer who has suffered some financial losses. And although their mother is alive, she never intervenes in the story—indeed, her only mention is as a frugal wife. Two sisters also appear in *The Orphan Milliners*; Henrietta, the elder, is, at nineteen, older than her literary predecessors, but her sister, Annie, is only fourteen years old. It is implied that the girls are of the middle class, both through the description of their lives before the death of their mother and by the fact that they have a wealthy cousin who provides the premiums for their apprenticeships and later provides Henrietta with her own shop. As in *The Young Milliner,* when it is decided that the girls must work, a position as a governess is first suggested, but neither sister has the education necessary. Needlework is then given as the only acceptable occupation. By focusing on middle-class women who work out of economic necessity, early writers were appealing to audiences, particularly feminine audiences, on two levels: presenting needlewomen as part of the "deserving poor," who merited both concern and help, and playing on readers' fears arising from the economic uncertainty of the period.

Just as the similarities in background arose from the authors' common desire to stimulate sympathy and interest in the protagonist, so the common desire to bring about reform created similarities in the descriptions of working and living conditions. A foremost concern of these writers was the long hours needlewomen had to work, particularly during the main social season, which ran from March through July, but also during the smaller one that occurred during November and December. In *The Wrongs of Woman*, Ann King has to work until two in the morning her first day in the millinery shop. And Toulmin's Henrietta receives a similar first-night education when she overhears two milliners preparing for bed after working until two o'clock: "'Poor Bessy!' said one, alluding to the girl who lay dressed upon the bed; 'two nights has she been up: thought she would have fallen asleep over that fancy ball dress. Well, I suppose our turn will come before the week is out; for though it is not the season, and I call it a shame to have such "long hours," *she* won't have "day hands" for this country order, so what is to be done?'" (281). The solution presented at the end, day hands, is undercut by the overall acceptance of the problem, creating a sense of helpless inevitability. The presentation of suffering young women who need help is a conscious design intended to appeal to a female readership which, because of its purchasing power, could affect a change.

In *The Young Milliner* late nights are shown to be a common occurrence; from the first, Ellen is shown having to work through the night in order to have a garment ready the next morning (68–71). And, like Toulmin's Henrietta, even early in the season Ellen must work without sleep. "'Though the season is not at the height, we have sat up three whole nights every week for some weeks past, and worked eighteen or twenty hours the other days'" (122), she explains to her friends Bessie and Mrs. Lambert, who are themselves slopworkers. At this point Stone points out the real cause of the seamstresses' hardships: the customers. Ellen continues her explanation:

> "Madame Mineau is not to blame . . . she cannot refuse the work; she dare not disoblige her customers."
> "Who is to blame, then?"
> "Why the ladies themselves. You cannot imagine, Bessie, how unreasonable they are; how little thought they have for us.
> ". . . they will delay ordering a dress till the last day, when they have known for weeks they should want it; and if Madame Mineau does but venture the most gentle and respectful remonstrance—oh! they step into their carriage at once, and drive to Madame Pelerin's or Mrs. Mode's, who have too much wit to demur . . ."
> "Yes: but the ladies do not know that."
> "They *must* know it, Bessie. Two or three ladies come together,—on a Saturday, perhaps,—and each order a dress, a full trimmed dress, and they must have them on Monday. . . ."
> "They don't think about it."

"They *ought* to think about it: they *ought* to think that if they— often unnecessarily—delay their orders till their milliner has as much work as she can do in the time . . ." (122–25)

Stone's assessment is supported by the 1843 *Second Report,* which recounts numerous instances of young women working through the night with little or no nourishment, occasionally for more than one night. According to the testimony of one dressmaker, "The two causes to which the present evils are to be referred are—1. The short time which is allowed by ladies to have their dresses made. 2. The disinclination of the employers to have sufficient hands to complete the work" (14:208). Emphasizing the impact of last-minute orders is a deliberate tactic by women writers appealing to a feminine audience. The placing of orders at millinery shops was one area in which women could actively participate in improving the working conditions of other women. Further, during the Victorian era, women were seen as the moral and spiritual guides for their families and, through the male figures they guided, for society. The responsibility of one class of women for the suffering of another class of women for morally questionable reasons such as pride and avarice was an issue sure to pique the interest of Victorian readers.

Similar arguments concerning the thoughtlessness of clients are presented in Paget's *The Pageant* and Tonna's *The Wrongs of Woman.* These writers, like Stone, place much of the responsibility on the women who patronize the shops, as Ann King's explanation to her doctor demonstrates:

> "It was in all the papers, sir, weeks and weeks before; and the time was fixed; but as some change might happen in the last fashions, the orders were put off to the latest; and then they were offered to those that would undertake them in the least time. A house employed by the family scrupled to break through Sunday, and wanted to begin a day sooner; but it would not suit, and Madame A. was delighted to undertake it. Such things as this are what give us the last blow when we are greatly weakened." (Tonna, *Wrongs,* 406)

Although Paget approaches the story from the perspective of the aristocratic young woman who visits the millinery house, his presentation is no less damning. A last-minute order is taken and, despite grave illness, Lucy Brooke is forced to work through the night, since the order is for the daughter of the woman who had obtained the apprenticeship for Lucy.

When Lucy subsequently dies of consumption, the young woman is forced to acknowledge that her thoughtlessness helped destroy the milliner's health. Toulmin presents a similar scenario in *The Orphan Milliners,* and again it is clearly the thoughtlessness of the client that is faulted, with an aside to the reader stressing the responsibility of women who order from millinery houses:

> "At a word, Madame Dobiere," said a fashionable looking personage,—"at a word, will you, or will you not, promise me the dress by six o'clock to-morrow?"
>
> "Really," exclaimed Madame in a hesitating manner, "really—I don't know—the time is so very short—if I had only had it yesterday"—
>
> "Oh! very well," returned the lady—"I would not be disappointed on any account. And I have no doubt Mrs. P—can make it up for me; in fact, I have been very particularly recommended to try her."
>
> "Well, ma'am," interrupted Madame Dobiere, dreading that her rival would take away a customer, "to oblige you, ma'am, I will undertake it—but I assure you we must work half the night."
>
> "Oh! nonsense, you always say that; I am sure I have often had a dress made up in less than four and twenty hours."
>
> Probably she had; and probably it never occurred to the thoughtless woman ... that she had on such occasions done her part in wearing out not only silks and satins, but youth, health, and life.... [A]nd well do I believe that many who seem cruel, are only—thoughtless. Alas! I fear that those among us who judge ourselves the most considerate, have sins of this kind, both of omission and commission, for which we must answer. (282–83)

The use of direct address to discuss responsibility, and the didacticism that deals not only with the practical aspects of social issues but also with the spiritual and moral ramifications, are uniquely feminine techniques in nineteenth-century fiction, and are frequently encountered in early seamstress literature.[4]

Along with the long hours, the workroom and sleeping conditions were addressed by authors. There are frequent references to the close confinement or stuffiness of the workroom in *The Young Milliner.* Tonna, however, is more specific:

... the accumulated breath of about thirty persons in a room, not indeed small for that number, but badly ventilated, together with the broad rays of sunshine streaming through the windows, and making visible a cloud of subtle dust ... [and at twilight] the blaze of gas-lights is shed upon every corner of the room, and with the increased heat comes the indescribable oppression, the giddiness, and nausea, produced by the fumes of gas in a confined, low-roofed space ... (403)

The description comes from an uninformed observer, Ann, during her first day at Madame A's. The next morning yet another concern about the lack of ventilation is presented: "Many [of the seamstresses] are suffering from asthma, and confirmed, advanced consumption, attended with bad coughs, the air respired by them must become foetid to a degree at once loathsome and injurious to the yet healthy victim of such influences." The unhealthy atmosphere is compounded by the fact that the seamstresses must sleep three to a bed (404). Again, Stone and Tonna based their presentation on testimony published in the 1843 *Second Report*: one woman who had been a milliner for several years and worked in four different establishments testified that "all the workwomen, in the season about 50, work in one large room. In the season, with the sun in the day, and the lamps at night, this place is extremely hot and oppressive. Several young persons have fainted at their work" (14:207). Other women spoke of the crowded, communal sleeping areas, with accommodations ranging from "4 or 5 young persons in the same sleeping-room" to an establishment where the women sleep in two rooms over a stable with eighteen in one room and ten in the other, "with only one window" (14:225, 226). For middle-class Victorians, the lack of privacy implicit in these descriptions would be almost as horrifying as the obviously unhealthy conditions under which women worked and lived.

Of equal or greater concern to authors were the moral conditions of the workplace. Exposure to drinking, innuendo, and questionable literature, and improper advances by men, were prime concerns. At other times walking unescorted to and from work, or even to and from church, leaves the seamstress open to unacceptable advances by men. The young woman in *A London Dressmaker's Diary* is exposed to drinking and gossip; when she refuses to participate she is branded a "little Methodist" and becomes an object of ridicule for the others. Less specific, but nonetheless damning in its implications, is Paget's behind-the-scenes look at the millinery shop in *The Pageant*:

> It was about ten o'clock in the morning of the day succeeding that on which our tale commences that a large, coarse-looking woman, haggard, and unwashed, with a dirty cap on her head, her hair *en papillotes,* and an old red silk shawl thrown over her shoulders, and partly obscuring a cotton gown of a large vulgar, tawdry pattern, entered the show-room at Mademoiselle Angelique's with a basket of the choicest flowers from Covent Garden market.... but the sweet smell of roses and lilies of the valley by no means overpowered the strong odour of brandy, with which the lady's own person was redolent....
>
> Does the reader desire to know who this person was? She was no other than ... the real proprietress of that establishment, which was nominally Mademoiselle Angelique's. (84–85)

The unspoken assumption is that a young woman could not work and live in an establishment owned by a woman of such questionable morality and remain morally strong herself.

Although Ellen in *The Young Milliner* is not exposed to drinking, she is often subjected to unwanted male advances—at a client's home, on the streets, and at work. Stone describes in some detail how an unscrupulous man could make life difficult for a seamstress. When Ellen is fitting Miss Godfrey at her home, the girl's father, although he does nothing specifically offensive, acts in a manner that makes Ellen uncomfortable and causes the younger men present to exchange "looks of disgust and contempt" (62). He has his valet investigate her background and later has her followed. At one point, when Mr. Godfrey accompanies his daughter to the millinery shop, he makes Ellen extremely self-conscious by fixing his "bold gaze" on her, and this awareness brings "a painful consciousness of a *double entendre* in Mr. Godfrey's remarks" (112, 113). But when Ellen asks to be released from serving Miss Godfrey in the future, Madame Mineau informs her:

> "A *modiste* must not mind trifles.... [Y]ou must expect to meet constant vexation from the caprice, the unreasonableness, and the total want of consideration, of people of fashion: and I could have told you then ... that there are other mortifications to which young dress-makers are too frequently subjected, and to which your pretty face would render you peculiarly liable.... [I]t is nonsense to conceal from you that your beauty will expose you to

many a bold gaze and fulsome compliment. It cannot be helped: good customers must not be offended." (118)

As Stone also reveals, although slopworkers did not deal directly with clients, lack of work and poor wages for what work was available made slopworkers even more susceptible to male advances than the women employed in millinery shops. In the case of Bessie and Mrs. Lambert, despite twenty years' experience on the part of Mrs. Lambert, the two women are not able to earn enough through sewing to feed themselves. When Bessie finally gives in to Mr. Godfrey's advances, it is with the understanding that her mother will receive enough money to buy food and avoid the workhouse.

In *The Wrongs of Woman*, Ann King is also exposed to undesirable and possibly compromising influences while working in a millinery shop. In this case, however, the influence is literature rather than male clients. While the women work they are read "a tale . . . where murder, and violence, and situations of fearful peril, and bursts of unbridled passion, at the expense of filial and conjugal duty, make up the exciting compound . . . a moral poison [which] sinks deep into their minds" (404). Like her predecessor Ellen Cardan, Ann has the moral strength to withstand temptation; not so her sister.

Frances King is also exposed to an immoral environment, one that eventually leads her to a fall into prostitution. Because Frances has a good eye for color, each day she is sent, unescorted, to a variety of merchants throughout London in order to match fabrics. She tells her father, "'If you see the sights and hear the sounds that I am forced to hear and see in the streets of London every day, you will think a modest girl could hardly be much lower abased'" (410). Her sister, Ann, agrees: "'She has been greatly exposed, by being sent out to the shops constantly, and has got too much accustomed to the flattering, familiar talk of the young men in that line. The gentlemen I heard of are quite of a different rank, and more dangerous to a girl so much off her guard'" (413). The problem is compounded by the fact that Frances is turned out every Sunday without a meal or a place to go, even in bad weather. She spends her Sundays with friends, and it is through these friends that Frances experiences "the temporary renovation that wine and other stimulating drinks supply" (414). Eventually her indentures of apprenticeship are canceled, within six months of expiration, and she is left with no hope of securing another position. After a short period as a slopworker, making shirts for three-halfpence, she becomes a prostitute in order to live.

Another concern for the early writers of works about women in urban millinery establishments was the seemingly inevitable destruction facing the needlewomen, either through fatal illness or prostitution. Many of the seamstresses interviewed for the 1843 *Second Report* spoke of women forced to leave the profession because of illness, and some who testified were ill themselves. Grainger remarks that when he met one woman at her home with her medical attendant: "She was in a most alarming state of illness, with symptoms of typhus fever. . . . [S]uch was her state that it seemed as if I were taking not her evidence, but her dying declaration. It is very doubtful if she will recover" (14:225). Grainger interviewed physicians who had worked with seamstresses as well. Particularly distressing was the testimony of Frederic Tyrrell, a surgeon to the London Ophthalmic Hospital, who discussed the dangers of excessive work in poor conditions. He argued that work with little rest, in poor light, was debilitating to a number of women; but much of his testimony focused on the harmful effects of working on mourning clothes. To illustrate his point, he told of a seventeen-year-old patient suffering from a total loss of vision, whose recovery he believed to be hopeless:

> The immediate cause of the disease in the eye was excessive and continued applications to making mourning. She stated that she had been compelled to remain without changing her dress for nine days and nights consecutively: that during this period she had been permitted only occasionally to rest on a mattress placed on the floor for an hour or two at a time; and that her meals were placed at her side, cut up, so that as little time as possible should be spent in their consumption. (233–34)

Thus it is not surprising that complaints about headaches and vision problems are common in seamstress literature, with one of the most effective portrayals of these maladies appearing a few years later in Elizabeth Gaskell's *Mary Barton*.

The format of *A London Dressmaker's Diary* presents an unusual opportunity to show the mental, as well as the physical, condition of a young woman in the millinery profession. The 10 November entry, almost five weeks into the diary, reveals the weary, confused mind of the seamstress:

> I am weak to such a degree as to be always tired. . . . Sewing stitch after stitch is not work for the mind; yet whenever it goes away, it is called back to attend to the everlasting repetition of the same. What can I do? . . . And the vagaries of my mind because its healthy

exertion is impossible! I believe I am not an idiot, only because I don't believe the things I fancy to be real! But may I not do so in time? I have already begun to take no notice of real things! I already laugh and cry at my own *things*! What makes idiots? They seem to believe and *see* what they only imagine. Long imprisonment makes people idiots—that is for want of mental employment—then I am getting to be an idiot! How shall I know when I am?—I dare not look at my father's chair for fear I should see him sitting in it: then I should know! (716)

Two weeks later, in her 25 November entry, the seamstress's depression and confusion reach such a point that she questions the reason for her own existence:

I will only write every other day. When I think of something to say, I get melancholy, for it's always the same thing: sewing, out of breath, cold, tired. Here is my life: I will ask it—Why did God make me? If I was made for the life I now lead, why have I more faculties than are needful for it?—I have been walking about the room a little, and now I almost feel inclined to scratch out the last lines. They frighten me. They shall stand, however; for they are true; and the matter rather concerns me. (718)

The final entry is dated six days later. The dressmaker can stand it no longer; she has written her father and is returning home.

In contrast to the almost immediate mental and physical breakdown shown in *A London Dressmaker's Diary*, *The Young Milliner* depicts the gradual—measured in months and years rather than days and weeks—breakdown of health caused by the long hours and unhealthy environment. For Ellen Cardan the first signs of illness pass almost unnoticed because they "had, as yet, no retarding effect on her usefulness" (288). The symptoms, however, soon become more marked: "Her hands became fevered, her lips parched, and her cheeks were sometimes deeply flushed, at others deadly pale, save a round spot on the cheek bone. Sometimes her breathing would seem affected, and she would almost gasp for a few minutes, and then burst out into an hysterical fit of crying, which would relieve her" (337–38). Finally Ellen experiences a fainting spell so severe that a surgeon must be called to revive her. The next day, having returned to work, she is startled and again swoons. Her condition is summed up in a letter from an old family friend to Ellen's minister at home: "'her friends ... have found her out too late, for it's little I know of things if she is not in a fast consumption'" (380–81). The assessment of Ellen's condition proves to be correct.

One of the strongest presentations of the hazardous conditions in millinery houses occurs in Tonna's *The Wrongs of Woman*. In the millinery shop where Ann King is apprenticed "many are suffering from asthma, and confirmed, advanced consumption, attended with bad coughs" (404). After six months Ann, complaining of severe pain in her side and back, sees a doctor: "'I was a strong, healthy girl when I came to town, as good as fourteen months ago; but coming at the season, I was forced to work immediately as hard as the oldest hands. It wore me out. I soon began to lose my appetite: I was too tired to sleep at nights; I had pain in the back, and shoulders, and limbs'" (406). When she again visits the doctor, after another six months, her condition is much worse. She tells the doctor: "'The pain, sir, in my chest is constant. I must stoop, because it seems to relieve the great pains in the shoulder blades; but stooping certainly makes my breath shorter. Palpitation of the heart comes on if I only change my altitude, or speak; and a mist is over my eyes, and choking in my throat and a very great sickness.... Then there is such a headache! grievous racking pains in the limbs, and you may see my right shoulder blade is growing out'" (406). Early writers did not exaggerate the frequency of death by consumption, as Edwin Chadwick's *Report on the Sanitary Condition of the Labouring Population of Great Britain,* published in 1842, demonstrates:

Deaths from Disease of Milliners and Dressmakers, in the Metropolitan Unions during the Year 1839, As Shown by the Mortuary Registers

Age	Number of Deaths	Average Age	Number of Deaths from Consumption	Average Age	Number of Deaths from Other Lung Diseases	Average Age
Under 20	6	17	4	18	—	—
20 to 29	24	24	17	23	1	33
30 to 39	11	34	6	34	1	33
40 to 49	2	45	—	—	1	40
50 to 59	4	54	1	58	2	55
60 to 69	5	64	—	—	—	—
Totals	52	32	28	26	5	41

NOTE: Out of fifty-two deaths in the year, forty-one of the deceased attained an age of twenty-five. The average age of the thirty-three who died of lung disease was twenty-eight.
SOURCE: Chadwick, 176.

Thus of the fifty-two milliners and dressmakers who were reported to have died in the Metropolitan Unions, thirty-three died of lung diseases, and twenty-eight died specifically of consumption. The average age of the seamstresses who died of consumption was twenty-six.

But there were health problems besides consumption and blindness. When Ann, in *The Wrongs of Woman,* begins working at the millinery shop she notices that the posture of the shop supervisor, the advanced hand, is deformed, but does not realize that spinal distortion is a common result of work in the millinery profession and one that, like consumption, she too will suffer. In the "Consequences" chapter of *The Wrongs of Woman,* Tonna verifies her presentation with medical testimony from the 1843 *Second Report:* "Distortion of the spine, and consequent projection of one shoulder, are very common" (416). Similarly, the women of Toulmin's *The Orphan Milliners* are all "pale and thin . . . many had weak eyes, and not a few suffered from distortions of the spine" (281).

III

A final concern for many of the early novelists, particularly women novelists, was the role other women played in the working conditions of seamstresses, and what role women could play in changing those conditions. In the closing chapter of "Dressmakers and Milliners," in *The Wrongs of Woman,* Tonna directly addresses her audience, asking them to encourage the owners of millinery shops to improve conditions, even if it means sacrifices on the part of patrons. Stone makes a similar address to women in the introduction to *The Young Milliner:*

> Fashionable ladies,—individually kind and good, and exemplary,— are collectively the cause of infinite misery to the young and unprotected of their own sex. Of the existence even of this misery, they are, it may well be believed, scarcely aware; of its frightful extent, utterly unconscious.
>
> Should this Narrative meet their sight, it is hoped that its appeal to their sympathy will not be made in vain. (ii)

Tonna believed that women could also influence conditions through their relationship with those in power—men. In the *Christian Lady's Magazine* she chastises her readers:

It is not that people can do nothing, but that they are not sufficiently roused to attempt doing any thing in the matter. . . . If a
lady on reading your pages finds her heart moved to go to some
male relation or friend who will listen kindly to her plea . . . [l]et
her take pen and paper, and simply set forth the fact that the
undersigned petitioners earnestly desire to call the attention of the
Honourable House to the deplorable conditions of the labourers
employed in our manufacturing districts. (17:285)

By presenting the female reader of *The Wrongs of Woman* with testimony
gathered by male parliamentary investigators, including male physicians,
Tonna was giving her reader the arguments and evidence necessary to persuade possible male skeptics. Thus upper- and middle-class women were
regarded as the main target of many writers of the early literature concerning seamstresses. The authors urged readers either to actively intervene
by boycotting houses that were known to subject seamstresses to harsh
conditions or to passively intervene by influencing male friends and relatives serving in Parliament.

Toulmin's approach to the role women could play in alleviating the conditions faced by seamstresses is different from her predecessors'. Although
she acknowledges the problems caused by the thoughtless client, they are
glossed over rather than stressed. For Toulmin, the women to be swayed
into reform are the owners of millinery establishments, for they are the
ones who actually make the decisions as to the amount of work done, the
hours kept, and the conditions under which the young women must live.
Although Tonna also deals with shop owners, her emphasis is different:
Tonna places the impetus for action with the client who would boycott the
shop, while Toulmin is concerned with the owner who would voluntarily
change the working conditions. The presentation of the call for change also
differs, for rather than breaking away from the narrative to urge reforms
as Tonna does, Toulmin makes her case in the story, concluding with the
image of the ideal shop owner: "Henrietta has been three years in business,
is considered the favourite milliner of L—, and is noted for her extreme
indulgence to the young people in her employ,—regulating their hours of
work, and making her arrangements with every regard to their health and
happiness" (285). Henrietta is thus established as a model to be followed,
and contrasted with the earlier, unfavorable portrayal of Madame Dobiere.
And the shift from overt pronouncements of responsibility and duty to the
more subtle inclusion of role models in the narrative carries over to later

novels. The presentation marks, in fact, the start of semiosis, with the "literal" meaning being frustrated and a "figurative" meaning being generated. The lack of overt references to factual materials, combined with the depiction of Henrietta as an idealized figure rather than an actual shop owner, would move Toulmin's story from a literal presentation to a figurative one. Further, readers are required to move a step beyond the literal because of the intertextual nature of seamstress narratives and artwork—with one work building on the information and images from previous works, with an artist writing or drawing, not from experience or testimony, but based on his or her predecessors' ways of textualizing experience or testimony.

The first truly paradigmatic presentation, though, occurred a few months before Toulmin's *The Orphan Milliners,* with Paget's *The Pageant.* Although concerned with the abuse of millinery workers, like many of the male writers who followed him, Paget shows equal or greater concern for other workers, in this case particularly those involved with mining. When Uncle Wat, the voice of reason in the story, visits with his niece, he expresses concern for the young milliner he sent to London under his sister's care; however, his discussion with his niece centers not on needlewomen, but on the sufferings of colliery workers. In fact, in the story itself, all but one of the notes referring to parliamentary reports deal with the investigation of women and children working in the collieries. (Paget does, however, append fifteen pages of testimony regarding London milliners to the end of the novel.) The implication is that the suffering and death of Lucy Brooke, the young seamstress, is but a minor representation of the general suffering of the working poor. The system of relationships that connects the seamstress to other workers signals the recognition of the possibility of using the seamstress as a paradigm for the working classes as a whole. Furthermore, *The Pageant* plays an important role in the history of social protest fiction generally: on 15 June 1844 Paget was tried for libel based on a statement he made in the introduction to his novel.[5] Within the introduction Paget had included excerpts of a letter whose source he refused to name. And so, despite the support of influential figures such as Lord Ashley, Paget lost his case. The extensive coverage in the press ensured that other writers were aware of Paget's trouble and the need for caution when writing about situations reported to them by others.

Another early work linking seamstresses with other workers is Tonna's *The Wrongs of Woman.* Although the presentations are literal rather than figurative, with dressmaking shown to be one of several occupations that abuse women and children, Tonna nevertheless continues to make the association between the "respectable" trade of dressmaking and other labor she first made in *Perils of the Nation*. Not only are the workers in the four sections of *The Wrongs of Woman* linked by geography, being from the same village, but there are cross-references among the stories and a number of formal links, such as the detailing of a typical day, recurring characters, and a concluding chapter of evidence gleaned from parliamentary sources. Drawing from her experiences in writing *Perils of the Nation* and an earlier industrial novel, *Helen Fleetwood*, Tonna supports her stories with documentation, including an evidential final chapter for each section: "Consequences" (part 1), "Corroborating Evidence" (part 2), "Authentications" (part 3), and "The Finale" (part 4). Also uniting the four sections are the types of occupations examined; each involves a non-textile industry investigated for the 1843 *Second Report*: dressmaking (part 1), screw-driving (part 2), pin-heading (part 3), and lace-running (part 4).

For Tonna, however, the most important link is that of the workers who are portrayed: women and children. According to Tonna, she is addressing "actual wrongs" (399) against those who she believes have been exploited in the name of progress, leading her to "repudiate all pretensions to equality with man" (397). As she concludes the work, Tonna's admonishment to her readers again unites the four sections, linking the impoverished middle-class seamstresses of the first section with the working-class women and children of the later sections:

> Ladies of England! under such circumstances as we have laid before you, are the materials of your daily attire prepared by manufacture and embroidery, the articles made up by dress-makers and milliners, and the very pins with which you secure them, formed to answer the purpose. At such price you make your toilet—we have gone no further than that one branch of the almost numberless productions of British industry, and we will not wrong you by any appeal—if such FACTS do not speak, all language is utterly in vain. (501–2)

The clothing image that unites the four chapters also links readers with characters. For as her title indicates, Tonna's concerns are the wrongs working women suffer at the hands of others, especially women, and what readers, especially women, can do to improve the conditions of these workers.

IV

While content was a major issue, writers of these early works were also concerned with the presentation of their material. The narrative of *A London Dressmaker's Diary* is marked by its unique and, for the time, radical attempt to capture the mental condition of needlewomen through an early form of stream of consciousness. While none of the other early narratives attempts anything so revolutionary, there are still signs of crafting, such as Tonna's attempt to unite four narratives involving the non-textile and needlework industries through the use of a common village in *The Wrongs of Woman*. As the narrator explains: "Wishing to avoid the admixture of fictitious narrative, yet to realize, as far as possible, the various situations in which female labourers are placed, we will suppose the inhabitants of a small hamlet in one of the midland counties, and not far from a town of considerable traffic, placing out their girls to such employments as their respective circumstances may render advisable or practicable" (399).

But one of the strongest indications of crafting is found in Stone's use of gradation in *The Young Milliner*. In the text are two alternating sets of comparison: Marian Godfrey and Ellen Cardan, and Ellen Cardan and Bessie Lambert. Together the three women form a spectrum with the rich but unthinking Miss Godfrey at one end, the desperately poor and misguided Bessie at the other end, and Ellen, who is poor but not starving, innocent rather than ignorant, as the mediating figure. An example of Stone's technique occurs at the close of chapter 6, with the abrupt juxtapositioning of Ellen and Marian at four o'clock one morning:

Twenty-five over-worked girls, with pale faces, heavy eyes, and aching limbs, threw down their work with a gesture of delight, and rushing to the table where the tea had been placed, bent eagerly over it, and sipped the homely beverage as if it were nectar. And sighing, as they replaced the emptied cups on the tray, they slowly returned to their places, snuffed the candles, and resumed their sewing.

Just then Miss Godfrey rejected the chocolate which her maid brought her.

"It is not good: it is very strange that they should make it so carelessly. . . ."

"I'm too much tired for any thing, . . . take care that the shutters and curtains are quite closed, that the light may not waken me: and don't come near me until I ring." (84–85)

Although jarring, the contrast is carefully made: Miss Godfrey has just returned from an event at which she wore a dress that Ellen and the other needlewomen had finished only the night before. Both have a warm drink; but for the needlewomen it is only a brief respite during a night in which they will get no sleep. For Miss Godfrey, on the other hand, it is an expected pleasure before a long and peaceful sleep. This abrupt collision of images is further emphasized by stylistic differences: the longer, frequently modified sentences describing the seamstresses echo their long evening of meticulous work, while the clipped, almost staccato diction of the sentences involving Miss Godfrey emphasize the childishness and careless energy of the idle rich.

This section of *The Young Milliner* contains an early version of what was to become a familiar contrast—the pampered client and the wretched seamstress. The image would be immortalized visually by works such as Richard Redgrave's "Fashion's Slaves" (1847) and *Punch*'s "Pin Money/ Needle Money" (1849) and "The Haunted Lady, or 'The Ghost' in the Looking Glass" (1863). Creating an ideological complex, a set of contradictory images with common bases used to subvert social hierarchies, these works often force readers to perform specific semiotic tasks.[6] Readers were expected to recognize the pun in "Pin Money/Needle Money," or understand that the plurality of Redgrave's *slaves* implies a lack of freedom on the part of the patron as well as the seamstress, or comprehend that the oppositions of ideological complex in the *Pictorial Times*'s "Slaves of the Needle" are also there by absence—the lack of men in the workroom as compared with the presence of men at the ball. Such contrasts also function as a major structural device in literary works such as Charles Rowcroft's *Fanny, the Little Milliner* and Reynolds's *The Seamstress*. As Kathleen Tillotson has argued,

> The "condition of the people," seen in the sharply antithetical terms of the "two nations," whether simply "rich and poor" or "employers and employed"—this theme came more and more to occupy novelists in the forties. Most novel-readers belonged to the other nation; the novelists were scouts who had crossed the frontier (or penetrated the iron curtain) and brought back their reports. . . . And always, the novelist reached readers unaware of government publications. (81)

And with these later writers there is a shift from interest in the seamstress herself to an interest in the working poor generally. Direct comparisons between the women of the two groups provided an effective measuring stick for reformers.

There is a discernible progression to the form taken by the early literature concerning seamstresses. First is the anonymous presentation of conditions in *A London Dressmaker's Diary* in November 1842, accurate but unsupported by any outside evidence, using only the genre—that of the diary—to lend credence to the narrative. Like *Diary*, Stone's *The Young Milliner* was written before the publication of the 1843 *Second Report;* but since the publication of the novel in 1843 followed that of the *Report,* Stone was able to add citations of the *Report* to support anything she thought her readers might question. And, unlike the author of *A London Dressmaker's Diary,* Stone follows up her description of conditions with a direct address to her readers giving possible solutions to the problems faced by seamstresses. Paget then combines the two techniques in *The Pageant,* using personal testimony in the introduction and excerpts from parliamentary reports in the story and its appendices; however, the introduction of workers from other occupations and the implied comparison of those workers with needlewomen indicates a move from the realistic toward the symbolic. A carefully documented call for action on the part of women who frequented millinery houses soon followed, with the publication of "Milliners and Dressmakers," part 1 of Tonna's *The Wrongs of Woman,* at the end of 1843. The subsequent publication of the remaining sections carried forward the alignment of the seamstress with the working poor. Finally, with the publication of Toulmin's *The Orphan Milliners* in 1844, the seamstress narrative moves to the presentation of conditions using neither the diary form nor documentation to ensure validity, and with no direct address to the reader calling for reform. Instead, narrative technique is used to create verisimilitude, and characters are used as role models, allowing the discourse to move from mimesis to diegesis.

V

Thomas Hood's "The Song of the Shirt," the "most famous blow for the downtrodden" (Price, 46), and considered by many to mark the beginning of seamstress literature, did not appear in *Punch* until December 1843, after the publication of numerous articles and four of the five fictional works listed above.[7] However, the impact of the poem was immense: its publication is said to have trebled the circulation of *Punch,* ensuring the new magazine's success (Spielman, 332–33). Moreover, it was quoted in nearly every paper, beginning with the *Times*, printed as catch pennies, dramatized, set to music, and even printed on handkerchiefs.

Most scholars trace Hood's interest in the seamstress to a 26 October 1834 *Times* police report on "a wretched-looking woman named Biddell, with a squalid, half-starved infant at her breast."[8] Contracted to sew trousers for Henry Moses, a slopseller, at seven pence a pair, out of which she had to supply her own needles and thread, Biddell had pawned several completed articles in order to buy some "dry bread" for herself and her two young children. In a second case before the same magistrate, and also reported by the *Times* that day, a "smartly-dressed" woman demanded the arrest of a young woman for pawning some shirts she had contracted to make for one pence each. The next day the *Times* ran a long leader and an article, "The White Slaves of London," both expressing outrage at the situations of these women. According to the leader, Biddell would have to work ninety-six hours a week, "16 hours every week-day, or nearly 14 hours every day including Sunday," to earn the "good living" of seven shillings—which Moses's foreman defended to the magistrate. Upbraid-ing the rich for "scandalously neglect[ing] their duty" and the middlemen who made a profit from the work, the leader concluded that a London seamstress was, from "every moral point of view, as much a slave as any negro who ever toiled under as cruel taskmasters in the West Indies" (4). The article presented the reader with a variety of facts concerning typi-cal working hours, conditions, and pay for slopworkers, concluding that "the wretched shirtmakers, in fact, finding they cannot obtain a subsis-tence by the starving wages allowed them, make away with the property, and being unable to redeem it, are either driven upon the streets to add to the hordes of miserable outcasts who infest our thoroughfares, or else become confirmed thieves, and end their days in a penal settlement or a model prison" (4). A week later, *Punch* reprinted the original *Times* report under the title "Famine and Fashion!" and added its own commentary, with the wish:

> Moses and his class were doomed to walk the streets of London arrayed in their choicest "slops" (blood-stained as the shirt of Nes-sus, but without its avenging qualities,) branded
> SEVEN PENCE,
>
> That men might know how they gained their sleekness! (203)

Punch then followed with a poem, "Moses and Co.," that attacks the thoughtless customer shopping for the most beautiful, least expensive garment without reckoning the human cost:

> All who would seek a spotless robe to wear,
> In breathless haste Moses should repair,
> Where *Holland coats* from two-and-three are shown
> By Hunger's haggard fingers neatly sewn.
> *York wrappers* that the Winter's blast defy,
> Made by a shivering wretch *too fond* to die;
> *Dress pantaloons* for Pleasure's gayest court,
> Though all were 'mid stark Desolation wrought;
> *Embroidered tunics* for your infant made,—
> The eyes are sightless now that work'd the braid;
> *Rich vests of velvet* at this mart appear,
> Each one begemm'd by some poor widow's tear;
> And *Riding-habits* form'd for maid and wife,
> All cheap—aye, ladies, cheap as pauper-life.
> For *Mourning suits* this is the fittest mart,
> For every garment help'd to break a heart.
> Then hasten all who mindful of the purse,
> For Moses' bargains braves the poor man's curse. (203)

The next week *Punch* published a review of *The Pride of London*, a book-length poem mocking the fashionable world, which wears clothing manufactured by Moses and Son. The review criticizes the products, customers, and owners, and concludes with a "humble imitation" reminding readers at what price such clothing is made:

> "But yon wretched woman, whose hunger is raging,
>   We'll make, if you please, sir, a sempstress of her."
> So the bargain was struck, and they hastened to get her;
>   She joyfully flew to her needle and thread.
> Said a *Voice*, "You are not the first tailor and sweater,
>   Who've ground down the bones of the poor for their bread."
>
> (249)

A week later, Hood's "The Song of the Shirt" was the lead piece in *Punch*.

Whether these articles and poems were Hood's inspiration, or whether Hood had been documenting the suffering of slopworkers for a number of years before the publication of "The Song of the Shirt" (Clubbe), the poem called attention to needleworkers as nothing else had; it was "perhaps of all poems in the decade the one to make the deepest impact on the largest number of people" (Dodds, 210). Its immediate impact on other writers and artists is demonstrated by Toulmin's use of the refrain in *The Orphan Milliners,* as the story's epigraph and as the caption to the opening illustration, and by Richard Redgrave's genre painting *The Sempstress,* exhibited at the Royal Academy, with lines from the poem in the catalog description, six months after the publication of Hood's poem.

The reaction of various critics to Redgrave's painting further illustrates Victorians' interest in and awareness of the plight of needlewomen (figure 2.3). The *Times* wrote, "the subject of this painting is one particularly of our time; vis, the miseries to which metropolitan needlewomen are subjected,

FIGURE 2.3   *The Sempstress,* Richard Redgrave, 1846. The FORBES Magazine Collection, New York ©All rights reserved.

and the motto is taken from Hood's admirable 'Song of the Shirt'" ("Royal Academy," 70). But the cautious praise of the *Athenaeum* reflects a more accurate view: "We shall on the present occasion further avert to Mr Redgrave's Illustration . . . of 'The Song of the Shirt,' as too sentimental. The real picture from the lyric would be too saddening if painted, and our artist has only reached a sort of theatrical and elegant sorrow" ("Fine Arts," 459). The response of the *Times* critic indicates that, to the Victorians, the suffering seamstress would not have been viewed as an artistic creation, but as a known figure. And, perhaps, the caution voiced in the *Athenaeum*'s review arises because Redgrave's portrait of the lone figure in her desolate attic room is not wholly realistic: a repeated complaint was the overcrowding of workrooms and sleeping areas.[9] In contrast, the illustration for Toulmin's story—with the workroom full of young women, heads bowed in concentration or eyes covered in exhaustion—would have been more familiar and more realistic. As T. J. Edelstein has pointed out, by using a single figure and ignoring the harsh conditions of the workroom Redgrave made "a conscious artistic choice" which "created a stronger empathy" and "clarified the iconology" of works involving the seamstress ("They Sang," 190). The creation of a stylized symbol, recognized by the *Athenaeum,* points up a division in the early portrayals of the seamstress: male writers and artists, especially those who came later, tended to use the seamstress to create stylized, theatrical works in which the needlewoman often functioned as a paradigm for the working classes generally, while female writers and artists of the day usually emphasized the bleak conditions and the role middle-class women played in creating these circumstances, resisting the idea of softening for effect the harsh situations faced by needlewomen.

The Symbolic Image

There is shirt making—baby linen—it's enough to make one smother the first baby one meets to think of it—then there's silk-embroidering, stay-making, dress-making. Then there's a cough, a consumption, a hospital, the parish, and a pauper's funeral. I believe that's some-where about a general catalogue of the whole business.

—James Rymer, *The White Slave*

By 1844 government reports and periodical articles, combined with the publication of *A London Dressmaker's Diary* and the novels of Stone and Tonna, had established the seamstress as a figure of hardship and suffering. Further pathos was created through illustrations such as the *Illuminated Magazine*'s "The Orphan Milliners" and the *Pictorial Times*'s "The Milliners and the Duchesses." And it is at this point that the seamstress was adopted as a symbol for the working classes as a whole. With the exception of Toulmin's *The Orphan Milliners*, in nine literary works dealing with seamstresses that appeared between 1844 and 1848—*The Orphan Milliners, Jessie Phillips,*[1] *The Sempstress, The White Slave, The Chimes,* and *Fanny, the Little Milliner* in 1844;[2] *Libbie Marsh's Three Eras* in June of 1847; and *Whom to Marry* and *Mary Barton* in 1848—the seamstress, although usually appearing as the title character, is shown as an illustration of or a spokesperson for the suffering of those around her, rather than in terms of her own suffering. She had become a working-class paradigm: her condition had become a representation of the condition of all workers.

With the change in focus from the seamstress herself to the larger issue of the working poor came several changes in the figure of the seamstress. Frances Trollope's *Jessie Phillips* serves as a transition from the tales concerning seamstresses and their circumstances to those using seamstresses to illuminate the circumstances of the laboring classes—specifically, in *Jessie Phillips*, the effect of the New Poor Laws on the rural poor, particularly women. A focus on women allows Trollope to begin the movement from the seamstress as an individual to the seamstress as a symbol of a larger group. Many of the common aspects of seamstresses established in the early narratives still appear in *Jessie Phillips*: the young seamstress is still a beautiful girl, with a sick (and therefore ineffective) mother, and is destroyed by the close of the novel. But it is also here that the major change in characterization first appears: Jessie is not of the impoverished middle class, but of the working classes. Yet Trollope appears to be concerned about the change in status, blurring the transition with frequent references to Jessie's "ladylike" nature (a device no longer considered necessary when Dickens published his Christmas story *The Chimes* a few months later).

The change in status is not without exception, however. The seamstress makes a brief return to the upper classes in James Rymer's *The White Slave* and Augustus and Henry Mayhew's *Whom to Marry*, and to the middle class in Charles Rowcroft's *Fanny, the Little Milliner*. But the resurgence is limited to a few novels, primarily written by men. Novelists such as Charlotte Brontë, when writing a work such as *Jane Eyre* (1847), might rely on the early portrayals of seamstresses that had established needlework as a respectable occupation for a middle-class female character.[3] But no attempt at bridging the social levels of subject and reader is made in either of Elizabeth Gaskell's works that followed, *Libbie Marsh's Three Eras* in 1847 or *Mary Barton* in 1848.

As shown in the earlier works, middle-class women who became seamstresses usually worked in large urban millinery shops such as the one depicted in *A London Dressmaker's Diary;* working-class women who worked as seamstresses usually worked out of their homes as slopworkers, as do the Lamberts in *The Young Milliner*. As illustrated both by the Lamberts and by Frances King in *The Wrongs of Woman*, the slopworker had a more difficult time procuring work and worked longer hours and was paid less than her counterpart in the millinery establishment. It was natural, therefore, that when the role of the seamstress changed from the subject to the vehicle of presentation, the type of seamstress also changed.

Thus there is no attempt to present Meg and Lillian in Dickens's *The Chimes* or Libbie Marsh in Gaskell's tale as anything but slopworkers.

I

But it is Richard Redgrave's painting of *The Sempstress* (1844) that first marks the turn from millinery shops to individuals doing piecework.[4] During the period preceding the exhibition of Redgrave's painting at the Royal Academy, the fiction, as well as the periodical reports and illustrations, had all focused on young women working in millinery houses. And while in these works one young woman might be highlighted, either as the main character in a story or as a focal point in an illustration, readers and viewers were always aware that she was but one among hundreds who were suffering—together. Even immediately after the exhibition of Redgrave's painting, R. B. Grindrod published *The Slaves of the Needle* (1845), a recapitulation of the findings of the 1843 Children's Employment Commission hearings, in which he had participated, that focuses on young women employed in millinery establishments. Although Redgrave's decision to isolate his seamstress was probably made for practical and aesthetic reasons rather than ideological ones, his work, nevertheless, was a departure from the established semiotic structure and had an impact on both the iconology and ideology of future representations.[5]

During the first half of the 1840s Redgrave exhibited a number of works portraying women who have been forced by economic circumstances—the death of the father usually is implied—to leave their homes and families: *The Reduced Gentleman's Daughter* (1840), *Going into Service* (1843), *The Poor Teacher* (1843), *The Sempstress* (1844), *The Governess* (1845). In all of these works the young woman is forced to leave the support and protection of her family behind, leaving behind as well the Victorian conception of her ideal place in society, to face an uncertain future without protection— specifically without patriarchal protection. Further, in all of the works the young woman is somehow, whether through placement or dress or lighting, separated from the other figures in the painting. But it is in the two works in which she is the sole figure, *The Poor Teacher* and *The Sempstress,* that her isolation is most effectively iconographic; without the protection of a father, a husband, family, or friends she is truly alone and defenseless. In *The Poor Teacher* Redgrave presented Victorians with a young woman, probably in mourning, alone in her in her small, dark room. She sits with a letter lying neglected in her lap, her eyes downcast and her expression melancholy, suggesting that she is thinking of people and events from the past. Perhaps the success of this work encouraged Redgrave to set his needlewoman alone rather than in a crowded workroom. While the isolation of the figures in *The Poor Teacher* and *The Sempstress* was clearly meant to evoke sympathy or pity from viewers, it also works as an iconographic device.

In *The Sempstress* the role of the patriarchy in the plight of needleworkers is highlighted by the garment the woman is sewing—a man's shirt. What might have been a loving task for wife, daughter, or mother now becomes a foreboding symbol, a circumstance that Redgrave highlights through his choice of quotation for the catalog. Rather than choosing a verse from Thomas Hood's "The Song of the Shirt" that might be seen as describing details from the painting, Redgrave chose the lines:

> Oh! men with sisters dear,
> Oh! men with mothers and wives,
> It is not linen you're wearing out,
> But human creatures' lives.

With these lines he calls attention to those held responsible for the sufferings of needlewomen, male customers, and reminds them that these women could be someone's sister, mother, or wife. While all needlework was underpaid, shirtmaking was notoriously so. That a young woman, who by Victorian standards should be under the protection of men, should die a painful death through starvation or consumption—or worse, fall into prostitution—making garments worn by men creates an irony that touched many Victorians. Fellow artist P. F. Poole wrote Redgrave, "If any circumstance could make me wage war against the present social arrangements, and make us go down shirtless to our graves, it is the contemplation of this truthful and wonderful picture" (Redgrave, *Memoir,* 45). Compounding the irony is the fact that many fathers or male guardians sent young women to work as seamstresses, since needlework was second only to teaching as the socially acceptable occupation for a respectable young woman forced to earn a living.

It is also of note that all of the women Redgrave portrayed in this group of paintings are displaced middle class—the social and economic class associated previously with seamstress literature and illustrations. Thus, although in *The Sempstress* Redgrave moved from the millinery shop to the home, he probably had no intention of changing from middle- to working-class laborer. Periodicals and novels had focused exclusively on economically reduced middle-class women, leading viewers of Redgrave's painting to assume, probably correctly, that the woman pictured was yet another distressed gentlewoman. According to the *Art-Union*, "The story is told in such a way as to approach the best feelings of the human heart: she is not a low-born drudge to proclaim her patient endurance to the vulgar world; her suffering is read only in the shrunken cheek, and the eye feverish and dim with watching" ("Royal Academy," 158). The response is telling. There is little in the painting itself to indicate class status; the room is sparsely furnished, the basin is cracked, a crust of bread is the woman's nourishment, and she is working by the light of a single candle—all indications of poverty but not of class. Nevertheless, the assumption is made that the figure is not "a low-born drudge," but, rather, one of what the Victorians termed the "deserving poor." Redgrave apparently realized, however, that of the various occupations middle-class women might enter, needlework was the most poorly recompensed. In details of setting, clothing, and food, *The Sempstress* delineates a much bleaker life than those portrayed in Redgrave's other works. And, although all the women in Redgrave's series are isolated and melancholy, it is only *The Sempstress* who is shown to be failing physically: her red-rimmed eyes, pale complexion, and gaunt face, combined with the medicine bottle on the mantle, tell viewers of the physical toll her occupation claims.

Whatever Redgrave's intention, and his audience's assumptions, his portraying the lone pieceworker, rather than a worker in a millinery establishment, opened the way for other such portraits. And while the numerous paintings that followed are equally ambiguous concerning social class, Redgrave's work nevertheless opened the door to visual portrayals of a subgroup of needlewomen who were primarily working class. Independent illustrations in magazines such as *Punch* adopted Redgrave's image of the lone worker—and his ambiguity regarding the worker's class. In the 1844 "Exhibition of the English in China," *Punch* uses the catalog for Mr. Dunn's Chinese Exhibition as a model for the creation of an exhibition of "the faces and fashions of the barbarian English . . . from high to low: numbered in cases as at Hyde Park Corner, and a catalogue of our good and bad qualities illuminates the darkened mind of the curious" (219). Among company such as "An English Peer," "The Literary Lord," and "A Member of the House of Commons" is "Case IV—A Sempstress" (figure 3.1). The illustration shows a lone woman sitting bent over, one hand covering her eyes, the other covering her mouth as if she is sobbing, reminiscent of figures in earlier illustrations such as "Slaves of the Needle." Prominently displayed in her lap is a shirt. The sharp angle of the upper-left portion of the sketch suggests the roofline of an attic room, and the table with teapot and cup allude to Redgrave's painting. The commentary accompanying the sketch begins with an ironic description of the healthy constitution of the seamstress and on her place in society, but then shifts to a typical mix of satire and reform highlighting what ladies do not do, but should:

> The women who live by needle and thread amount to many thou-
> sands; and are easily known by the freshness of their complexions
> and the cheerfulness of their manners. Indeed, nothing shows the
> humanity of the barbarians in a more favourable light than the
> great attention which is paid by the rich and high to the com-
> forts of their milliners, dress-makers, and sempstresses. Women of
> noblest title constantly refuse an invitation to parties rather than
> press too hardly upon the time of those who have to make their
> dresses. Indeed, there is what is called a visiting Committee of
> Ladies, who take upon themselves the duty of calling, not only on
> the employers of the needle-women to inquire into the comfort of
> the workers, but of visiting the humble homes of the women them-
> selves to see that they want nothing that may administer to their
> healthy, reasonable recreation. Hence there is a saying in England,
> the life of a sempstress is as the life of a bee; she does nothing but
> sing and make honey. (220)

Although the caption, "Case IV—A Sempstress," separates the sempstress from dressmakers and milliners, suggesting a separate category of worker, the commentary includes references to both milliners and pieceworkers. Visiting employers to inquire about working conditions indicates a focus on the middle-class millinery shop worker, yet visiting homes to see to liv-ing conditions indicates an interest in working-class pieceworkers. But it is the inclusion of the needlewoman in the series—with personages readily tied to national identity, members of the aristocracy and the arts—that attests to her position as a figure who was fascinating to Victorians and readily identified as being English.

Such blurring of classes continues in the artwork into the late 1840s. For example, a few artists develop the iconographic pattern first seen in the *Pictorial Times*'s "The Milliners and the Duchesses," where comparative views of needlewomen and their clients are presented. Some, like John

Leech's "Pin Money/Needle Money" (1849) are straightforward comparisons: on one page a young woman, in a richly appointed room, sits at her cluttered dressing table holding a length of ribbon while her maid arranges her hair; on the facing page a young woman, in a dark, bare room, sits at a table sewing a shirt (figure 3.2). Yet the neatness of the seamstress's attire and her presentation in general point to a more elevated class status than her poverty would indicate, suggesting a comparison based more on economics and character than on birth. Underlying even an obvious comparison, then, is a subtle commentary on the industry of the needlewoman as compared with the indolence of the client, and the warning that social position is not a certainty. The comparison of the two women—the former with full, rounded features and well dressed, the latter with thin, pinched features and thinly clothed—and of their settings is heightened even further by the contrast of light and dark in the two sketches.

A little less obvious is George Cruikshank's comparison in "Tremendous Sacrifice" (1846). Part of the *Our Own Times* series, a collection focusing on the issues of the "Hungry 'Forties," the cartoon shows a seemingly

CASE IV.—A SEMPSTRESS.

FIGURE 3.1   "Exhibition of the English in China—Case IV—A Sempstress," *Punch* 6 (1 June 1844): 220.

unending procession of needlewomen climbing into a huge meat grinder that churns out clothing and is operated by a demonic figure who gleefully watches the march of money bags appearing from under the grinder. Dividing the picture is a curtain, on the other side of which is the "Cheap House" sales room, crowded with women buying garments. Bubble captions provide the ironic commentary, with two seamstresses saying, "I understand that it is impossible to get a liveing [*sic*] at this work." "So I have heard. Never the less, we *must* try." Their conversation is contrasted with the comment of a customer on the other side of the curtain hiding the grinder—"I cannot imagine how they can possibly be made for the price!!" As do many reformers, Cruikshank indicts middle- and upper-class women who search for bargains without counting the human toll.

By far the most subtle comparison is found in Redgrave's *Fashion's Slaves* (1847). Redgrave's choice of an accompanying quotation for *The Sempstress* had first presented the possibility of viewing the seamstress in terms of the employer/employee relationship; in the later work, Redgrave

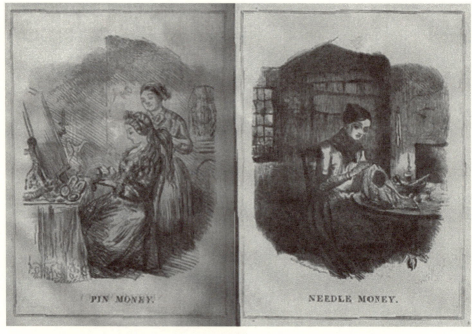

FIGURE 3.2   "Pin Money/Needle Money," John Leech, *Punch* 17 (23 December 1849): 240–41.

visually opposes a demure milliner with an impatient client (and, interestingly, an unsympathetic maid). At contrast are the dark simplicity of the milliner's dress and the white richness of the client's, as well as the lack of color in the dressmaker's face and the healthy pinkness of the client's. But more importantly, the pose of the figures—the upright stance of the dressmaker, head bowed, holding the box strap, compared with that of the reclining, barefoot client, imperiously pointing to her clock—differentiates between the genteel industriousness of the milliner and the shrewish laziness of the client. Thus, whether overtly or covertly, the noble suffering and strength of character of the poor seamstress was compared to the sometimes willful ignorance and idleness of the wealthy clients.

Two of the most dramatic visual presentations are periodical illustrations: the *Illustrated Magazine*'s October 1844 illustration for "Death and the Drawing Room, or the Young Dressmakers of England" and *Punch*'s 1848 cartoon "'A Shroud as well as a Shirt'" (figures 3.3 and 3.4). "Death and the Drawing Room" was written "with no purpose of affording mere information or the gratification of curiosity, but with an earnest wish to drive people out of their strongholds of indifference and calculating policies, and, by bringing home to their feelings the suffering which is now remote and hidden, to make them rouse themselves and say, 'These things shall exist no longer'" (97). The article is primarily a series of excerpts from Grainger's 1843 report to Parliament. It ends by lauding members of the aristocracy who have subscribed to the "Association for the Relief and Protection of Young Persons Employed in the Dress-Making and Millinery Departments in London" and praising Lord Ashley's attempts to control the length of work days and terms of apprenticeships. It is the illustration that is unique, however. One of the first to visually confront the high mortality rate of the profession, the artist presents a skeleton in bonnet and skirt carrying a large hatbox into a drawing room. The incongruity of the skeletal rib cage, arm, and hand in what would otherwise be a typical presentation of a milliner delivering goods to a client is startling and effective.

But, as Hood's poem had indicated, female customers were not solely responsible for the sufferings of seamstresses. For the writers and illustrators of *Punch,* the responsibility of the male customer for the conditions faced by needlewomen presented numerous opportunities for lampooning. In December 1844, "Song of the Cheap Customer" appeared, attacking the unthinking attitude of customers determined to find the best garment at the least price, even if it "encourage[s] oppression and vice" (255). Describing the "starvation in stitching" that results from

FIGURE 3.3 "Death and the Drawing Room, or the Young Dressmakers of England," Kenny Meadows, *The Illuminated Magazine* (October 1844): 97.

the shirt for whose purchase I pay
From a couple of shillings to three,
Wrought by famishing Need at a farthing a day,

the poet forces the reader to acknowledge responsibility rather than regard it as "their employers' look-out." Many of the pieces in *Punch* are as concerned with awakening the customer to his or her responsibility as with revealing the conditions in which seamstresses worked and lived.

The illustrators for *Punch* were among the few graphic artists to focus on the plight of the women who most commonly made shirts—the slopworkers. But even they usually did so only when an exceptional case came to the public's notice, and then only symbolically. With "'A Shroud as well as a Shirt,'" *Punch* is calling attention to a court case similar to the

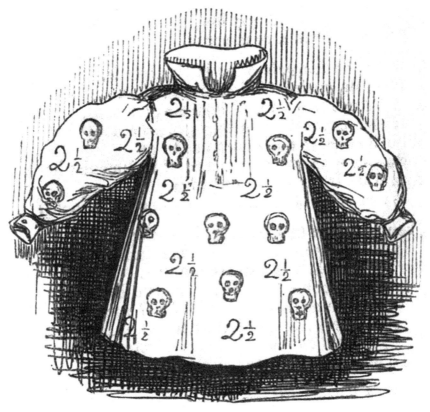

FIGURE 3.4   "'A Shroud as well as a Shirt,'" *Punch* 15 (19 August 1848): 76.

one that inspired Hood to write "The Song of the Shirt" five years earlier, a similarity of which *Punch* reminds readers in both the cartoon title and caption. According to *Punch,* Emma Mounser, "a wretched-looking woman, but who, from her manner, had evidently seen much better days," was charged with unlawfully pawning seventeen shirts she had been hired to make. Testimony revealed that she helped support her husband and two children on her earnings: she was paid two pence per shirt, and after buying her needles and thread the most she could earn was four pence a day. Further testimony disclosed that the shirts sold for one shilling each, but that "the competition in such business was so great" that the company "could not afford to pay more than the present rate." The cartoon is a pattern for a 2½-pence shirt scattered with skulls and the price. Although such visual works kept the sufferings of the seamstress before the public, unlike much of the seamstress literature from the same period, they did little to address the sufferings of other members of the laboring classes. Thus, even when dealing with working-class seamstresses, the visual arts remained focused on the seamstress herself, never growing to envelop the laboring classes generally.

II

During the second half of the 1840s the discourses of the visual arts and literature begin to separate. Although the writers continue to use details from art, especially from *The Sempstress,* in their descriptions, the literature increasingly focuses on needlewomen who are clearly working class. In contrast, while the artwork almost exclusively focuses on women working alone in their homes, and illustrations still accompany stories and articles, visual representations still suggest that needlework is an employment for the distressed middle class: although women may be shown working alone or in subservient situations, the dress and the presentation of the seamstresses would have suggested to Victorians a refined manner.

But even in narrative literature, the change in class was not absolute, nor did it happen overnight. For example, in Mark Lemon's two-act melodrama *The Sempstress,* the class of the heroine is unclear, since her family seems to be displaced middle class but her sweetheart is of the working classes. Although Lemon, then editor of *Punch,* claimed inspiration from Hood's "The Song of the Shirt," there is little presentation of the difficulties facing needlewomen of any class in his melodrama. Instead the play illustrates the suffering that can result from avarice and greed. Perhaps inspired by the play's program illustration, which depicted the familiar attic room with the seamstress hard at work—although this time attended by her father—the reviewer for the *Athenaeum* suggests that another source is Redgrave's painting. He complains, however, that "the embodied representation of Mr. Redgrave's picture would have been more impressive without speechmaking: nor does the presence of an imbecile old father and a desperate husband add to the wretchedness: the blank solitude of monotonous misery, hopeless, protracted, and wearing, is a more saddening spectacle than intense anguish, sudden and transient" ("Music and Drama," 533–34). While Lemon's play obscures the issue of class, much as do the artists of the period, most writers maintained an explicit class status in their portrayals.

In *The White Slave*, Rymer's protagonist, Millicent, at first appears to be an exception to the equation between middle-class women and millinery shop workers. She begins her career as a seamstress by sewing shirts at home with the Widow Mitchell, yet throughout the novel Millicent's class is indicated through forms of address and through description. She is always referred to by the widow and Tom, her nephew, as "Miss Manning" or "Miss Millicent," and is immediately recognized by landladies and shopkeepers as someone who has fallen on hard times rather than a born member of the laboring classes. Although she is revealed first to be the child of an army officer and then to be the daughter of an earl, Millicent's brief period as a slopworker allows Rymer to illustrate the hardships faced by all needlewomen. Tom tells her of his sister's suffering and death as a seamstress in a millinery shop and Millicent herself soon gives up shirtmaking to try working at a millinery shop. Similarly, in *Fanny, the Little Milliner,* Rowcroft's protagonist and her friend, Julia, appear to be exceptions, with Julia in a millinery shop and Fanny working at home. But both are of the upper or middle classes by birth, and in the case of Fanny by adoption as well. It is not surprising, therefore, that Julia works in a millinery shop and Fanny, even though she is employed at home, works directly for the millinery shop that employs her adoptive mother. Both *Fanny* and *The White Slave* were written in 1844, a transitional year for seamstress narratives, so the blurring is not surprising. It is also of interest that, unlike the majority of social protest writers, the authors of these two books are men. Similarly, four years later in *Whom to Marry,* the Mayhew brothers create a slopworker who is the daughter of an earl, but disowned for marrying the gardener's son. Perhaps it was the desire to portray the seamstress as worthy of patriarchal protection, or even worthy of male interest, that caused these male writers to socially elevate their heroines—not just to the middle class but even to the aristocracy, in the case of Rymer and the Mayhews, and the upper-middle class for Lemon and Rowcroft.

On the other hand, neither was the equation of working-class heroine with slopwork without exception. For example, although she works out of her home, Jessie Phillips's duties are enlarged by her rural existence, encompassing many duties that in urban areas are associated only with millinery houses. It is in *Mary Barton*, though, that the clearest exception is made. Gaskell attempts to reason away any doubts on the part of the reader that the daughter of a factory worker could secure a position at a millinery house. Gaskell shows that, although Mary's working-class father is unable to gain her a position in a millinery house, applying by herself Mary is taken on because "her beauty ... made her desirable as a show-woman" (63). And Gaskell balances Mary's character with that of Margaret, also a working-class seamstress but one who is a slopworker. It is Margaret whom Gaskell most often shows at her needle. The scenes involving needlework usually show Mary helping Margaret in the evenings, with any discussions of working or health conditions, including the inevitable blindness resulting from long hours and poor lighting, centering around the experiences of Margaret, the working-class slopworker:

> "Mary! do you know I sometimes think I'm growing a little blind, and then what would become of grandfather and me?... last autumn I went to a doctor; and he did not mince the matter, but said unless I sat in a darkened room, with my hands before me, my sight would not last me many years longer. But how could I do that, Mary?... There now, Mary," continued she, shutting one eye, "now you only look like a great black shadow, with the edges dancing and sparkling."
>
> "And can you see pretty well with th' other?"
>
> "Yes, pretty near as well as ever. Th' only difference is, that if I sew a long time together, a bright spot like th' sun comes right where I'm looking; all the rest is quite clear but just where I want to see.... I suppose I'm going dark as fast as may be. Plain work pays so bad, and mourning has been so plentiful this winter, I were tempted to take in any black work I could; and now I'm suffering from it."
>
> "And yet, Margaret, you're going on taking it in; that's what you'd call foolish in another."

"It is Mary! and yet what can I do? Folk mun live . . ."
She took up her sewing, saying her eyes were rested now, and for some time they sewed on in silence. (85–86)

Fifty pages later, Margaret is totally blind. Although Margaret soon gains employment as a singer, and ironically is better paid than she was as a seamstress, she is now handicapped and deprived of what was considered a normal life: if her blindness does not preclude marriage, the traveling involved in her singing career will.

Although Jessie Phillips and Mary Barton are both exceptions to the equation of working-class seamstresses and slopwork, it is likely that in both instances the exception occurs for literary reasons. In *Jessie Phillips* the central issue of the novel is the effect of the New Poor Laws on the rural poor and women in particular; therefore, Trollope uses an accepted symbol of the working woman, the seamstress, and places her in a rural situation. And it is the rural setting that allows Trollope to blur social standings and use an image associated with the middle class as representative of the working classes. But Gaskell's placement of Mary Barton in a millinery establishment four years later stems from a different motivation. The acceptance of slopworkers by readers was no longer a cause for concern, as Gaskell's own *Libbie Marsh*, published the year before, had demonstrated. But placing Mary Barton apart from the rest of her class allows her to act as a distanced observer and creates a sense of objectivity in the presentation of working-class conditions for the reader.

Because of the change in the status of the seamstresses being portrayed, there are also some changes in setting. Slopworkers were employed in their homes. For writers dealing with the urban poor, such as Dickens and Gaskell, the profession provided an ideal entry into the working-class neighborhood and home. Gaskell uses this entry in *Mary Barton*:

> [Berry Street] was unpaved; and down the middle a gutter forced its way, every now and then forming pools in the holes with which the street abounded. . . . [W]omen from their doors tossed household slops of *every* description into the gutter; they ran into the next pool, which overflowed and stagnated. Heaps of ashes were the stepping-stones, on which the passer-by, who cared in the least for cleanliness, took care not to put his foot. . . . You went down one step even from the foul area into the cellar in which a family of human beings lived. It was very dark inside. The window-panes

were many of them broken and stuffed with rags . . . three or four
little children [rolled] on the damp, nay wet, brick floor, through
which the stagnant, filthy moisture of the street oozed up; the fireplace was empty and black; the wife sat on her husband's chair and
cried in the dank loneliness. (98)

The poverty and unsanitary conditions would have been unfamiliar to
Gaskell's middle- and upper-class Victorian readers, who were protected
from such scenes by building facades hiding the alleyways and tenements.
And it was also important that neither Mary Barton nor Margaret live
there, since such squalor would have been so horrifying and repulsive to
readers that they would have mentally distanced themselves from those
portrayed. Yet by placing the accepted figure, the seamstress, amid those
experiencing the worst effects of poverty, Gaskell acquaints her readership with the seamstress's suffering in a non-threatening, sympathetic
fashion.

Setting is also a key element in the message Frances Trollope is trying
to communicate about the poor, but hers is a different issue; thus her use
of the rural setting creates a different set of circumstances. In many ways
Jessie Phillips has more in common with the middle-class needlewomen of
the early narratives than she does with her working-class urban counterparts. For although she does not work in a millinery house, and is not
exposed to exactly the same kind of detrimental influences as Ellen Cardan
in *The Young Milliner* or the King sisters in *The Wrongs of Woman,* she is
nevertheless faced with a familiar situation: an ambiguous social position,
leading to being compromised by a client's brother.

Jessie is definitely of working-class status, yet her beauty and personality have made her an extremely popular companion to young women of the
upper class. The rural setting further complicates the matter; class boundaries were not as obvious or as closely observed in the country as they were
in the city. It is not surprising, then, that when Frederick Dalton flirts
with Jessie, he entertains the possibility of one day marrying her, and that
when he promises marriage as a part of his seduction Jessie believes him.
For Jessie, however, all social status is lost when, seen in an embrace with
Dalton at a ball where she is working, she is compromised. Once she has
lost her tenuous grasp on social status, marriage to Dalton is no longer a
possibility, and, more importantly for Trollope, Dalton no longer has any
responsibilities toward her. The repercussions of her loss of character are
first brought home to Jessie by the actions of the Lewis sisters:

She was shewn, as usual, into the drawing-room, where the two young ladies were employed . . . Both ceased their occupations as soon as Jessie entered, and the younger turned herself round from the instrument, apparently to look at her, while the elder received the basket from the hands of the pale sempstress, but for a minute or two not a word was spoken by either. There was something in this very painfully unlike the manner in which poor Jessie used to be received by the good-humoured sisters. . . .

"If you have any work to be done, Miss Lewis, I shall be very happy to undertake it."

"I have no work whatever to be done: we have neither of us any thing," replied Miss Lewis, repeating her nod, and at the same time resuming her occupation; while Lucy, who had never before failed to honour her pretty favorite with a little village gossip, whenever an opportunity occurred, uttered not a word, and, perceiving that her sister thought it time that the interview should end, turned herself round again in her chair, and resumed her practice of "*We met, 'twas in a crowd.*" (161–62)

Jessie's loss of character is not the only consequence of her seduction—she is pregnant. And it is in dealing with Jessie's pregnancy that Trollope succeeds in merging the image of the seamstress with that of the working classes.

For Jessie the impact of her social class on her pregnancy is twofold, with both effects tied to the Bastardy Clauses of the New Poor Laws. First, since she has been compromised she can no longer obtain work in order to support herself—let alone a child—and, as a member of the working classes, she must go to the workhouse for support. Since, until this point, the reader has not seen Jessie in situations or settings that linked her with the working classes, placing her before the Board of Guardians and in the workhouse has much the same impact as facing the reader with the same possibility. Second, because Jessie is of the working classes, Dalton has no responsibility toward her or her child. Until the passage of the New Poor Laws in 1834, the father of an illegitimate child could be required to either put up some kind of security so the child would not become a burden on the parish or pay the mother for the child's support. But since all the proof that was necessary to file a claim was the mother's statement, taken under oath, legislators became convinced that the law could become a vehicle for blackmail or revenge. The New Poor Laws completely reversed the situation:

an unwed mother became solely responsible for her child; the father had no responsibility to her, the child, or the parish. If a mother could not support herself and the child, they were to go to the workhouse. As a lawyer explains to Jessie when she seeks support for her child:

> "[Y]ou may stand all day swearing that one man or another is the father of your child, and no more notice will be taken of it than if you whistled. If it turns out, indeed, that you can't manage to maintain it yourself, and that it is actually and *bonâ fide* thrown upon the rate-payers, why then *they* may look about them, if they like it, and if they can prove, without any help of yours, mind you, that this one or that one is the father, why then, by bringing forward their proof, they may make him just pay the workhouse charges, and no more. But *you*, and the like of you, have no more to do with it than the man in the moon." (255)

The experience is again heightened by the reader's ambiguous vision of Jessie's social status. By blurring Jessie's social position, Trollope is able to create an empathetic reaction and persuade an uninformed, possibly skeptical audience of the injustices of the New Poor Laws. For it is soon apparent that the dominant issue of Trollope's narrative is the New Poor Laws, with their centralization of relief through workhouses and the shielding of upper-class men from responsibility for support for bastard children; the seamstress is merely the vehicle. Indeed, it was in terms of its purpose rather than its literary quality that contemporary reviewers dealt with the novel. The *Athenaeum* dismisses it as "the old tale of the Lamb and the Wolf" (956), while *John Bull* accuses Trollope of having "sinned grievously against good taste and decorum" by dealing with a matter "not perhaps the very best subject for a female pen" (732).

But the use of the seamstress as a symbol for the laboring poor is problematic, here and in much of the seamstress literature. As Sally Mitchell argues, Trollope's dilemma is that "she wanted to create propaganda for legal change and the law could not be changed by praising women's strength but by pitying their weakness and arousing the chivalry of male legislators" (25). Further, by relying on emotions such as empathy and sentimentality to convey their messages, artists and writers ran the risk that "this creation of a sympathetic, emotional reaction in the viewer would tend partially to satisfy the urge to reform ... to assuage concern while they incite it" (Edelstein, "They Sang," 184). Perhaps this is why early reformers such as Tonna and Stone limited themselves to dressmakers and milliners and what their customers could do to relieve their plight. In such literature, chivalry or other forms of patriarchal protection are not at issue; what is important is how women are being exploited by other women, and what women can do to relieve the situation. With the move to representation of the entire laboring class, however, any solutions now involve men— relief for the working classes was only possible through changes put in place by factory owners or by legislators, both male groups. Advocating protectionism—including the belief that there should be laws designed to compensate for the inherent physical and intellectual inferiority of women, and to protect them so that their superiors could not take too much advantage—was a way to garner pity for the laboring poor. It banished fears of revolution, and thus became a tool in industrial reform. In the earlier works the desired emotional response was sympathy and perhaps empathy, now it had become pity.

III

In *The White Slave,* Rymer also used the seamstress as a symbol of the working classes. But his work compromises between the hardships of the seamstress and those of the working poor in a much different way than Trollope's. In his preface, Rymer takes up the analogy between worker and slave that had been established a decade earlier by reformers such as Oastler, and he demonstrates how the seamstress comes to be a central figure in the equation:

> Our object in the composition of *The White Slave* was to call popular attention to the sufferings of a large class in London, whose miseries are not considered by saints of Exeter-hall, or the mock-philanthropists who make after-dinner speeches at the Freemasons'-tavern, because it requires the sufferer to have a black skin before his claim to be "a man and a brother" can be admitted.
>   . . . [W]e wished to convince the public that there were white slaves in London a great deal worse off than the black slaves in Africa. . . . Who knows but the evangelical lady who snuffles and groans at Exeter-hall, and subscribes her guinea for the suppression of slavery, may have made some poor creature a real white slave on account of the dress with which she has decked herself to look well in the sight of Heaven? (iii–iv)

Although Rymer alludes to early labor rhetoric, he is nevertheless aware of middle-class fears and prejudices. His use of an upper-class heroine appeases those fears and prejudices while fitting well with his decision to write a melodramatic romance. Further, Rymer's use of an impoverished young woman from the upper classes allows him to present a variety of stories as people try to dissuade her from trying to earn a living as a seamstress. Although the second half of the novel sinks into a romantic melodrama that never allows Millicent to return to her profession, the first half solidly equates her sufferings and misadventures with those of the poor generally. For example, as Millicent begins working on her first batch of shirts, a conversation between the widow and Millicent expands to encompass an entire class and then return to the seamstress:

> "Ah, my dear, winter is the most severe of all for the poor white slaves of London to be employed in. They want more of the comforts of life than in summer, and they are not able to work so many hours."
>
> "I fear this will be a dreadful winter to many," replied Millicent; "God help the poor."
>
> "Ah, if he don't, few else will."
>
> Millicent was right; that winter was dreadful to many ...
>
> The evenings were long and the days short; small comfort have the wretched in London at such a season, and at such a time; darkness soon envelops them, and where to fly for refuge they know not. We can indeed be but little surprised at the crimes committed in this vast city, when we think of the immense amount of human suffering that is buried—for such is a proper term—in the tumult of society. Want and poverty stare one in the face when it is really sought, there is an abundance of it—abundance! Aye there is more than the easy-doing and self-satisfied giver of a few pence, and contributor to the poor's rates can possibly, or perhaps, ever will give credence to....
>
> The night was dark and very cold; sharp gusts of wind clung round the hapless passenger, who shrunk from the encounter that none would willingly brave; and in those parts of the great city, where none but the poor and abject live, its inclemency appeared to increase, just as the means to meet it decreased....
>
> Such was the season at which our poor suffering heroine commenced her work, and although she was intent upon doing as much

as she possibly could, she found herself much behindhand when the day closed—she had earned about threepence from ten o'clock in the morning until sunset. (60–61)

The allusion in the passage's first line to "white slaves of London" is one that would have been easily recognized by Victorian readers as referring to seamstresses. But the passage's movement from the sufferings of needle-women to the sufferings of the poor generally would also have reminded readers that even earlier the analogy had been made concerning the working classes as a whole. Thus through the voice of the narrator the discourse moves from mimesis to diegesis, shifting from a literal portrayal of one group to a larger classification, of which needleworkers are a subgroup.

Millicent herself experiences very few of the hardships associated with needlework. She is turned away from the workhouse for damaging a shirt in her very first bundle and is kidnapped from a millinery house the first day she works there. But her desire to earn a living by some means other than service and her ignorance of the trade provide several opportunities for those employed as slopworkers and dressmakers to explain the problems and hardships in the profession. Tom tells how his sister, apprenticed to a fashionable dressmaker for whom she worked sixteen hours a day for eight shillings a week, was worked to death within a few months. The Widow explains how prices are set and the meanings of terms such as *open contracts,* and a young woman at a millinery house warns Millicent not to allow herself to be compromised by accepting loans or lodgings from less-respectable employers. Because these discussions center around the hardships of women employed in or by millinery houses, the reader often feels on familiar ground as the horrors of earning a living by sewing are recounted; thus the attitude of employers toward needlewomen who do not work in shops comes as a shock, to both Millicent and the reader.

As a slopworker she is considered fallen, morally as well as economically. When she goes to the warehouse to pick up a bundle of shirts it is assumed by the manager that her younger brother is her illegitimate son. When the Widow addresses her as "Miss Manning" he responds: "'Miss, indeed! . . . D—n me, that's good. Miss, indeed! oh, oh, oh! I like that, a miss making a living by shirts, oh, oh!'" (59). The man's response is not unrealistic; reports such as Henry Mayhew's *London Labour and the London Poor* (1849–1850) documented for Victorian readers that many slopworkers turned to prostitution in order to survive. And sketches such as John Everett Millais's "Virtue and Vice" (1853) made the temptations all too clear. Here a poor, tired young needleworker is faced with the alternative to her sparse life in a garret—a garishly clad prostitute. The face of the streetwalker is more demonic than feminine, and in her cloak pocket is a theater program showing the word *Haymarket*, a reference to the London district where young prostitutes solicited customers. Objects in the room point to the young seamstress's situation: tacked on the wall is a flyer entitled "Distressed Needlewomen" and beside the chair is a bundle of shirts addressed to Moses and Son.[6] The coin that the prostitute is offering the seamstress thus becomes a problematic gift; it is unclear whether the prostitute is offering charity or temptation. Both the implication that a prostitute would be economically secure (and meritorious) enough to offer charity and the suggestion that needlewomen suffer sufficiently to make prostitution an attractive alternative would have distressed Victorians. Thus many reformers felt the need to establish that many slopworkers would resist such temptations, choosing to starve or succumb to consumption or blindness rather than fall into prostitution. For many Victorians this attitude was necessary if those aligned with the laboring classes were to be seen as "deserving poor" and worthy of aid.

Perhaps this is why Henry and Augustus Mayhew create a slopworker who is the disowned daughter of an earl when offering an example of a destitute, abused, working-class wife in *Whom to Marry*. Like the other writers of the period, the Mayhews are focusing on a larger issue, but in this instance one of gender rather than of class: the impact marriage, particularly a bad marriage, can have on a woman's life. Because of the book's broader scope, the slopworker is one of several women whose marriages are examined, rather than the focus of the narrative. Likewise, because the audience for whom the novel and its lesson are intended is of the upper classes, it is important that the women whose marriages are portrayed be of those classes as well. Nevertheless, the Mayhews' portrayal of the slopworker is interesting, both because of its similarity to other texts and, more importantly, because of Henry Mayhew's series in the *Morning Chronicle* the following year.

In the novel, the first encounter with the slopworker occurs when, in the process of preparing her trousseau, the narrator employs a seamstress to make some gowns. Although the needlewoman's poverty is not overt, the reader's attention is immediately drawn to the fact that, although it is the dead of winter and a heavy snow lays on the ground, the seamstress "wore a summer gown, that was so thin that it made me shiver to look at it, while the only covering that she had to her shoulders was a rusty-black silk scarf" (43). The needlewoman's full story does not come out until the narrator visits her home when she is late returning the work. The daughter of an earl, the needlewoman was turned out by her parents when she married the gardener's son. Now the woman supports her son and husband through slopwork. The description of the family's miserable living conditions is reminiscent of the details of Redgrave's work, but also prefigures many of the descriptions that would appear a year later in Henry Mayhew's series:

> She lived in a miserable court running out of Tottenhamcourt-road; and as I went up the dark and close-smelling staircase to her second-floor, I trembled at finding myself in such a place. When I entered the room, I don't know which struck me most—the wretchedness or the cleanliness of the apartment. In one corner stood a bedstead, and from the thin fold of the sheet, which was turned down over the patchwork counterpane, I knew directly that there was not a blanket upon it. In another corner, her invalid son lay stretched upon a mattress on the ground, with an old flannel petticoat wrapt round his limbs to keep him warm. Across the room, on a string suspended from wall to wall, hung a few stockings, and other articles of wearing apparel, to dry. There were but two wooden chairs; one with its broken back roughly mended with string, way by the sick boy's side, with a cap on it, while the other, by a deal table, and close to the small shovelfull of fire in the grate, was the seamstress herself. (*Whom to Marry,* 44)

The use of the feminine, upper-class, first-person narrator is an effective device: the intended audience of the narrative's object lesson was women such as the narrator; thus the idea, so horrifying to the narrator, that the daughter of an earl could be brought to such circumstances would have precipitated a like response in Mayhew's readers. Further, the narrator can ask questions that allow the needlewoman to explain the horror of her marriage, and why she does not leave it: "'I could not—he would not leave *me,*' she answered; '*that* was all I wanted—all I asked of him. But no, he knew he was entitled to all I earned, and that I must work if it was only for my child; so as he was too idle to keep himself, he was all but too glad to be kept by me.... Often and often have I fled with my child ... but the hound has tracked me out so soon, that I now see how foolish it is to hope ever in this life to be rid of him'" (47–48). The use of the upper-class, unmarried heroine who witnesses scenes from the lives of these women, supported by the fictional testimony as to the suffering that can result from a misalliance, creates a sense of verisimilitude while allowing readers to maintain a sense of objectivity and distance. Yet, conversely, this sense of realism is combined with an underlying sense of excitement and sensationalism that is a result of the voyeuristic nature of using the narrator as a surrogate for the reader. And although this specific episode involves a marriage whose problem, it is implied, stems from a misalliance of classes, other marriages presented over the course of the novel demonstrate that abuse takes many forms and is not restricted by class. For the Mayhew brothers and their readers, the point is not that many slopworkers, or even many working-class women, are supporting abusive husbands from whom they cannot escape, but that many women in general are trapped in bad marriages.

In contrast, Rowcroft, like Rymer, uses the seamstress to represent the working classes in *Fanny, the Little Milliner.* And the previous establishment of the figure of the middle-class seamstress allows Rowcroft, like Rymer, to use her as an observer rather than a participant in the hardships faced by the working classes. From the very beginning of the narrative, the reader is aware that Fanny is the daughter of a viscount, legitimate though unacknowledged, spirited away by circumstances. And in her role of seamstress, Fanny epitomizes the character established in the early novels: she is of the middle class and impoverished, young and beautiful, as is her frequent companion and fellow seamstress Julia Makepeace. Although both remain virtuous, Julia is faced with temptation when a young aristocrat follows her home from work and subjects her to unwanted advances. Furthering the standard representation, Julia is an orphan and early in the novel Fanny is seemingly left an orphan. Although Rowcroft does spend some time presenting the conditions of seamstresses, his portrayal tends to act more as a reminder of previously established conditions surrounding milliners and dressmakers rather than an in-depth presentation of the particular problems faced by these two kinds of needlewomen. Last-minute orders and late nights are taken as a matter of course, and when Fanny's adoptive mother dies, it is "[b]y selling nearly every article of furniture which Mrs. Sidney had possessed, [that] Fanny was enabled to pay the expenses of the funeral" (249).

When Fanny is used as an observer rather than a participant, the hardships of needleworkers are highlighted, as when Julia tells Fanny of a young seamstress who is dying of starvation. Yet it is by concentrating on the dying girl's wages that Rowcroft moves from needlewomen in particular to the working classes generally, since in the Victorian era the need to earn a living removed the seamstress from the gentility of the upper classes and placed her marginally in the laboring classes. To demonstrate the hardship faced by women forced to earn their living by needlework, the two girls are shown trying to discover why the dying girl could not support herself. They begin with the girl's wages: "'All that she could earn, with all her work, extra hours and all, was only eight shillings a-week! Without father or mother to take care of her; and without relations; all dead! she lived entirely by herself. . . . And obliged to dress genteelly, that she might not discredit the establishment. Just think; what could she do with eight shillings a-week?'" (113). The girls then begin tallying up all the expenses that a seamstress encounters—food, lodging, candles, clothes—and comparing them to the dead girl's wages:

> "The whole comes to ten shillings and fourpence halfpenny," reported Fanny.
> "Gracious! that's more than eight shillings a-week!—more than she has to lay out. . . . Let me see: she must have bread, and potatoes, and a bit of meat; and lodging, and fire; and some clothes and shoes; and soap and candles. What do those things come to?"
> "Eight shillings and eightpence halfpenny." (116)

The girls continue to figure, dropping out extras such as meat and potatoes, and finally get the costs within the salary, but are horrified at the results:

> "[S]he can have nothing but dry bread to eat, and not enough of that; and nothing for accidents."
> "My dear Fanny, it is impossible to live on that. To have nothing but dry bread to eat, and to be obliged to work hard besides; sewing all day, and every day, and for fourteen and sixteen hours a-day; and sometimes obliged to work on Sundays." (117)

The situation is given further emphasis when Fanny reminds Julia, "her fate may be mine—or yours" (117). Since the reader has come to know and appreciate the two young women, the idea that they would, in all likelihood, face such a future is horrifying and underscores the message that this is the fate of all seamstresses.

The real focus of the novel, however, is the general conditions of the working classes, not a particular segment of the group. Rowcroft uses

Fanny's experiences, those that separated her from her father and those that eventually return her to him, to bring these conditions before the reader. Early in the novel, when setting the stage for the uprising that separates Fanny from her family, Rowcroft presents the state of mind of the poor in a discussion between a young, well-read laborer and an older, more traditionally minded laborer. A meeting of disgruntled workers that same evening reinforces and gives detail to the generalized discussion. In this meeting the complaint of a woman who has lost her husband and children is recounted in detail. Rebecca captures the attention of both workers and readers when she presents her case against the upper classes:

> "Who could bear, as I have borne, to see my little children, one by one, pine, and languish, and die! When they came home from that horrible mill, where hard-hearted savages grind down children's bones to make money for themselves, how I have wept over their strained and wearied limbs and their little fleshless bodies, and cursed their cruel task-masters for their selfishness!"
>
> "But even that work, Becky, was better than none."
>
> "No, it was worse than none; it was a living death! None but little helpless children would submit to such wicked treatment. And why do they submit? Because they are weak and helpless, and have none to stand up for them. And I, their mother, was weak enough, and fool enough, and wicked enough to sacrifice my own offspring for the sake of the miserable pittance which they earned by the sacrifice of their childhood, of their health, and of their lives! . . .
>
> "Eighteen-pence a-week—that's what they give them; and some of those poor pennies often muleted by the knaveries practised on the children. Eighteen-pence a-week for six days' work of fourteen, sixteen hours a-day!" (45–46)

Later, as the various characters begin to gather for the resolution of the novel, another presentation of the laboring poor is made. A discussion again occurs between the young man and old worker of the earlier chapter, but the events of the novel have reversed their responses to and expectations of the ruling class. The old man's situation shows that the position of the working man has changed little in the seventeen years that have elapsed in the novel, and for many workers conditions have worsened rather than improved:

"Now that we are old and can work no longer, and I applied to the workhouse to take us in to shelter us, what did they say? Yes, they would take us in, but I and My dame mustn't be together! . . . It's not the starving that they have in the workhouse, nor the confinement, though that's hard enough to bear they tell me; but it's the parting a man from his wife that angers me. And why do they do it? Because we are poor and can't help ourselves. I never was against the rich before, but always the contrary; and I tried to still the labourers . . . when they were after violence; but this beats all. What do the rich suppose we poor people will do? Bear it? No; I can tell them they won't bear it." (292–93)

The cruel working and living conditions of laborers and the lack of understanding that the rich show toward the poor are the central focus of the novel; however, Fanny is never shown as experiencing destitution or hardship of the kind discussed. She is a removed observer. By keeping her aligned with, but separated from, both the upper and working classes, Rowcroft creates a situation in which Fanny is free from all blame attached to the upper class and untainted by the sufferings of the working classes. This allows the middle- and upper-class Victorian reading audience to sympathize with her but not to pity and dismiss her.

Similarly, Elizabeth Gaskell immerses a seamstress in the working classes and has her function as an observer rather than a participant in *Mary Barton;* however, there are some fundamental differences between *Mary Barton* and narratives such as Rymer's and Rowcroft's. For, unlike Fanny, Mary Barton is a product of the working classes; both her parents were factory workers, but her position as a seamstress has set her apart from others of her class. When the mill lays off workers, she observes their hardships, but does not experience the same degree of suffering herself. Surrounded by those for whom hard times mean a nightmarish cellar life and slow starvation, Mary experiences hard times as the loss of tea at work, the selling of furniture, and the possibility of having to move to a smaller abode. Thus although Mary Barton is aligned with the working classes, as compared to Fanny, who is aligned with the aristocracy, a sense of objectivity is preserved. For by having Mary observe the sufferings of the laboring classes, rather than experience them herself, Gaskell distances her protagonist from the issues, yet allows her to be sympathetic to them. This detachment creates a feeling of empathy in readers; they see the suffering along with Mary Barton and respond with equal sympathy. And thus Gaskell, like Rowcroft and Trollope, uses the image of the seamstress as a device, a means of presenting the conditions of the larger group to which she belonged, the working classes.

IV

Accompanying the change in focus is a change in method. The works using the seamstress as a symbol for a larger group or issue do not use parliamentary evidence or documentation in the manner of Charlotte Elizabeth Tonna, nor do they refer their readers to such sources as did Elizabeth Stone. Now any overt presentation of evidence is woven into the narrative as a presentation of detail. Such use of factual material also changes in terms of content; the material chosen deals with the conditions of the poor as a whole rather than the seamstress in particular. For example, although Frances Trollope's *Jessie Phillips* is not actually documented, it does incorporate information published in parliamentary reports, such as the selection of the Board of Guardians, the conditions of the workhouse, and the possible repercussions of the bastardy clauses in the New Poor Laws. Although the novel's closing suggests active research on the part of the novelist (Trollope writes of "a multitude of communications urging various and contradictory modes of treating the subject" and of "information which has been earnestly sought for by the author, and eagerly given by many" (352), there is no attempt to actually cite sources of information.

Likewise, Charles Dickens's *The Chimes* lacks overt documentation. Not only would such an approach have been out of character for Dickens, but also the nature of the plot precludes the use of such devices. As in his earlier work *A Christmas Carol,* Dickens transports his main character, in this case a messenger named Trotty, into a frightening future determined by the character's lack of Christmas spirit. This phantom future presents Trotty, and Victorian readers, with the worst conditions that could befall slopworkers, in this case Trotty's daughter, Meg, and Lillian, the daughter of Will Fern, a fellow laborer:

> In a poor, mean room; working at the same kind of embroidery which he had often, often seen before her; Meg, his own dear daughter was presented to his view. . . .
> Ah! Changed. Changed. The light of the clear eye, how dimmed. The bloom, how faded from the cheek. Beautiful she was, as she

had ever been, but Hope, Hope, Hope, oh where was the fresh Hope that had spoken to him like a voice!

She looked up from her work, at a companion.... [Lillian speaks:] "Such work, such work! So many hours, so many days, so many long, long nights of hopeless, cheerless, never-ending work—not to heap up riches, not to live grandly or gaily, not to live upon enough, however coarse; but to earn bare bread; to scrape together just enough to toil upon, and want upon, and keep alive in us the consciousness of hard fate! Oh Meg, Meg!" she raised her voice and twined her arms about her as she spoke like one in pain. "How can the cruel world go round, and bear to look upon such lives!" (208–9)

A few pages later Trotty again sees his daughter, now fallen on even harder times:

His daughter was again before him seated at her work. But in a poorer, meaner garret than before: and with no Lillian by her side.

The frame at which she had worked, was put away upon a shelf and covered up. The chair in which she had sat, was turned against the wall. A history was written in these little things, and in Meg's grief-warn face. Oh! who could fail to read it!

Meg strained her eyes upon her work until it was too dark to see the threads; and when the night closed in, she lighted her feeble candle and worked on. (217–19)

Meg continues working until she is interrupted at half past midnight. The visitor is Lillian, who, as implied, has become a prostitute, but has returned to Meg to tell her she is loved, and to ask forgiveness, before dying at Meg's feet. But Dickens saves the most horrific for last. At the end of his dream Trotty sees Meg as a widow with a young child, unable to find work and thus unable to buy food or pay her rent. Finally, in despair, she takes the child and jumps from a bridge into a river.

Meg's attempt to drown herself and the child in the Thames was derived from the case of Mary Furley, tried and sentenced for infanticide on 16 April 1844. Furley and her two sons had been living in a workhouse, where the eldest child was shaved by a drunk barber who nicked the child's head in several places, leading to severe infection. When the infection on his head cleared up, the child's eyes became sore and "an eruption" appeared over his entire body. Furley blamed the latter on poor food, but was unable to obtain anything better in the workhouse, so she left. First she made shirts, but "as they only allowed 1 3/4d. for a shirt, and by working hard she could only make three shirts a day," she decided to seek other work. She took what money she had to buy the materials to make caps to sell, but when she arrived at the store she found her purse had been lost or stolen. Her aversion to reentering the workhouse was so great that she, while holding her youngest child, jumped off a bridge. A boatman saw her and pulled her out; she was alive, but her infant was dead. In his jury summation, Justice Maule argued that he could "see no cause or provocation which could bring the crime under the denomination of manslaughter ... The crime was not altered at all by the fact of her having attempted her own life at the same time that she destroyed that of her infant." The jury returned a guilty verdict, and the judge sentenced Furley to death (*Times*, 8). Dickens's immediate response was the ironic "Threatening Letter to Thomas Hood, from an Ancient Gentleman, by favor of Charles Dickens," published in *Hood's Magazine and Comic Miscellany*:

Ah! governments were governments, and judges were judges, in my day, Mr Hood. There was no nonsense then. Any of your seditious complainings, and we were ready with the military at the shortest notice. . . . Then, the judges were full of dignity and firmness, and knew how to administer the law. There is only one judge who knows how to do his duty, now. He tried that revolutionary female the other day, who, tho she was in full work (making shirts at three-halfpence a piece), had no pride in her country, but treasonably took it in her head, in the distraction of having been robbed of her easy earnings, to attempt to drown herself and her young child; and the glorious man went out of his way, sir—out of his way—to call her up for instant sentence of Death; and to tell her she had no hope of mercy in this world—as you may see yourself if you look in the papers of Wednesday the 17th of April. He won't be supported, sir, I know he won't; but it is worth remembering that his words were carried into every manufacturing town of this kingdom, and read aloud to crowds in every political parlour, beer-shop, news-room, and secret or open place of assembly, frequented by the discontented working men; and that no milk-and-water weakness on the part of the executive can ever blot them out. Great things like that, are caught up, and stored up, in these times, and are not forgotten, Mr Hood. The public at large (especially those who wish for peace and conciliation) are universally obliged to him. (409–10)

Dickens's letter helped fan a public outcry and Furley's sentence was eventually commuted to seven years' deportation. But Dickens realized that the case was not an isolated one; the conditions that drove Mary Furley to desperate measures were faced by an increasing number of women. By alluding to her story in *The Chimes*, Dickens reminded his readers of her plight, and the possible sufferings of other working-class women, and kept the lack of understanding and the injustice she experienced an issue after the case had faded from the newspapers.

But it is not the specific plight of the seamstress that is at the heart of the story. More important to Dickens was the attitude of the middle and upper classes toward the poor. In Alderman Cute, a caricature of London politician Sir Peter Laurie, he satirizes those in power who are full of knowledge and advice, who "put down" anything they cannot deal with:

> "Now, I give you fair warning," [Cute tells Meg,] "that I have made up my mind to Put distressed wives Down. So, don't be brought before me. You'll have children—boys. Those boys will grow up bad, of course, and run wild in the streets, without shoes and stockings. Mind, my young friend! I'll convict 'em summarily, every one, for I am determined to Put boys without shoes and stockings Down. Perhaps your husband will die young (most likely) and leave you with a baby. Then you'll be turned out of doors, and wander up and down the streets. Now, don't wander near me, my dear, for I am resolved to Put all wandering mothers Down. All young mothers, of all sorts and kinds, it's my determination to Put Down. Don't think to plead illness as an excuse with me; or babies as an excuse with me; for all sick persons and young children (I hope you know the church-service, but I'm afraid not) I am determined to Put Down. And if you attempt, desperately, and ungratefully, and impiously, and fraudulently attempt, to drown yourself, or hang yourself, I'll have not pity for you, for I have made up my mind to Put all suicide Down!" (98–99)

Dickens was equally harsh on wealthy patrons of charities who contributed for power and prestige rather than out of kindness. When Trotty, a poor porter, delivers a message to Sir Joseph Bowley, his reception is a lesson for Dickens's readers—not only does "the Poor Man's Friend and Father" deliver a sermon on the improvidence of the poor in falling behind on the rent, he then neglects to pay Trotty for his service. Dickens's message is clear: it is not enough for the rich and the powerful to talk about helping the poor, nor are the problems of the poor such that they can be easily fixed through judicial means, a system established by those in power to serve the powerful. Thus, although the two seamstresses are important to the story, they are vehicles for the moral point of the story rather than main characters. The seamstresses are relegated to supporting status and their existence is shown as if it were commonly known, without explanation or documentation.

Similarly, Gaskell, the wife of a Unitarian minister who worked among the poor in Manchester, uses information garnered from parliamentary reports without specific references, suggesting common knowledge. But Gaskell balances this evidence with personal observation to create her narratives. In *Libbie Marsh's Three Eras,* which appeared in *Howitt's Journal* during June 1847, details are often used as an aid in characterization rather than to set a scene. For example, with Libbie Marsh as observer, Franky Hall is first seen in terms of his illness, the result of an accident:

> Upon the blind she saw, first unconsciously, the constant weary motion of a little spectral shadow, a child's hand and arm—no more; long, thin fingers hanging down from the wrist, while the arm moved up and down, as if keeping time to the heavy pulses of dull pain.... now and then [that incessant, feeble motion] did cease, as if the little creature had dropped into a slumber from very weariness; but presently the arm jerked up with the fingers clenched, as if with a sudden start of agony. (462)

Such injuries were detailed at length in parliamentary reports and Gaskell knew some maimed and disabled children among the poor to whom she and her husband ministered. Further, the emphasis of the tale is not on how the boy came to be in this condition, but on how he and those around him live with the results. This approach suggests the story is based on Gaskell's own experiences and observations, which could have included visiting and ministering to such a family, rather than government reports or periodical articles, which concentrated on conditions and accidents in the factories. In contrast, in *Mary Barton* the issues surrounding the poor are set equal with characterization, resulting in a greater use of detail and a larger reliance on documented evidence. Thus scenes such as the Davenport cellar are lifted from parliamentary reports concerning sanitary conditions, while twists in the plot such as the murder of Harry Carson are taken from newspaper stories. But as did Dickens, Gaskell used the information without documentation, suggesting that Gaskell assumed readers would recognize the information and the sources.

Enlarging the focus of the seamstress novel also resulted in formal changes in such basic elements as the titles of the novels, more specifically the subtitles. Early writers focused on the sufferings of an individual, usually specified in the title, and therefore did not need to establish a context or explain a relationship by using a subtitle. When writers began to use the seamstress as representative of a larger group, however, subtitles were used to guide the reader toward the larger interpretation from the beginning of the work. Rowcroft's *Fanny, the Little Milliner,* subtitled *The Rich and the Poor,* is typical. The reader is prepared by the subtitle, so that the lengthy discussions between characters concerning the plight of the poor, the responsibilities of the rich toward the poor, and the lack of understanding the classes have for each other come as no surprise. Similarly, Rymer's *The White Slave: A Romance of the Nineteenth Century* establishes a context and approach: the term *romance* prepares the reader for the melodramatic adventures and the chivalric rescue of the nineteenth-century equivalent of the damsel in distress—the seamstress. At times, however, authors had difficulty determining the parameters to be defined by the subtitle. Thus a work like Trollope's *Jessie Phillips* has two subtitles.[7] The first, *A Tale of the Present Day,* appears on the title page and forces the reader to view the situation presented as a current problem rather than one that has passed or a fantasy about what could happen in the future. The second subtitle, *A Tale of the New Poor-Law,* occurs, with the title, on the first page of the story. This second subtitle, then, points to the novel's overriding concern, establishing a context and telling the reader which issues in the text should receive particular attention.

Changes in content also led to changes in characterization. Like the early writers who encouraged women to perform actions that would improve conditions for seamstresses, later writers using the image of the seamstress to represent the working classes also sought to inspire action from their readers. But unlike Tonna and Stone, who often digressed to directly address and exhort their readers, these later writers presented their arguments through dialogue and, much like Toulmin in *The Orphan Milliners,* established models for their readers to emulate. For instance, with the character of Martha Maxwell, Trollope shows rather than tells her female readers what to do. After Jessie Phillips is compromised, Martha Maxwell, unlike the other women of the community, continues to bring Jessie sewing to be done and encourages her to plan for the future. At one point the narrator voices some of the doubts that would have arisen concerning Miss Maxwell's actions: "Whether Miss Maxwell was consummately wise and perfectly right in making this visit, or rather in saying all the comforting words she did in the cause for it, is another affair. It is extremely possible that many very sensible persons may think this doubtful" (173). However, the tone, especially of the last sentence, suggests irony, since in *Jessie Phillips* the three characters exhibiting sense are Ellen Dalton, Martha Maxwell, and Captain Maxwell, her father. And Trollope's portrayal of Martha is one of a mixture of kindness, wisdom, and strength—a balance not found in any other character. Martha, then, can be viewed as an ideal character, a character to be held up as an example to emulate, even if not overtly marked as such. And in case her reader is not inspired by the character of Martha, or the reader is male, Trollope also supplies arguments presented to Martha by her father, to provide further awareness and impulsion into action:

> Often had Martha listened to the indignant eloquence of her father (for on that theme the blunt veteran could be really eloquent) as he pointed out . . . the impolitic as well as hateful cruelty of this most *uneven-handed* legislation. . . .
>
> "Setting aside the obvious and horrible injustice of thus making one responsible for a fault committed by both, let us look," he would say, "at the wisdom, justice, and humanity of the choice which has selected the woman as sacrifice . . . the victim of the short-sighted policy of her country, which . . . has decreed that a weak woman (that is to say a weak *poor* woman) who has committed this sin shall atone for it by being trampled in the dust, imprisoned in a workhouse with her wretched offspring . . . And how fares it the while with the privileged seducer? Why, he, being of the sex which make the laws, is so snugly sheltered by them that there is no earthly reason whatsoever why he should not go on in the course he had begun, and thank the gods that he is not a woman." (203–4)

Trollope's goal is that these words will have the same effect on the reader that they do on Martha:

> Making her think that if in days of yore every English maid and matron felt it her duty to testify her abhorrence of the offence from which they vaunted themselves more free than the females of any other nation on the globe, the violent change which had taken place in the law of the land called loudly for a corresponding change in them. It was no longer reprobation, but mercy that was called for towards the erring creatures whom this newborn tyranny had selected as the helpless scape-goats of the whole community. (204)

By making Martha the listener and respondent to these comments, Trollope seeks both to repeat her presentation of Martha as a role model, and to ensure that even if readers do not emulate her in deeds they will do so in thought.

In *Fanny* the impulse to stimulate reform no longer rests with women, but with men. The change is attributable to two factors: first, enlarging the scope of the problem from the particularly feminine plight of the seamstress to the more general problem of the working classes makes women far less effective or involved advocates for reform. Second, the novel was written by a man, making the urge to seek a way for women to participate in reform less likely. Taking into consideration the latter point, it is not surprising that the only shown method of assistance open to women is Lady Sarum's membership in "a benevolent association of ladies of rank and influence, desirous of alleviating the hardships, privations, and temptations to which the class of young females in the employment of milliners and dressmakers is particularly exposed" (181). It is Lord Manley who is set up as a model of behavior, and it is in his discussions with other male characters that Rowcroft's arguments about the conditions and the treatment of the poor are voiced.

In contrast to the other writers, Gaskell, in *Mary Barton*, separates argument and action. Some of the most articulate and moving arguments concerning the conditions faced by the laboring classes are presented by the workers themselves, particularly John Barton. But these same men meet and decide to call attention to their frustrations through violence. By drawing the short straw John Barton becomes the man who must commit the murder, and thus the spokesperson for the cause is forced into an action that cannot be condoned. Rather than weakening Gaskell's presentation, the division between argument and action helps demonstrate her premise: that there must be reciprocation; laborers and owners must work together. For without reciprocation neither worker nor mill owner will survive, as John Barton comes to realize on his deathbed and Mr. Carson through the death of his son. For Carson it becomes:

> [t]he wish which lay nearest to his heart . . . that none might suffer from the cause from which he had suffered; that a perfect under-standing, and complete confidence and love, might exist between masters and men; that the truth might be recognized that the inter-ests of one were the interests of all; and as such, required the con-sideration and deliberation of all; that hence it was most desirable to have educated workers, capable of judging, not mere machines of ignorant men; and to have them bound to their employers by the ties of respect and affection, not by mere money bargains alone. . . . (460)

In *Mary Barton*, then, it is only at the close of the novel, when worker and owner come to an understanding, that the presentations of argument and action come together.

V

With the second wave of novels—*Jessie Phillips; The Chimes; The White Slave; Fanny, the Little Milliner; Libbie Marsh's Three Eras;* and *Mary Barton*—there is a movement away from the particular sufferings of the seamstress toward the larger sufferings of the working classes. And with the broadening of scope come changes in the portrayal of the seamstress, in her setting, and in the presentation of argument. It was a change destined to be short-lived, however. Nonfiction works, such as Grindrod's *Slaves of the Needle,* continued to focus primarily on the findings of the 1843 *Report,* while visual artists never ceased concentrating on the seamstress as an individual, even when illustrating novels that used the seamstress symbolically. For example, only two of Phiz's illustrations for Rymer's *The White Slave* address Millicent as a seamstress; the rest center around melo-dramatic moments in the romantic narrative.[8] Yet the two illustrations that do portray Millicent's life as a seamstress capture key points concerning the lives of millinery workers. The first is an illustration of Millicent applying for work at a millinery shop. The condescension of the women to whom Millicent is applying is clear, as is the misery of the women bringing in finished garments on the other side of the picture. The second image is the familiar one of the seamstress sewing a shirt by the light of a single candle, although in this case she is not alone—her younger brother lies asleep at the bottom of the sketch. The illustrations for *Fanny* are similar in that the majority simply highlight particularly melodramatic or highly comical moments in the story. In fact, it is only the elaborate title page that illustrates the life of the seamstress or her place in society—at least her place in the society of this novel. At the center of the etching, encircled by laurels, is Fanny, carrying a milliner's box. On the left, in a vertical line, are four small scenes of life among the rich; further left is an elaborate grape vine. On the right, in a vertical line, are four small scenes of life among the poor; further right is a thorny vine. Underneath, and slightly to the right, is a rural scene. This etching encapsulates Rowcroft's intent, and the intent of most of the writers of this time, that the seamstress serve as an intermediary between the rich and the poor. The rural scene reminds readers of a past lost to industrialization, and suggests that those who were respectable farmers become the destitute and homeless under industrialization. Such portrayals were only partially effective, since they tended to evoke pathos rather than sympathy, a sense of pity divorced from its social context, allowing viewers and readers to expend their emotions and walk away. Yet it was not the ineffectiveness of the portrayal or the lack of response that spurred the next alteration in presentation, the move to graphic nonfiction. In 1849, Henry Mayhew began publishing his series of articles on the working classes, *London Labour and the London Poor,* in the *Morning Chronicle.* The interviews with seamstresses that appeared in the series detailed once more the hardships faced by these women. The writers' discourse never again paralleled that of the visual artists, although both again focused on the seamstress's plight in the hope of raising the public's consciousness and improving the needlewoman's situation.

Emigration and the Secular Saint

As to the vessel's side we throng to look our last at thee,
    Each sunken eye is dead and dry—what cause have we for weeping?
We leave no homes behind us, no household ties had we;
    In one long coil of heavy toil our hours went creeping—creeping. . . .

Lift up your hearts, my sisters! and to the fresh sea air,
    Oh wan and weak, give each pale cheek, till it forget its sorrow:
Our yesterdays were gloomy—but our to-day is bright and fair—
    And loving powers will guide the hours of our uncertain morrow.

          — "The Needlewomen's Farewell," *Punch*

Henry Mayhew's series of letters in the *Morning Chronicle* on the working classes in London, particularly the letters concerning slopworkers published during November 1849, once again brought the working and living conditions of the seamstress before the public eye. Previous literature and visual presentations had conditioned Mayhew to see the needlewomen he visited in a particular way, as demonstrated by his language, much of which echoes popular literature such as Hood's "The Song of the Shirt." Nevertheless, unlike the 1843 *Second Report of the Children's Employment Commission*, Mayhew's series spurred the upper classes to actively seek some method of relief. Although Mayhew's series included both slopworkers and dressmakers working in millinery houses, the letters concerning slopworkers and needlewomen (letters VI through XI) ran from 6 November until 23 November 1849, while the two letters concerning women employed in millinery establishments (letters LXXV and LXXVI) were not published until October 1850. Thus writers publishing during 1850 were affected by the earlier letters concerning slopworkers, rather than those dealing with milliners and dressmakers. And it was these women to whom reformers applied their common solution: emigration.

But while Mayhew's letters renewed public sympathy for and interest in seamstresses, they also created a seeming equation between slopworkers and prostitution, an implied connection at odds with the semiotics of emigration, which emphasized marriage and family. To Mayhew, prostitution was so much a part of needlework that letter VIII (13 November 1849) even contains a section with the heading "Prostitution among needlewomen." In this section Mayhew examines a topic that is frequently mentioned in his other interviews, but not explored in detail—why employment in needlework seemed to inevitably lead to prostitution:

> During the course of my investigation into the condition of those who are dependent upon their needle for their support, I had been so repeatedly assured that the young girls were mostly compelled to resort to prostitution to eke out their subsistence, that I was anxious to test the truth of the statement. I had seen much want, but I had no idea of the intensity of the privations suffered by the needlewomen of London until I came to inquire into this part of the subject. (*Unknown Mayhew,* 147)

Mayhew uses the testimony of two slopworkers to document the connection between needlework and prostitution, but in such a way that he elicits a pitying response from readers:

> But the poor creatures shall speak for themselves. . . . The first case is that of a good-looking girl. . . .
>
> "I was virtuous when I first went to work, and I remained so till this last twelvemonth. I struggled very hard to keep myself chaste, but I found I couldn't get food and clothing for myself and my mother, so I took to live with a young man. . . . I am now pregnant by him. . . . I was very fond of him, and had known him for two years before he seduced me. . . . He told me if I came to live with him he'd take care I shouldn't want, and both mother and me had been very bad off before. He said, too, he'd make me his lawful wife, but I hardly cared so long as I could get food for myself and my mother.
>
> "Many young girls at the shop advised me to go wrong. . . . There isn't one young girl as can get her living by slop work. . . . I am satisfied there is not one young girl that works at slop work

that is virtuous, and there are some thousands in the trade.... [N]o one knows the temptations of us poor girls in want. Gentlefolks can never understand it.... To be poor and to be honest, especially with young girls, is the hardest struggle of all." (*Unknown Mayhew*, 148–49)

Mayhew then recounts another story, "one of the most tragic and touching romances ever read." In his introduction to the tale, he stresses the physical and mental agony of the girl as she tells her story, "her face hidden in her hands, and sobbing so loud that it was with difficulty I could catch her words ... tears oozing between her fingers." Although he has already detailed, through the testimony of inspectors, middlemen, and workers, as well as with charts, the insufficient pay and the expenses involved in slopwork, Mayhew has the young woman begin there:

"I used to work at slop-work—at the shirt work—the fine full-fronted white shirts; I got 2 d. each for 'em. There were six button-holes, four rows of stitching in the front, and the collars and wrist-bands stitched as well. By working from five o'clock in the morning till midnight each night I might be able to do seven in the week. These would bring me in 17 d. for my whole week's labour. Out of this the cotton must be taken, and that came to 2 d. every week, and so left me 15 d. to pay rent and living and buy candles with. I was single, and received some little help from my friends, still it was impossible for me to live. I was forced to go out of a night to make out my living. I had a child, and it used to cry for food. So as I could not get a living for him myself by my needle, I went into the streets and made out a living that way. Sometimes there was no work for me, and then I was forced to depend entirely upon the streets for food. On my soul I went to the streets solely to get a living for myself and child. If I had been able to get it otherwise I would have done so.

"I am the daughter of a minister of the gospel. My father was an Independent preacher, and I pledge my word solemnly and sacredly, that it was the low price paid for my labour that drove me to prostitution." (*Unknown Mayhew*, 149–50)

The girl's story continues for several columns: she gave up prostitution, tried to enter a workhouse but was turned away because she did not have an order, was temporarily rescued by a woman when she and her son were huddled in a doorway during a snowstorm, and tried to commit suicide but was stopped by a policeman. She entered a workhouse where she was separated from her child, then was finally able to obtain a position in service, but her son remained in the workhouse. She ends her testimony with the warning that "if I had a girl of my own I should believe I should be making a prostitute of her to put her to slop work. I am sure no girl can get a living at it without, and I say as much after thirteen years' experience of the business. I never knew one girl in the trade who was virtuous; most of them wished to be so, but were compelled to be otherwise for mere life" (*Unknown Mayhew*, 147–52). Readers would be horrified that the daughter of a minister would have been so reduced, but they would find that her background, when supported by her apparent shame and grief, added validity to her testimony. Mayhew's assurance that, because of the "startling nature" of her testimony, he inquired among several sources in order to corroborate her story would not only add legitimacy, but increase the horror for readers.

Building on the narratives Mayhew recounted, the *London Journal*, during February and March 1850, ran a four-part narrative by J. P. H. entitled "The Slave of the Needle." The story is in many ways a standard seamstress narrative. The opening paragraph encompasses both verbal representation of the standard seamstress illustrations (hands clasped, face turned toward heaven) and the city/country dichotomy, while the third paragraph designates the seamstress as one among the many laboring poor. Later paragraphs enumerate her hours of labor (bolstered by a stanza of Hood's "The Song of the Shirt") and the poor monetary returns, including a table listing her minimal living expenses—the story supports Mayhew's seeming conclusion that to be a slopworker and survive one must also become a prostitute. Yet the story also suggests that, although the sins of these women are unforgivable to society, the women are victims whose sins will be expunged in the eyes of God. The second installment begins by establishing the seamstress as a "victim to our present social arrangements" who is "buried in a living grave of cold and hunger." As the mother of the young needlewoman gasps out her last breath, she warns her daughter, "I have stitched my life away, and the last threads are in my hands.... When I am gone, think of me, and pray, when evil men cross your path, and evil thoughts crawl like serpents into your mind, pray, my child, or your beauty will be your curse.... [F]or this is an awful town, and sin stalks unblushingly through every street" (395). In the third section we are told how Watkins, the middleman, "uniformly selected his victims from among the slaves of the needle, over whom he exercised despotic sway" and that the "very excess of her innocence" placed the young seamstress in danger of seduction. In the fourth section it is clear that the young woman has been seduced, yet the writer's reaction to her state is mixed. First we are told, "For a woman once fallen there is no hope—the gates of the hell into which she has been coaxed by fraud and artifice are closed upon her for ever." But then, many lines later, we are told, "In the abstract, between herself and her Maker, she was as spotless as a finely polished mirror; but to her fellow-creatures—men careful of their families, and women proud of their unblemished chastity, those prosperous beings who are privileged to be critics in morals by their education and auspicious circumstances—she was fallen and degraded—a lost spirit driven from the paradise of hope to wander as an outcast in a world where every thing to her, of all others, was cold and repelling" (27). In the end, the young woman drowns herself. But with her death she transcends her life: throughout we have been told that Victorian society bears a responsibility for her demise—through the uncertain economy that caused her father's bankruptcy, through the constant search for the lowest prices that resulted in her starvation wages, through the double standard that allowed her employer to seduce her and others like her under his employ without fear of recompense. In the same way, the description of the woman's "fellow-creatures" suggests that those who judge her do not see themselves as equals but as superiors looking down on her from positions of ease, far removed from want or temptation. Like many of the writers who immediately followed Mayhew, the author of "Slaves of the Needle" felt the need to expatriate the "sin" of the seduced: these women fall because society drives them to it, they are destroyed by society and become martyrs to society.

Other stories worked to establish needlewomen as deserving of help. For example, the third installment of Miss H. M. Rathbone's inspirational series "The Routine of Daily Life," simply entitled "The Sempstress," focuses on a widowed mother who tries to support herself and her daughter through needlework. The story emphasizes the carelessness of many of the woman's clients—they set up appointments but cancel them after she arrives, and do not compensate her for her time or lost wages—as compared to the industry of the seamstress. Further evidence of the family's integrity is gleaned through repeated references to the daughter's attending school. The installment is very brief, approximately two double-column pages, and relies on established motifs in portraying the hardships of earning a living through needlework: long hours, poor pay, lack of food. The story ends with the miraculous return of a son, believed killed in service overseas, who rescues his mother from a life of poverty. Combined with the portrayal of the woman's patience and industry, the closing sentence of the story establishes her as a religious model: "Such was the somewhat romantic ending to poor toiling Mrs. Carter's hard day's work, and her heart was lifted up in mute thankfullness [sic] to the Almighty, protector of the *widow and the orphan,* for His great mercy" (308). Thus she is aligned with biblical parables of sacrifice and reward, and offered to readers as a reminder to be charitable.

Even for Victorians who still regarded needlework as a respectable occupation for middle-class young women forced to earn a living—usually separating these women from the working-class stigma associated with slopwork—the language of seamstress literature would often suggest that an economic fall could lead to a moral one. For example, the language used in Anne Marsh's *Lettice Arnold* quickly draws the reader into the complexity of the economically displaced middle-class seamstress. When Lettice walks, unescorted, to deliver completed work to a client, the narrator comments that "the things she found it the most difficult to reconcile herself to in her fallen state were the scoffs, and the scorns, and the coarse jests of those once so far, far beneath her" (42). This "fallen state" is not a moral one, as the usage might suggest, but strictly an economic one; nevertheless, both the narrator and the characters repeatedly use the term *fallen* when speaking of Lettice. In fact, when it is discovered that Lettice has been working on the trousseau for an old schoolmate, and is invited to share her breakfast, we are told, "She felt as if there would be something of a presumption in accepting the invitation. She had become so accustomed to her fallen condition, that it seemed to her that she could not longer with propriety sit down to the same table with Catherine" (58). The terms *presumption, fallen condition,* and *propriety* carry the connotation that Lettice's economic fall, specifically her fall to the level of slopworker, is equivalent to a moral one. Thus for Victorian women the economic uncertainties that might have made it necessary for them to earn a living would displace them not only in terms of class, but also in terms of morality; earning a living moved them from the private sphere of domesticity and placed them in the public sphere of employment.

And the public nature of needlework—the showing of clothes in a shop or delivering of goods unescorted—made the women associated with it especially vulnerable. As Luce Irigaray argues in *This Sex Which Is Not One,* "How can one be a 'woman' and be 'in the street'? That is, be out in the public, be public. . . . We come back to the question of the family: why isn't the woman, who belongs to the private sphere, always locked up in the house? As soon as a woman leaves the house, someone starts to wonder, someone asks her; how can you be a woman and be out here at the same time?" (144–45). For Victorian needlewomen, it would not just be their gender, their femininity, that would be compromised when they became "public" and entered the workplace, it would be their respectability.[1] The *Punch* cartoon "The Great Social Evil" (1857)—in which one woman, encountering another walking alone in the rain, asks, "And how long have you been gay, Fanny?"—illustrates that just her being on the streets unescorted indicated to Victorians that a woman was a prostitute.[2]

For many Victorians, the link with prostitution made seamstresses undesirable applicants for emigration. Thus, for those who saw emigration as the only workable answer to the distress of dressmakers and slopworkers, it was important to depict seamstresses, particularly slopworkers, as women of high moral standards. Considering this need to disprove the seeming correlation between needlewomen and prostitution, and to encourage the support, especially financial, of the upper classes, the move to portray the seamstress as a martyr to urban society, a kind of secular saint worthy of attention and support, was a logical step. A few advocates, such as Gustave Doré in his illustration to Moxon's 1870 folio edition of Hood's poetry, take the concept to extremes. In the illustration for "The Song of the Shirt," Doré shows a seamstress diligently working in her attic room while two putti wait in the window to carry the martyred woman to heaven. However, few other illustrators were as immoderate.

I

During this period, in the few literary works that portray needleworkers but do not deal with emigration, there is an emphasis on the saintly character and the suffering martyrdom of needlewomen equaling that of many of the visual portrayals. In *Lettice Arnold*, the title character is a clergyman's daughter who, at her father's death, with her mother and sister, has fallen on hard times. In an attempt to keep the family together while earning a living, the mother has moved the family to London. When the story opens, the mother has died and the two sisters are on the verge of starvation. Interestingly, Marsh ties the ability and the willingness to work to character: Lettice is an excellent seamstress who is willing to work long hours; she is also saintly in character. Myra, the sister, does not have the skills to do fine needlework and is unwilling to work long hours; she is also spoiled, petty, and selfish. Since the two women are sisters and share their occupation, the implication is that Victorians should not sweepingly condemn or generally pity slopworkers, but, rather, look on them as individuals and respond to them according to their individual characters and situations.

In constructing her portrait of Lettice, Marsh incorporates the seamstress's established semiotic system, drawing from a number of sources, to create a woman of exceptional character. For example the scene in which Lettice is introduced owes much to previous presentations, both verbal and visual:

> It was now half-past twelve o'clock, and still the miserable dip tallow candle burned in a dilapidated tin candlestick. The wind whistled with that peculiar wintry sound which betokens that snow is falling; it was very, very cold—the fire was out, and the girl who sat plying her needle by the hearth ... had wrapped up her feet in an old worn-out piece of flannel, and had an old black silk wadded cloak thrown over her to keep her from being almost perished. The chamber was scantily furnished, and bore an air of extreme poverty, amounting almost to absolute destitution. One by one the little articles of property posted by its inmates had disappeared to supply the calls of urgent want. An old four-post bedstead, with curtains of worn-out serge, stood in one corner; one mattress, with two small thin pillows and a bolster that was almost flat, three old blankets, cotton sheets of the coarsest description, were upon it: three rush-bottomed chairs, an old claw-table, a very ancient, dilapidated chest of drawers, at the top of which were a few battered band-boxes,—a miserable bit of carpet before the fireplace, a wooden box for coals; a little low tin fender, a poker, or rather half a poker, a shovel and tongs, much the worse for wear, and a very few kitchen utensils, comprised all the furniture in the room. What there was, however, was kept clean; the floor was clean, the yellow paint was clean, and I forgot to say, there was a washing-tub set aside in one corner. (24–26)

The list convinces the reader that she is aware of everything in the little eight-by-ten room, and the ending indicates that, despite the extreme poverty and endless work, an effort is made to keep what is there clean.

For Victorians this would be an important indication of character, and in the semiotic systems surrounding needlewomen cleanliness is next to godliness. The use of details repeatedly incorporated by preceding artists and writers, and part of a proven sign system associating the seamstress with religion and suffering, would aid in quickly establishing Lettice's character. In terms of her suffering, it is significant that it is long after one o'clock in the morning when she finally finishes her sewing.

The physical description of Lettice, although she is not yet named, is equally important. The narrator goes to great lengths to point out that she is rather plain, not a typical storybook heroine whose life would "be diversified by those romantic adventures which *real* life in general reserves to the beautiful and the highly-gifted" (26). In all, we are told, her appearance is "more than redeemed to the lover of character in countenance, rather than beauty." Her features show her to be "patient," "resigned," "earnest, composed, busy, and exceedingly kind" (27). Finally, we are told, "She was so much occupied with the sufferings of others, that she never seemed to think of her own" (28). When she is dressing to deliver the garments she worked on until late in the night, we find that Lettice cannot afford both food and fire, has no shawl, and needs a new bonnet. Yet when she enters the richly furnished home of her customer we are told: "She must needs be what she was,—a simple-hearted, God-fearing, generous girl—to whom envious comparisons of others with herself were as impossible as any other faults of the selfish" (37). But the most telling description occurs when Mrs. Danvers, Catherine's godmother, compliments Lettice on her willingness to work: "To work for her living had never lessened her in her own eyes; and she had found, with a sort of astonishment, that it was to sink her in the eyes of others. To deny herself everything, in food, furniture, clothing, in order to escape debt, and add in her little way to the comforts of those she loved, had ever appeared to her to be noble and praiseworthy" (78). This passage, and others like it, show that much of Lettice's suffering comes from a society that devalues independence and service among women, and establish Lettice as one who suffers for others—either so that others might benefit or because of the hypocrisy of others.

The question of what the middle and upper classes could do to help alleviate the sufferings of needlewomen is also dealt with in Marsh's novel. Influenced by earlier writers such as Stone and Tonna, Marsh presents two role models, Mrs. Danvers and Catherine, for middle- and upper-class readers. Not only does Mrs. Danvers dine simply and dress in a manner "conventual in its simplicity," spending the money she saves on the poor, but she also visits the poor, patients in hospitals, and prisoners. But it is the situation of needlewomen that "peculiarly excited her compassion, and to their welfare she had especially devoted herself" (51). Not only does she encourage her friends to allow more time for gowns made at shops, she also personally hires slopworkers for her own clothes, avoiding the use of a middleman, so that the needlewoman receives a larger wage for her work. She also encourages her friends to hire slopworkers directly, and often visits the needlewomen's parishes in order to find particular women to recommend to her friends. It is on such a visit that she encounters Lettice and her sister. In contrast, Catherine's character allows Marsh to introduce an uninformed figure to whom information can be given, and thus presented for readers. Also, Catherine quickly begins to imitate Mrs. Danvers, especially where her childhood friend is concerned. Not only does Catherine find Lettice a position as a companion, for her parents, she also encourages Mrs. Danvers to find Myra a position in a well-run millinery shop. There is a clear implication that without the intervention of Catherine and Mrs. Danvers, Lettice would soon have starved to death despite her hard work, and Myra, Lettice's sister, would probably have been reduced to prostitution. Thus it is the intervention of the upper-class women that prevents the needleworkers from becoming victims of industrial society.

Marsh also draws on previous sources in her presentation of wages—having Lettice explain to someone who is outside the occupation how much she earns and what she must spend for lodging, food, supplies, and fuel. More important symbolically, however, is Marsh's use of the city/country dichotomy. Catherine, the client to whom Lettice recounts her life, is a wealthy young woman who knew Lettice as a child. When Lettice asks if she remembers the parsonage, Catherine replies affirmatively: "The tiny house, all covered over with honeysuckles and jasmines. How sweet they *did* smell. And your flower-garden, Lettice, how you used to work in it. It was that which made you so hale and strong, aunt Montague said" (71). To those familiar with the iconology of the seamstress, country life is healthy, and urban life, if one is forced to work, is destructive. This, along with the association with flowers, places Lettice in the category of saintly martyrs who have been forced to leave a paradisiacal rural life for the evils and physical suffering of urban life. Indeed, Mrs. Danvers makes the association clear when she tells Catherine:

> "You have only seen life upon one side, and that its fairest side— as it presents itself in the country. You cannot imagine what a

dreadful thing it may prove in large cities. It cannot enter into the head of man to conceive the horrible contrasts to be met with in large cities—the dreadful destitution of large cities—the awful solitude of a crowd. In the country, I think, such a thing as this hardly could have happened,—however great the difficulty may be of helping those who still preserve the delicacy and dignity with regard to money matters, which distinguishes finer minds. But in London, what *can* be expected? Like lead in the mighty waters, the moneyless and friendless sink to the bottom. Society in all its countless degrees closes over them: they are lost in its immensity—hidden from every eye—and they perish as an insect might perish amid the myriads of its kind, unheeded by every other living creature." (102)

With this speech, the loneliness and danger of urban life for the working poor—especially for women displaced from the middle class—is made clear. The speech also suggests how the seamstress could become a victim, a martyr, of urban society.

As a Mrs. Murphey of Manchester testified to the Children's Employment Commission in 1843, "[t]he apprentices in London very often come from the country and have no friends in town" (206). Implicit in both the literary and the visual representations of the seamstress languishing in the city is that she has left a happy, full life in her rural home and now pines for family and friends. "The Seamstress" in *Eliza Cook's Journal* frames descriptions of the sufferings of urban needleworkers with those of a pleasant bucolic life:

> Tripping over the stile, one Sabbath summer morning, came a village girl, her sunburnt face half-shaded by a knitted bonnet, dimples showing upon her cheeks and chin, lips rosy and full, eyes sparkling with life and health, her whole frame radiant with rural beauty and vigour. . . . Rosie, whom we last saw entering the village church. . . . Can this be the girl whom we found so bright and glowing with hope only six months ago? It is! For poor Rosie now leads the familiar life of a London seamstress, and she has already stamped upon her features the accustomed miseries of her class. (17)

In the city Rosie wastes away until her family finds her in a charity hospital, "a feeble remnant of womanhood—pale, wasted, almost ghastly," and returns her to her home in the country. The story ends on a Sunday, much like the one on which it began, closing with Rosie's thankful prayer "for rescuing her 'from the deep pit, and from the miry clay'" (19).

In contrast to the direct comparisons of the literature, painted works can only allude to this city/country dichotomy. The most effective image incorporated by visual artists was that of a flower. Hood had used the flower image in "The Song of the Shirt" to suggest the seamstress's gentility and fragility, and to refer to her rural origins:

> Oh! but to breathe the breath
> Of the cowslip and primrose sweet—
>   With the sky above my head,
>   And the grass beneath my feet,
> For only one short hour
>   To feel as I used to feel.

It is little surprise then that Victorian artists, who consistently used Hood's poem for their titles or as an accompanying catalog quotation, would recognize the effective simplicity of the flower. In one of the best-known seamstress paintings, *The Sempstress,* Richard Redgrave places a weak, spindly potted plant on the windowsill. The symbolism is twofold: on one hand it points to the futility of the needlewoman's attempt to create some aspect of her past life in her new, urban environment; on the other, it demonstrates that the industrial city is unable to support healthy life of any kind, and that, like her flower, she will wither and die in that environment. According to Edelstein, the flower "symbolizes the struggles of the lone shirtmaker against the growing tangle of impersonal forces that comprised the Victorian city. She becomes both an image of oppression to be fought against yet also a source of catharsis for her audience because she evokes an immediate emotional response and alludes to a greater world beyond this one" ("They Sang," 106). Throughout the Victorian age writers and artists used the seamstress, either through her life generally or with objects such as a flower, to symbolize the struggles of life in the depersonalized industrial city. Feeling torn away from the old cultural traditions, "battered and adrift in a feelingless world" (Altick, 96), Victorians responded to an iconography that expressed the city/country dichotomy that seemed to control their destiny.

A more overt martyrdom is shown in the *London Journal*'s "Slaves of the Needle." In this series, presenting Victorian readers with a young woman who is gradually worn down by the unscrupulous behavior of the middleman who supplies her work, each installment shows the conditions of the young slopworker as being a little more dire. In the first installment we are told that when the women presented their work to the middleman for payment, they "implored to be paid, not an increased sum, but the bare amount previously bargained for and allowed; but the man found so many faults with this collar and that collar, this band and that band—the seams were crooked, the necks awry—and so many faults were pointed out that many of the poor creatures became frightened, and, to escape from such a place gladly took what was offered them" (378). In the second installment the young girl's mother dies, while in the third the villainous middleman tries to seduce her. A neighbor rescues her, but, addressing the middleman, draws a comparison that presages the young girl's eventual destruction: "Leave us one flower in this little hell for us to gaze at, and think of youth and innocence once again before we die. Away! and may your slumbers be haunted by the ghosts of the dead—of the girls with Thames mud dripping from their hairs!" (412). Like the flower alluded to, the young girl cannot survive in the city. By the fourth installment she has been seduced and, as foreshadowed in the neighbor's curse, she drowns herself in the Thames. As Sally Mitchell points out, for feminist reformers, "Successful martyrdom provides a subversive triumph: since women are morally and emotionally finer than men, men's power can be attacked by bringing them to their knees with guilt and remorse and consciousness of their failings" (9). "Slaves of the Needle" provides an example of such an approach: the story is never specific concerning the economics of sweated labor, thus the message is not that the seamstress is worked to death, or that she needs wage protection; the seduced woman is destroyed because a man takes advantage of her innocence and her gender. Such treatment excludes the young woman from the doctrine of self-help advocated in works such as *Lettice Arnold;* rather, she is a social problem, an innocent destroyed by, martyred to, a patriarchal society that must protect her from itself.

II

To the Victorians emigration was the great social panacea. To move those lacking work, food, and shelter to new frontiers that theoretically offered an abundance to those industrious enough to get there seemed an ideal solution. In 1848, *Punch* published "Here and There; or, Emigration, a Remedy," a diptych suggesting emigration as a solution to the poverty of families among the working poor. On the left a destitute family stands dejectedly in front of a wall along which a variety of notices have been posted: "meeting," "charter," and "illegal" are all legible. But most forbidding is the large notice that frames the two adults: "Caution / All Vagrants." On the right the same family is shown prosperous and happy in their new home. Dirty rags have been replaced by neat clothing; gaunt features are now filled out. What is most distinctive, however, is that the starving, homeless family is now not only in a home, but is shown preparing for a meal. There is a surplus of food, and the father, who had been holding a starving child, is now carving a roast while the mother places another platter of meat on the table. Such visions answered the Victorian need to find an economical resolution that did not necessitate personal involvement or an expenditure of energy on the part of the upper classes. During the same period Caroline Chisholm had, with the support of Lord Ashley and Sidney Herbert, established the Family Colonization Loan Society, an organization primarily interested in aiding entire families and that loaned emigrants the balance needed for passage after they had contributed the maximum amount possible. Later, a strong argument for middle-class emigration, especially that of single females, was presented with the publication of Edward Gibbon Wakefield's *A View of the Art of Colonization* (1849). The coincident appearance of Mayhew's and Wakefield's works brought a logical reaction from the media and upper classes: emigration was the solution to the seamstresses' problems.

Punch was not slow to take up the crusade. Only weeks after the publication of Mayhew's letters concerning slopworkers, *Punch* opened its eighteenth volume with a discussion of female emigration examining a variety of viewpoints—commercial, cynical, alarmist, domestic, naturalist, and its own: "It is lamentable that thousands of poor girls should starve here upon slops, working for slopsellers, and only dying old maids because dying young, when stalwart mates and solid meals might be found for all in Australia. Doubtless, they would fly as fast as the Swedish hen-chaffinches—if only they had the means of flying. It remains with the Government and the country to find them wings" (1). In the same issue *Punch* ran the poem "The Needlewomen's Farewell" accompanied by the diptych "The Needlewoman at Home and Abroad" (figure 4.1). The poem highlights the struggles of slopworkers, including Mayhew's picture of the almost inevitable fall into prostitution:

> And so we strove with straining eyes, in squalid rooms, and chill;
> The needle plied until we died—or worse—oh, Heaven, have
> pity!—
> Thou knowest how twas oftener for want we sinned, than will—
> Oh, nights of pain and shameful gain, about the darkling city!

But in the last three stanzas, emigration offers hope of "suffering stayed" and of food, work, and marriage (14). The John Leech illustration on the facing page makes the contrast between a needlewoman's life in the two countries even stronger: in England she is in the city, where she must brave her way through the wind and cold in tattered rags, tempted by notices for "cordial gin," and accosted by a policeman; in Australia she is in the country, surrounded by plump, happy children, with plenty of food, and an attentive husband.

The contrast is heightened by the use of vertical and horizontal lines. In "At Home" the shading is done with vertical lines and all the figures are standing, each shaded to highlight the vertical, especially the policeman. The only horizontal line is the dark arm of the beadle reaching out toward the seamstress. In "Abroad" the shading is horizontal and the woman is seated. While the husband and one child are standing, they are placed on

FIGURE 4.1   "The Needlewoman at Home and Abroad," John Leech, *Punch* 18 (12 January 1850): 15.

either side of the seated figure and within the cabin in such a way that the three figures create a diagonal line from bottom left to top right rather than a series of verticals. Further, the diptych incorporates two standard dichotomies of the semiotic system surrounding needlewomen: that of city/ country and that of employment/domesticity. In "At Home" the open street suggests the impersonal nature of the figures' moment of intersection, an indifference among the figures associated with urban life and—because of the disconnection from domesticity and family—with women working outside the home. In contrast, the wall of the cabin in "Abroad" creates a sense of enclosure suggesting unity and cohesiveness achievable only through domesticity and idealized by the rural setting.

During 1849 four other emigration societies were founded, with Sidney Herbert's Fund for Promoting Female Emigration specifically aimed at financing the emigration of London's distressed needlewomen. During 1850, several journals advocated emigration for impoverished, unmarried women, and needlewomen in particular. On 5 January, both *Eliza Cook's Journal* and the *Penny Illustrated News* ran articles concerning the employment of women, specifically mentioning seamstresses, and promoting emigration. "The Employment of Young Women," which appeared in *Eliza Cook's Journal*, opens with what was, for many Victorians, a central concern in the larger issue of women and work: "that the proper sphere of the woman is the Home—that her highest duty is to minister to the domestic well-being there—that, as the nurse and moral teacher of the youth, the refiner and comforter of man, the mother, the wife, and the housekeeper, she is labouring in her truest and holiest vocation." Readers are reminded that, for many Victorian women, "this is but a beautiful theory, and yet very far from being realized in practice" (145). The article then compares the plight of working- and middle-class women in England who are forced to work through economic circumstance with those of America and France. Blaming the English woman's "want of education," the article stresses that American and French women are able to run their own businesses, save money, and marry. Two professions are singled out, teaching and sewing, with the heaviest condemnation falling on dressmaking. The article first argues that it is "probable" that a better education, "with an eye to utility rather than exhibition" (146), would open up other employment opportunities for middle-class women. Almost as an afterthought, the concluding paragraph introduces the idea of emigration to either the colonies or America "for those who would find remunerative employment" (147). Although seen as a less attractive alternative to education and marriage, emigration is nevertheless presented in enthusiastic terms: "America has been called 'the paradise of women;' and the inducements which that country, as well as our own colonies hold out to the thousands of unemployed young women in this country, are certainly worthy of their serious regard and consideration" (147).

In contrast, the illustrated article in the *Penny Illustrated News,* the first number of a series entitled "The Labour Question: An Exposition of the Social Condition of the Working Classes," focused exclusively on "The Needlewomen of London," although it used the category to include drawn-bonnet making, shoe binding, brace making, and shirt making. The illustration incorporates much of the standard iconography—the attic room, the candle, the pitcher, the shirt—although there are two women working. One woman diligently plies her needle while the other looks off in seeming consternation with a hand to her throat, suggesting shortness of breath or coughing, a variation on the symbols suggesting illness. Quoting extensively from Mayhew's letters in the *Morning Chronicle,* the article concludes with the thought that there "are hundreds of single young women, unable to obtain better employment. For those of them who have not made their misery perpetual by falling into sin there is hope. Mr. Sydney [*sic*] Herbert has attracted the attention of the public to the most natural means of relief by recommending emigration" (83). Concluding with statistics indicating a surplus of unmarried women in Great Britain and a deficit in Australia, the article implies that the solution of emigration will also lead to marriage, and it ends with the promise to follow up in future numbers with "such information respecting the colonies as may be relied on for its accuracy; and to familiarise the people with the aspect of their natural scenery and products" (83).

Soon, on 25 February 1850, the first shipload of seamstresses left for Australia. On 17 August 1850, the *Illustrated London News* devoted the entire back page of its first supplement to the "Emigration of Distressed Needlewomen." Comprised of two large etchings, "Emigrant Needlewomen on Deck" and "Emigrant Ship Between Decks," with three one-inch columns of text between, the page celebrates the "glorious instance" as made possible by the care and concern of the upper classes for the laboring poor. Such action, described as "an interesting feature in the English character," is the result of "some of the most distinguished votaries hav[ing] employed themselves in works of active benevolence." And the needlewomen are described as "rescued from the very depths of poverty and suffering, and all more or less objects of deep commiseration" (156). The top illustration foregrounds a sailor stowing rope while numerous men and women mill around the deck; the bottom illustration shows a number of women stowing goods or sitting on benches along the side while two gentlemen look on. Although there are a number of boxes and the number of women implies a certain amount of crowding, there is also a sense of cleanliness and order and a suggestion of privacy from the draped curtains hanging overhead. The illustrations suggest large numbers of emigrants, but there is also a sense of spaciousness on the ship, especially above deck, which suggests all can be accommodated—perhaps countering rumors of overcrowding and unsanitary conditions.

With the combination of renewed public interest in and a seeming solution for the plight of needleworkers, it is hardly surprising that the year 1850 saw an unprecedented number of literary works concerning seamstresses, a number never again to be repeated. And in terms of visual representations, as T. J. Edelstein has demonstrated, emigration was second only to the seamstress herself as a popular Victorian social theme: it "was inoffensive; it presented a solution rather than a problem, a solution which had been implemented by many and questioned by very few. The visual imagery of the emigration theme, moreover, emphasized its positive aspects. The inviolate nature of the family, and the promise of a better life beyond; both are central to the iconology of the emigration theme" ("But who," 231). This iconography offered Victorians the opportunity to return to a semiotic system with which they were comfortable—woman as wife, mother, moral center of the home—rather than acknowledge that not all women could fit within that system.

Emigration first had been mentioned in connection with the seamstress in 1846 by Rowcroft in *Fanny, the Little Milliner.* The matter is brought up twice, both times by Lord Manley, and both times it is dismissed as impractical. Two years later Gaskell shows Mary Barton and her husband, Jem, emigrating to Canada, but not because of Mary's profession; they are emigrating in order to escape the notoriety caused by Jem's murder trial. Their emigration is not an occupational relief then, but a perpetuation of the association of emigration with convicts and other undesirables.[3] Nevertheless, by 1850 illustrators and writers were presenting emigration as the one way to save urban slopworkers from inevitable destruction—physical, moral, or both.

Gaskell's interest in emigration and her impression of it as a way to gain a fresh start probably sprang from personal experience. Ministering with her husband among the poor in Manchester, she was familiar with the lack of options facing the working poor once they were in trouble. The founding of Chisholm's emigration society, which concentrated on the skilled working class and lower-middle class, received much publicity and no doubt seemed to Gaskell a way for people to escape the hardships of urban industrialization. Gaskell, however, appears to have been more lenient concerning the moral standards being applied to potential emigrants. A specific example of her interest in emigration, particularly as a means of starting over for a young woman whose life seems to have begun a downward spiral, can be found in her letter to Charles Dickens dated 8 January 1850:

> I am just now very much interested in a young girl, who is in our New Bayley prison. She is the daughter of an Irish clergyman who died when she was two years old; but even before that her mother had shown most complete indifference to her;... and when she was about 14, she was apprenticed to an Irish dress-maker here, of very great reputation for fashion. Last September but one this dress-maker failed, and had to dismiss all her apprentices; she placed this girl with a woman who occasionally worked for her, and who since succeeded to her business; this woman was very profligate and connived at the girl's seduction by a surgeon in the neighborhood who was called in when the poor creature was ill. Then she was in despair, & wrote to her mother, (who had never corresponded with her all the time she was at school and an apprentice;) and while awaiting the answer went into the penitentiary.... I want her to go out [to Australia] with as free and unbranded a character as she can; if possible, the very fact of having been in prison &c to be unknown on her landing. I will try and procure her friends when she arrives;... She is a good reader[,] writer, and a beautiful needlewoman; and we can pay all her expenses &c.... (*Letters*, 98–99)

Yet, Gaskell is asking for help only because she sees no other possibility.

Ironically, Gaskell generally did not favor emigration for women who had become prostitutes, not because she felt it would not be in the best interests of the emigrant societies, but because it might not be in the best interests of the women. Instead, as Elsie Michie has pointed out, she preferred that the women be placed in private homes in England, as was the protagonist in her novel *Ruth*. But on this point Gaskell could find little support: her letter to Dickens indicates that she had written earlier about establishing a home similar to Urania House, a "house for homeless women" supported by Dickens, but he was unwilling to lend his support to Gaskell's project unless it was connected with an emigration scheme (98). Further, much of the horror expressed over *Ruth* centered not on Ruth's seduction or her illegitimate child, but on the fact that she lives in a private house and serves as a governess after her "fall."

A. Stewart Harrison's "The Iceberg," a story in Dickens's *Once a Week,* further illustrates the difficulties women faced once it was known that they were "ruined." In the story a sailor searches for his sweetheart, who was seduced while he was at sea. When he finally finds her, making shirts in Manchester, "'she was dreadfully thin, and her eyes bright and far back in her head'" (404). He pays her back rent and takes her and her infant son back to her home. But as he tells the curate, there is a problem getting work: "'[N]obody would employ her here, as she had lost her character, and that her father and mother could not keep her, though she might live with them.'" He then asks the curate to serve as a go-between, "'paying her to make shirts for a man in Liverpool.... He'd pay sixpence each for the making of the shirts'" (409). Thus it is only through the intervention of a man of impeccable character that the young woman can get a job, and only if the client has no contact with her. Such reactions were not unusual, presenting seemingly impenetrable barriers for the young women, barriers that Gaskell hoped to break down.

Gaskell's letter, however, is significant in terms not only of her work but also of that of Dickens. Not only did Dickens support and actively involve himself with Miss Burdett Coutts's Urania House, he was already acquainted with Caroline Chisholm and her program, discussing her society in the first issue of *Household Words* and subsequently publishing articles she wrote concerning emigration. Indeed, as Elsie Michie argues, "Because [Gaskell's] 'Lizzie Leigh,' the story of a working woman's 'fall' into prostitution, was positioned as the first article in a volume of *Household Words* that ended with a series of letters praising the benefits of emigration, the whole issue appeared to argue in favor of Dickens's position that emigration was the solution to the problem of prostitution" (87–88). At the time he received Gaskell's letter, Dickens was writing *David Copperfield,* which appeared in serial from May 1849 until November 1850, and the letter apparently led him to a combining of Chisholm's concept with the situation Gaskell described. The novel ends with the emigration of two families, the Micawbers and the Peggottys. Micawber's rise to the magistracy and Peggotty's success as a sheep farmer illustrate the wisdom of Chisholm's idea of family emigration, while the saving of Little Em'ly from further moral corruption echoes Gaskell's intent.

Because *David Copperfield* was serialized, however, it was not the first example of seamstress emigration presented to the Victorian reading public. The first to appear was *Lucy Dean; the Noble Needlewoman,* written by Eliza Meteyard and published under the pseudonym Silverpen, in *Eliza Cook's Journal* from 16 March until 20 April 1850. Meteyard's picture of emigration is based on a blend of Chisholm's work and Wakefield's *Art of Colonization,* and it is presented as a possible salvation for distressed needlewomen. Lucy Dean, like most of the seamstresses in the fiction immediately preceding and those interviewed by Mayhew, is a slopworker. And although she has work to do, she does not have the money to purchase thread or candles, let alone bread, and so cannot work. It is when she is trying to raise money by selling her brother's songbird that Lucy first hears of emigration and Mary Austen, a character modeled after Caroline Chisholm. The reader, however, is made aware of the possibilities offered by emigration before beginning the story. Meteyard prefaces her story with two epigraphs from Wakefield. The first stresses the need to inform the working classes of the possibilities offered by emigration. The second argues the important role women play in shaping the communities formed through colonization:

> In trade, navigation, war, and politics—in all business of a public nature, except works of benevolence and colonization—the stronger sex alone take an active part; but, in colonization, women have a part so important that all depends on their participation in the work. . . . [I]n every rank, the best sort of women for colonists are those to whom religion is a rule, a guide, a stay, and a comfort. You might persuade religious men to emigrate, and yet, in time, have a colony of which the morals and manners would be detestable; but, if you persuade religious women to emigrate, the whole colony will be comparatively virtuous and polite. As respects morals and manners, it is of little importance what colonial fathers are in comparison with what the mothers are. It was the matrons more than the fathers of the New England Pilgrimage, that stamped the character of Massachusetts and Connecticut; that made New England, for a long while, the finest piece of colonization the world has exhibited. (312)

Through these quotations from Wakefield, Meteyard introduces three themes that are stressed throughout *Lucy Dean:* the need for the working classes to receive information concerning emigration, preferably from others who have emigrated; the need for emigrants to raise the fare necessary to emigrate; and the need for women who were both virtuous and religious to emigrate.

There are many similarities between Chisholm's program and emigration in Meteyard's story, primarily concerned with the Victorian concept of women as the domestic and moral center of the new communities. From the beginning it is stressed that Lucy will need skills other than needlework. The first thing Mary Austen asks is: "'Could you wash, cook, bake, do you know how to provide a comfortable dinner, and nurse a child?'" When Lucy answers affirmatively, Austen replies: "'This is well, for these are chief points . . . in all womanly life, . . . but much more needful ones, to those who seek a new country'" (329). The second similarity between the story and Chisholm's program is the emphasis on religious and moral purity. In the same interview Austen explains: "'A woman, useful, religious, and chaste, is more worthy of success, and more likely to succeed in a new country'" (230). The third parallel is that Lucy herself must earn as much of her own travel money as possible. Chisholm's society differed from other emigration programs in that it was not wholly philanthropic and stressed the concept of self-help. In Meteyard's story, Lucy earns eight pounds and four shillings toward the fifteen pounds necessary, with the rest made up by donations. A final similarity is the emphasis on the moral efficacy of female emigration. Chisholm "believed passionately in the ideal of the feminine civilising mission" (Hammerton, 101) and believed wives and children to be "God's police," able to turn male emigrants from "murmuring, discontented servants" to "loyal and happy subjects of the State" (Chisholm, 30–31). This correlation between female emigration and salvation marks the beginning of the movement toward the iconographic representation of the seamstress as a secular saint.

When discussing possible emigration with Lucy, Mary Austen repeatedly states that women can aid other women through emigration. At first this appears to be a variation on the message of Stone and Tonna, whose novels call for upper-class women to help needlewomen by boycotting certain establishments and being prudent in placing their orders. But rather than looking for organizational or financial support from upper-class women, Meteyard sees the possibility of needlewomen aiding needlewomen—an expansion of Chisholm's self-help ideal. Austen demonstrates this concept when she promises to aid any woman whom she believes "would go forth to the colonies, with the determination to work, not only for herself, but to pave a way for others of her sex, less fortunate, or less courageous. Such a woman might achieve immeasurable good" (329). It is an image furthered by Lucy's return to England to spread the message of emigration.

When she arrives in Australia, Lucy finds it idyllic, filled with agricultural beauty and the promise of aesthetic richness:

> They had left their own land in the prime of summer, and now the same season, or rather earlier summer, though a degree hotter and drier than their own, met them on the beautiful park-like plains and sheep-runs which lie to the north and east of Adelaide. These plains, overspread with grass, and lightly timbered with the beautiful mimosa, gum, and acacia trees, soon lead to the cooler regions of the chain of hills which, stretching from the extreme southern point of Cape Jervis on the south, and extending as far north as has yet been explored, contain those vast mineral resources, which will yet make Australia not only a wonder amongst nations, but will give, through the power of using metals in architecture, and impetus to a new and forthcoming era in the arts, unseen yet but by the few who have a ken into the coming ages. (362)

For the English emigrants, Australia represents an earthly paradise, a land that has escaped the horror they left behind in England—industrialization. Once in Australia Lucy quickly begins her work. Not only does she provide a model of modesty and industry for other female settlers, she is soon traveling among the communities seeking funds "for the assistance of those distressed women whom she had promised to help as soon as she had power" (378). Thus through her role as behavioral model, her letters home, and her raising of funds, Lucy becomes the prophet of a new paradise.

III

But not everyone was equally impressed with the emigration scheme for the relief of needleworkers. During the latter part of 1849 and early 1850 a debate was carried out in the press over the wisdom of Sidney Herbert's Fund for Promoting Female Emigration. During the month of December the *Spectator* ran four articles on Herbert's plan. While generally supporting female emigration, the articles demonstrate that it would not solve the problem of unemployment or low wages for seamstresses. The first, "The Needlewomen and Their Rescue" (8 December 1849), defends Herbert's scheme against attacks in the *Morning Chronicle,* on the premise that the writer had attacked out of jealousy rather than from any actual complaint with the program (1158–59). On 15 December the *Spectator* published two articles concerning Herbert's project. "Quiet Thoughts on Emigration" is a letter to the editor by X that, under the guise of clarifying the difference between colonization and emigration, presents emigration as a means of fulfilling the biblical command to "Increase and multiply, and replenish the earth, and subdue it" (1182). The second article, "The Great Woman Market," is again a defense of Herbert's program. After presenting population statistics showing that women age fifteen to thirty-five outnumbered men by over seventy thousand, and that in London alone it was estimated that over ten thousand women were unemployed, the writer argues that while it is unlikely that the emigration of a number of needlewomen might improve conditions for those remaining, it is better to help a few than to ignore the problem (1184). A third article, "Needlewomen's Rescue—Ministerial Hopes" (29 December 1849), again states that, while Herbert's plan is good, it is not a cure for the problem presented by urban needleworkers. Also presented are explanations showing why Herbert's program is better than many of those previously tried, and a defense against attacks in other journals, the *Globe* specifically (1232).

Whereas the *Spectator* was cautious, tempering its praise for Herbert's program, some newspapers were more outspoken concerning the problems they saw in the plan. For many, the problem appears to center around the emigration of single women, usually unaccompanied, rather than families and couples. For example, in 1848 *Reynolds's Miscellany* published a six-part account in favor of working-class emigration, Edwin Roberts's "The Life of a Labourer or, Six Episodes of Emigration," telling its audience: "The world is wide, and there is an over-abundance of room for all, and we cannot think of the dreadful destitution existing *now* among the poorer classes in our own land, without fervently hoping that *emigration* upon a gigantic scale may be adopted by those in power, as a means of ameliorating the condition of all men; and giving to the wretched a chance of happiness elsewhere, which they in vain seek for *here*" (395). Accompanying the series was Henry Anelay's "The Emigrants," showing Stephen Gwyn, the protagonist, and his family on their way to Australia, sitting on the deck, entertained by a sailor's story. Both the illustration and the story emphasize the positive possibilities emigration offered to emigrant families, while ignoring the possible hardships. However, a year later, when the issue involves single, middle-class women, *Reynolds's Political Instructor* issues "A Warning to the Needlewomen and Slopworkers." In his article, George W. M. Reynolds emphatically rejects Herbert's program:

> A more scandalous proceeding was never initiated by that patrician class which is so heartless in its oppression and so base in its duplicity towards the sons and daughters of toil. This gilded pill which a parcel of titled and reverend quacks are endeavouring to cram down the throats of starving Englishwomen, is entitled a "Fund for Promoting Female Emigration;" ... I conjure the needlewomen and slopworkers to put no faith in the promises held out: I warn them—emphatically, earnestly warn them against yielding to the representations set forth in such brilliant colours and in such an apparently Christian spirit
>
> ... Miserable enough ye are in your own country, poor women!—I know it well: but ten thousand times more miserable still would ye find yourselves on board the worthless old emigrant-ships in which it is proposed to pen you up like so many sheep,—ten thousand times more miserable when turned adrift in some colony at the end of the world, and with the harrowing conviction that you have been basely juggled into accepting a change of condition only too well calculated to prove that even in the lowest depths of wretchedness there is a lower deep still! (66)

Although much of Reynolds's attack is based on who is sponsoring the plan—the aristocracy and clergy—he also voices many of the fears of those considering the program: the conditions of the ships and of the land to which they would emigrate. Until this time Australia was generally considered a wasteland, a place to which convicts were transported. Indeed, Reynolds uses this past transportation as part of his argument against Herbert's program: "The Society's Prospectus shows that in the Colonies there are more males than females ... But of what class does a large proportion of the male population of Australia consist? Of the banished felonry from England!" According to Reynolds, any relief for urban needleworkers must come from "an alteration in the laws which *make* the millions poor, and *keep* them poor too, in order that the few may be rich now and grow richer as time moves on" (66).

But Reynolds's attack against the emigration of needlewomen was not limited to articles in his newspapers. One week after the appearance of the first installment of *Lucy Dean*, Reynolds began publishing *The Seamstress* in his miscellany. It was to be part of a larger series entitled "The Slaves of England." Reynolds's work differs greatly from that of Meteyard, both in its handling of the seamstress and in its search for a way to relieve her condition. For in her first installment Meteyard had briefly dealt with the hard conditions under which needlewomen worked and their abuse by middlewomen, and glowingly presented a solution—emigration. Reynolds, in turn, concentrates on the plight of the seamstress, its causes, and what could be done in England to relieve the situation. Emigration is mentioned only as a means of getting rid of unsavory characters—Lovel, a forger and murderer, and his common-law wife.

Reynolds's story is strongly influenced by the many portrayals of seamstresses that precede it, and is, in many ways, a return to the earlier seamstress narratives. The plot of the novel is reminiscent of those of Rowcroft's *Fanny* and Rymer's *The White Slave*: like Fanny and Millicent, Reynolds's heroine, Virginia, is the offspring of an alliance between the aristocracy and the middle class, which is broken for social and monetary reasons, although Virginia, unlike either of the earlier heroines, is illegitimate. In each of the three stories the parents have lost contact with their child, and in both *Fanny* and *The Seamstress* the daughter unknowingly encounters one of her parents through her work. Finally, each of the three heroines falls in love with a young nobleman encountered while working for her parent, and in each case the love affair appears doomed because of social inequality, until the end when the girl's parentage is revealed. Thus all three novelists use the image of family and paternalism to set up a vision of social paternalism, with the seamstress functioning simultaneously as the offspring of the upper classes and a representative of the laboring poor.

It is with his ending, however, that Reynolds departs from his two male predecessors. Where Rowcroft and Rymer end on positive notes—the young women are reunited with their families and saved from the destruction of needlework—Reynolds's heroine is found too late. Rymer ends his narrative with the call for readers to "Join up in a more glorious cry of emancipation than ever issued from the lips of would-be philanthropists, and let us insist upon looking at home, and doing something for the liberation from bondage of our own *White Slaves*" (254). Reynolds's last paragraph invokes similar images, but with a much darker tone:

With regard to the establishment of Messrs. Aaron and Sons, would to heaven we could announce that the earth had opened and swallowed it up, or that the red right arm of Jehovah had hurled the avenging thunder-bolt upon its roof! But it is not so. That establishment still exists and the system whereon it is based flourishes more than ever;—and while poor Virginia, one of the countless victims of that diabolical system, sleeps in the silent grave, the toils of the *White Slaves* whom she has left behind her are still contributing to the colossal wealth accumulated within the walls of that Palace of Infamy. (46)

In the course of the narrative it becomes clear that, while Reynolds believes that class reconciliation is the necessary key to relieving the sufferings of the laboring poor, he does not believe the upper classes will act altruistically. To him, then, the solution is clear but unlikely.

Rowcroft and Rymer, however, are not the only literary sources Reynolds uses; he also borrows from a later novel, *Mary Barton*. Not only does Reynolds use biblical allusions, such as that of Dives and Lazarus, but he also combines a story about a working-class seamstress with a murder mystery involving the girl's father. Like that of *Mary Barton*, the original thrust of *The Seamstress* was an investigation of social conditions—as the title of the series, "The Slaves of England," indicates. The fourth installment, however, ends with the attempted murder of the duchess, and the story of the seamstress is not introduced again until the beginning of the seventh installment. The split between social novel and *roman policier* has been considered a serious weakness in Gaskell's novel, since the detective story overwhelms the social issues in the last half of the novel. And Reynolds apparently recognized that the introduction of the murder mystery had also pulled his narrative away from its original focus, for beginning with the eighth installment he renamed the work *The Seamstress: A Domestic Tale*,[4] eliminating the series title. But unlike *Mary Barton*, Reynolds's novel does not end with the unraveling of the murder plot. Rather, he returns to graphic descriptions of the hardships faced by needlewomen and slopworkers. Thus, instead of having a novel that divides into two parts—social novel and *roman policier*—Reynolds attempts to use the social novel as a frame for the detective story, creating a stronger sense of structure in the work.

Reynolds's most important sources, however, predate the work of both Rowcroft and Gaskell. The opening of the novel is set in January 1844 and uses the imagery of Hood's "The Song of the Shirt," published in December 1843, and Redgrave's *The Sempstress,* first exhibited in 1844, for setting and characterization. Reynolds opens with a description of the seamstress's room: "That back attic—for it was nothing more—was as scrupulously clean as the nicest sense of female tidiness could render it ... Upon the floor was stretched the humble bedding—a flock mattrass [*sic*] and one thin blanket, with a pair of sheets as white as snow. A small deal table, a solitary chair, a basin and ewer, a candlestick, a little moveable cupboard, and a piece of broken looking-glass hanging to the window ..." (129). This is an amalgamation of the room described in Hood's poem, with its single table, broken chair, and blank wall, and the one shown in Redgrave's painting, a small attic room with a single window, lighted by a candle, with a table holding a broken basin and pitcher, a chair, the low bed, a cupboard, an empty fireplace, and a clock showing two-thirty. Even the time correlates, for Reynolds's seamstress hears the clock strike two and calculates that it will take another half hour to finish her work (130).

The Seamstress is also a mixture of the characteristics of the seamstress narratives of the early 1840s and those of the works of the late 1840s. As in the early works, there is a concentration on the seamstress herself and her working conditions, and an attempt to explain why the conditions are so hard. At one point Reynolds even includes statistics, much as Stone and Trollope cited parliamentary reports. But like the later works, Reynolds's story is firmly embedded in the working classes—as indicated by the original series title, "The Slaves of England"—with a wide gap existing between the working classes and the aristocracy. But unlike either set of preceding works, Reynolds sees no possible solution to the problems of the needle-workers. According to Reynolds, any solution must come from legislative reform, but he despises those in power and so has no faith in the legislature. To him the fact that nothing has been done indicates that nothing will be done.

The blending of an in-depth study of the seamstress with that of a working-class setting also allows Reynolds to cover material never before discussed at length. Of primary interest is his discussion of the securing of work through middlewomen. Middlemen and middlewomen do appear in other works—Annie Lee is seduced by the unscrupulous middleman, Watkins, in "Slaves of the Needle," and *Lettice Arnold*'s Mrs. Danvers avoids using middlewomen when contracting work so that the needlewomen are better compensated for their work—but in both cases no explanation of the system is given. And while Lucy is shown trying to procure work through a middlewoman in the first installment of *Lucy Dean*, Meteyard, like the others, does not attempt to explain the system or discuss the hardships that resulted from exploitation by the system. However, when Reynolds begins his series the next week, he goes to great lengths to show the reader how the system operates. By having Virginia, the young seam-stress, deliver a finished garment to the various levels of the middlewoman system, Reynolds demonstrates both how the system works and why needle-workers starve despite the cost of the garment to the customer. Virginia delivers a dress to her contact, Mrs. Jackson, and is paid three shillings and six pence. As a favor to Mrs. Jackson, she then delivers the dress to Mrs. Jackson's contact, Mrs. Pembroke, who gives her the seven shillings Mrs. Jackson was to be paid for the garment. Mrs. Pembroke then requests that Virginia deliver the gown, with a bill for fourteen shillings, to the milliner who originally requested the work. The milliner also has Virginia deliver the dress, this time to the customer, with a bill for four pounds and four shillings. When Virginia questions another seamstress about the system, she, along with the reader, receives a lengthy lesson in suppression through economics:

> "Madame Duplessy employs a middle-woman, because it saves trouble in the first instance — and secondly because the result is to keep down the price of the work thus put out to be done.... [T]he more hands it passes through, the better she is pleased, because the earnings of the wretched needlewomen who do the work are diminished in proportion. By thus keeping down the wages of the needlewomen, the great houses ... can from time to time reduce the prices paid to the middle-women.... The result is that your earnings, Virginia, will continue to grow less and less: but I ques-tion whether Madame Duplessy will lower her prices towards her aristocratic customers.... Mrs. Jackson crushes you — Mrs. Pem-broke grinds Mrs. Jackson — and Madame Duplessy keeps a tight hand over Mrs. Pembroke.... Now, were Madame Duplessy left to fight the battle of labour's value direct with *you* who did the labour, she would be pretty well at your mercy — because you could charge her at least a guinea for the work which she charged the Duchess four guineas for: and, however discontented Madame Duplessy might be at such a charge on your part, she has not the time to run all over London to ascertain who will work cheaper for her than you." (163–64)

The middlewoman system was, to Reynolds, at the heart of the economic problems faced by needlewomen; therefore, when he returns to the harsh conditions faced by needleworkers at the close of the novel, he also returns to the issue of middlewomen:

> She is employed on work that is more remunerative though much harder than that of shirt-making. For the middle-woman, or "sweater," by whom Virginia was engaged, found that the young creature would prove a more serviceable and valuable slave at trousers-making than at shirt-sewing. . . .
>
> But why could not Virginia, who was so proficient with her needle, obtain the best and most delicate work from the mantua-makers and milliners, instead of the coarse slop-work of the delectable Messrs. Aaron and Sons?—or why, at all events, could she not procure the work direct from the establishment itself, instead of through the hands of a middle-woman? All these points have been discussed and explained in a previous chapter; and the same system which in the first instance rendered Virginia the slave of Mrs. Jackson, now enchains her to the service of one of the numerous "sweaters" who farm the work of Messrs. Aaron and Sons. . . .
> (541–42)

Reynolds then proceeds to give an account of Virginia's wages as compared to the cost of the shirts, and the costs of necessities such as rent, food, and supplies—again reminiscent of Rowcroft and the list compiled by Fanny and Julia—based on figures presented by Mayhew in letters X and XI of his series for the *Morning Chronicle*. For these two letters Mayhew interviewed a variety of needlewomen, investigators, and employers; he also presented a table calculating the income (breaking down the earnings, deductions for trimmings, and clear earnings per week) of a group of slop-workers over a four-year period. Not only did his findings demonstrate how seasonal and how low the earnings of slopworkers really were, they also showed that earnings had actually dropped over the four-year period (*Unknown Mayhew*, 164–67).

Reynolds builds the image of Virginia as suffering victim, turning her into a martyr of a system established by the middle class in order to prey on the working classes. As she succumbs to consumption, Virginia is increasingly described as saintly: from presenting the "resigned meekness of a saint" (369) to displaying looks "full of the martyrised sweetness and resignation of a saint" (370), and finally demonstrating, on her deathbed, "the mingled meekness of an angel and resignation of a martyr-saint" (44). Adding to the image of Virginia as saint is her unflagging moral integrity. Reynolds makes it clear that such virtue is unusual: "And if our humble heroine remained pure and spotless in the midst of contamination—in the midst of temptation—in the midst of sorrow, suffering, and crushing toil,—she must be regarded only as an exception to the rule, and not as a type of her class in this respect. With pain and indignation do we record the fact that virtue in the poor seamstress is almost an impossibility . . ." (356). Yet, despite his disclaimer, the very fact that Reynolds portrays his seamstress as resisting moral temptations indicates to readers that there are needlewomen who remain virtuous, choosing physical suffering and possible destruction over moral or spiritual destruction.

When presenting readers with shocking material or information that might be considered questionable, Reynolds, like earlier novelists, uses known sources to back up his presentation. But unlike Stone and Tonna he merely presents the statistical data without naming the source. For example, Reynolds opens the fifteenth installment with a chapter entitled "The Temptations of the Seamstress," in which he uses statistics to demonstrate the seeming inevitability of the needlewoman's fall into prostitution: "Of the thirty thousand females living in London ostensibly by the needle and slop-work, not less than twelve thousand are *under* twenty years of age;— and nine-tenths of those poor girls are plunged by stern necessity into the vortex of vice before they scarcely know what vice means! Eighty thousand daughters of crime walk the streets of London . . ." (356). But Reynolds does not reveal the source of his statistics—Mayhew's *London Labour and the London Poor.*

The influence of Redgrave's *The Sempstress* is again seen in Reynolds's selection of illustrations. The opening sketch, drawn by Henry Anelay, is actually two pictures separated by a pair of scissors and other sewing equipment—pincushion, thimble, thread, and pins (figure 4.2). On the left a lone seamstress is shown working, while on the right is a drawing room scene with a number of well-dressed women. To readers familiar with Redgrave's painting the similarities of the figure on the left would be unmistakable: the lone figure in a room lighted by a single candle, a window, one chair and table, an empty fireplace, a mattress on the floor, and a broken basin and pitcher. Equally notable would be the differences: the young woman is beautiful rather than haggard, and a contrasting scene is used on the right—a crowded ballroom, lit by chandeliers, filled with richly dressed ladies. The contrasting scenes—the single candle compared with the bright chandelier; the single figure with the crowd; the cracked walls and empty room with the opulent wallpaper and fine fixtures; and the plain, modest, dark dress with the variety of ornate, lavish dresses—would recall earlier diptychs. Earlier diptychs such as the *Pictorial Times*'s "The Milliners and the Duchesses," or *Punch*'s "Pin Money/Needle Money," established another iconology associated with the seamstress, the contrast of the needle-worker with her client. Anelay and Reynolds use the seamstress/client dip-tych again in the fourth installment to the novel, borrowing the title from the *Pictorial Times,* but isolating single figures: on the left, "The Seam-stress," modestly dressed in a dark, pin-tucked dress with a demure white collar and tie, her hair in a neat roll, and her eyes downcast; on the right, "The Duchess," in an ornate, décolleté gown, her hair decorated with strings of beads and feathers, looking straight at the viewer with a proud, sensuous expression. Adding to the impact of the comparison, in Reynolds's narrative the duchess turns out to be Virginia's mother, who abandoned her because she was illegitimate.

FIGURE 4.2   "The Seamstress," Henry Anelay, *Reynolds's Miscellany* 4.89 (23 March 1850): 129.

The influence of Redgrave's portrayal can also be seen in Reynolds's presentation of Virginia's saintliness. Aside from Lucy Dean, Virginia is the first fictional seamstress to live alone—all others live at the millinery house or with relatives, and even Lucy Dean originally lived with her brother and sister until he died and she ran away. The isolation of the seamstress was unusual in literature, but common in painting. Edelstein comments on the traditional association of the single figure with the images of the saints, arguing that through this association the seamstress becomes a secular symbol of urban martyrdom. Contending that Redgrave's work builds on previously established iconographic systems of sainthood and martyrdom, she demonstrates how the imagery was developed and carried on through the nineteenth century: "The sympathetic response of the viewer was reinforced by the vocabulary of symbols, which assumed meaning through constant repetition; the single figure, the candle, the shirt, the flower, all emphasize the roll [*sic*] of the seamstress as a martyr to society" ("'But who,'" 301). From the first issue, then, Reynolds was using the association created by Redgrave and his followers to suggest the saintly character of Virginia. Indeed, of the fifteen Anelay illustrations that accompanied *The Seamstress,* fully half involve either Virginia or Julia, her neighbor and fellow seamstress, many documenting the hazards of the occupation, such as long nights, unescorted walks, and illness. Those that focus on Virginia always emphasize the qualities that set her above others in the narrative. In the opening diptych she is the suffering martyr to stylish society; in a later diptych her modesty is compared to others' pride and sensuality; and in the closing illustration, her deathbed scene, her pillows form a halo around her head as she grasps the hand of the young lover who has found her too late. In this final illustration, she and the other three figures in the room—her long-lost parents and her suitor—form a triangle of which she is the apex, their focal point and the viewer's, as she pronounces a kind of benediction on them and on society:

> But when she cast her dewy eyes around and met the looks that were fixed in unutterable sadness and blank despair upon her, she experienced a sudden revival of the Christian spirit of resignation which had animated her soul ere the development of the varied and exciting scenes of the last hour. In the deep despondency which had seized upon her father and her mother, and in the frantic wildness of the affliction to which Charles had become prey, the poor girl beheld a motive for exercising all her own moral courage

and arming herself with all the fortitude which she could possibly summon to her aid. In silence her soul spoke for a few moments,— fervently she prayed, although her lips moved not;—and it seemed as if a responsive voice came whisperingly from the celestial spheres—a voice full of heaven's own blessed melody and which she alone could hear,—breathing hope of eternal bliss in the angel state that was approaching!

And thus was it that with a smile of ineffable sweetness upon her lips,—a smile which was nevertheless mournfully compatible with the deep and touching pathos of the scene,—she said, "Weep not for me, dear parents—weep not on my account, beloved Charles: I am going to another and happier world!" (43–44)

The Anelay illustrations underscore Reynolds's presentation of Virginia as a martyr to urban Victorian society, suffering immense deprivation, physical hardships, and a painful death in order to temper her character into that of a saint. The opening and closing illustrations emphasize the martyr/ saint imagery, while the illustrations between emphasize the suffering, either directly or through comparison with other characters. Furthering this reading of Virginia's character is the effect she has on those she encounters: meeting her causes them to look into their lives, to admit past failings, and to try and rectify faults or problems, leaving them better able to cope with whatever befalls them.

Emigration and the portrayal of the seamstress as a martyr/saint are also present in two other works published during 1850: August saw the publication of both Charles Kingsley's *Alton Locke, Tailor and Poet* and the anonymous short narrative *Ellen Linn, the Needlewoman* in *Tait's Edinburgh Magazine.*[5] In *Ellen Linn* the picture of emigration, while favorable, is more cautionary than in *Lucy Dean,* especially concerning the ability of the poor to pay their own passage costs. The tale centers around Ellen's inability to earn enough money to feed herself and her grandmother while awaiting assistance from her lover, Tom Cripps, who has emigrated to Australia because of the lack of work in England. After the failure of her employer's business Ellen cannot secure enough work as a seamstress to support her grandmother and herself, let alone pay emigration costs. Tom's letters to Ellen during his first year in Australia are "rather discouraging than otherwise; for, like many other emigrants, he had imagined that almost on his first landing money would pour into his lap; and not finding this to be the case, he had felt much disappointment" (466). At the time of the story, however, he has written to say things are improving and he will be writing again soon and sending money. But he does not write again until after two vessels have left, since it has taken him that long to earn enough money for her passage. In the meantime Ellen suffers a physical and mental breakdown from which she never recovers, and "to the day of her death she remained an idiot" (470). To the author of *Ellen Linn,* emigration is a positive step toward relieving the conditions faced by the working poor, but it is not a solution. It is also made clear that emigration cannot work on a strictly self-help basis, but must be supported by the upper classes. Indeed much of the blame for Ellen's breakdown is placed on the thoughtlessness of Mr. Fishlock, a clergyman who was a "gentleman of respectability" (466):

> He had been absent from home when Ellen's letter had arrived there, and being shortly expected by his family, they had not forwarded it to him. On his return he set about making the necessary inquiries and applications for Ellen; but whilst thus occupied he did not deem it necessary to write and tell her that he was so doing. He did not reflect that her letter had lain some time already at his house, and that she might be anxiously awaiting for an answer. He was a benevolent and kind-hearted man, but in common with many other amiable and well-intentioned people, he was of dilatory and procrastinating habits. He had deferred writing from day to day. . . . He had also made inquiries about Ellen's obtaining a free passage to Australia, and had intended at once to write to her; but being obliged to go to London on business, in two or three days, he thought it better to see her herself upon the subject, as the short delay could not, he imagined, make any difference! Had he, then, written one line to give her hope, it would have enabled her to bear up against her sufferings—it would have cheered her broken spirits; but now—(470)

Thus the rich must not only contribute funds, they must make an effort to communicate with those they wish to help, to consider the feelings and situations of the poor. The need for greater understanding across class boundaries is shown earlier in the text, when Ellen observes a wealthy woman who for several days is also waiting for the postman. Watching the woman Ellen notes the similarity of their situations, despite the difference in their socio-economic condition, and realizes "that the high-born and the lowly were sisters of affliction!" (467). Ellen's understanding and sympathy for the wealthy woman emphasizes Mr. Fishlock's thoughtlessness and makes it appear all the more damning.

Although the martyr/saint image is not as strong in *Ellen Linn* as it is in the other works of 1850, it is present nevertheless, particularly in terms of the seamstress as a martyr to industrialized urban society. "As if stung by a serpent," Ellen recoils when sexually propositioned while begging for money to buy bread. The introduction of the serpent image with the rejection of sexual temptation has unmistakable biblical overtones and places Ellen on a higher moral plane than the people around her. This elevation receives immediate reinforcement through Ellen's reaction to the sight of women pawning clothing in order to buy gin: "A cold shudder seized the starving girl; and she felt that, wretched as she was, and sunk in life, she was not degraded—that abject as was her present situation she had not forfeited her self-respect—that shame and infamy could not be coupled with her name" (468). Ellen's strong sense of morality is accompanied by the starvation and mental agony she suffers. When Ellen applies for work, she is informed: "we have no demand for ready-made articles. The last shirts you made I have still on hand; it is impossible, therefore, to give you any more work when it don't pay; you must seek elsewhere" (467). The lack of work, and the suffering it brings, make her a victim of supply-and-demand economics and of the laissez-faire approach that dominated Victorian politics as well as business.

Compounding her own hunger and despair is the suffering of her grandmother. When her grandmother falls ill, Ellen is told that some nourishment would improve her condition, but Ellen has no money for food. And in the delirium that follows, her grandmother, imagining that Ellen's mother is present, accuses Ellen of maliciously letting her starve: "'Hush, Mary, don't let them hear! they'd kill poor we if they could. And yet I cared for her as I did for ye, Mary.... But she is ungrateful; she won't work: she's wishing for our death, she and Tom. Do ye know Tom? He's bad, or he wouldn't let poor we starve. Aye, starve! do ye hear?'" (469). The combination of mental and physical suffering brings about Ellen's collapse; it is this suffering, when combined with her moral strength, that shows her to be a martyr to the injustices of society.

A similar image of the seamstress as a suffering, saintly martyr, but with stronger religious overtones, is presented in the eighth chapter of *Alton Locke*. As early as the chapter title, "Light in a Dark Place," there are indications of the saintly character of the young seamstress whom Locke and

Sandy Mackaye visit. The setting is reminiscent of Hood's "The Song of the Shirt," but even poorer—with no bed or table, only a broken chair by a cold fireplace. In the room are an old woman, two young women sewing, and a third girl apparently sleeping. It is the third girl on whom attention is focused. She is the only person described in detail—smallpox marked, hollow eyed, and emaciated—and it is soon apparent that she is dying of consumption. When she speaks her voice is "faint" and "unearthly," and her topic is salvation and saving others, particularly her sisters, from temptation. In this brief episode, Kingsley also alludes to emigration as a means of salvation for needlewomen. One of the young seamstresses says: "'Oh! if that fine lady, as we're making that riding-habit for, would just spare only half the money that goes in dressing her up to ride in the park, to send us out to the colonies, wouldn't I be an honest girl there?—Maybe an honest man's wife!... Wouldn't I mend my life then!'" (92). Although the issue is not discussed, within the context of the novel the message is clear: legislative reform will not bring social reform, but emigration offers the working poor a chance to start a new and richer life; however, in order for any emigration plans to succeed, the rich will have to sponsor the poor. Thus, although the presentation is brief, Kingsley incorporates both themes then associated with needleworkers—the hope of emigration and the martyrdom of the saintly young needlewomen forced to remain in urban England.

IV

In their zeal to create sympathy and generate funds for emigration, writers did not deny the reality presented by Mayhew's study. In all the works published during 1850 the likelihood of a slopworker's falling into prostitution is shown. But the writers tempered this seemingly inevitable fall through the presentation of cruel circumstance, vows of love, and calls for compassion. In Dickens's *David Copperfield* Little Em'ly's fall is tempered first by sympathy, when she is verbally attacked by Rosa Dartle. For even if readers felt much the same as Miss Dartle, the venomous attack, combined with Em'ly's own remorse, would have created sympathy for Em'ly, as would her claim that Steerforth had "'used all his power to deceive me, and ... I believed him, trusted him, and loved him!'" (615). As Sally Mitchell explains in *The Fallen Angel: Chastity, Class, and Women's Reading, 1835–1880*, for Victorians there was a distinction between a seduced woman and a fallen one: the former was "the helpless victim of a superior male," while the latter was "capable of sin and therefore responsible for her own destiny" (x). These two presumptions were also the basis for much of the argument favoring the emigration of women, since "the expansion of chastity to first—and perhaps only—place on the list of woman's virtues depended on two underlying presumptions. The first is the concept of woman's place; the second ... of woman's special nature" (x–xi). As one seduced, Em'ly has a claim to virtue in terms of her nature, if not in terms of her place. Thus for reformers who believed that emigration could relieve the competition for work among seamstresses, it became vitally important that the association between needlewomen and prostitution be allayed by characterizing seamstresses as victims of seductions rather than independent women who consciously decided to sin. Such victimization could be portrayed as arising out of innocence and thus mitigated, allowing the women to function as the moral center of a home and family in Australia. And since Dickens advocated the emigration of reformed prostitutes who had entered homes such as Urania House, it is hardly surprising that by the close of the novel Em'ly has become, while not a saint, a kind of ministering angel to the settlers in Australia. She is "'fond of going any distance fur to teach a child, or fur to tend a sick person, or fur to do some kindness tow'rds a young girl's wedding ... patient; liked by young and old; sowt out by all that has any trouble'" (744). Her portrayal shows the benefits of emigration and suggests that many times it is environment, rather than personality, that is responsible for a woman's fall into prostitution.

The circumstances surrounding the fall of Nelly, Lucy's sister, in *Lucy Dean* are similar to those of Little Em'ly—leaving home out of love for her seducer, and with the expectation of marriage. Readers familiar with Mayhew's series would also recall the young woman interviewed in the eighth letter, who was seduced by a tinman who promised marriage, but whose sister "made mischief" between them. The young woman Mayhew interviewed had known the father of her child for two years before the seduction, and her mother believed them to be married. The young woman tells Mayhew that "[h]e could make 14s. a week. He told me if I came to live with him he'd take care I shouldn't want, and both mother and me had been very bad off before" (*Unknown Mayhew*, 148). This motivation also parallels Nelly's story, for as Nelly explains to Mary Austen, compounding her affection and expectation of marriage was a desire to improve the living conditions of her family:

> "All this sorrow first came about, not through an evil disposition, or a love of finery, but because I who loved all within our poor

home as dearly as human creature could, wished to lift them out of the sordid, abject, debasing misery of the needlewoman's life; a life than which London city holds none more dreadful. And in going away with Lawrence's friend, the son of a wealthy organ-builder, under a promise of marriage, I thought to go back, as it was promised, a happy young wife, willing and able to assist them through my husband's goodness." (361)

Thus there is an element of sacrifice in her fall. And although Nelly is forced to prove herself worthy before emigrating to Australia, once removed from the scene of her moral decline and placed in the promising atmosphere of Mary Austen's home, like Em'ly she proves to be a model of redemption. Meteyard, however, does not trust the reader's ability to see that this redemption is not an isolated example but is possible in many cases. So, through Mary Austen, she announces to the reader: "'The grave is no fit ending to human tragedies like these, my poor one; for if we, as women, despair of helping our sister woman, what can men do? No! it is only through labour—honest self-help, that those standing can raise the fallen'" (331).

In contrast, works such as *The Seamstress, Ellen Linn,* and *Alton Locke* concentrate on the circumstances leading to a needlewoman's decline into prostitution rather than her possible redemption. The strongest picture of breakdown of virtue by poverty is found in *The Seamstress.* In his portrayal of Julia Barnett, Reynolds presents the most detailed explanation of a needlewoman's fall—surpassing even Stone and Tonna:

"I did not make society as it is: I was born into it such as it is— I was compelled, willing or unwilling, to yield to the circumstances arising from its false, its vitiated, its unjust condition and influence. . . . Poverty—cold—disappointment—hunger—crushing toil—and rags,—these are enemies which strike at the most rigid virtue.

"... I, too, have experienced the hardship of oppressive labour, and the horrors of starvation! . . . I have worked, indeed, till my back has ached and the pain has spread all over my body, . . . until my eyes have grown dim, and my brain has reeled. . . . I have worked in the cold until my limbs have been rigid as if with paralysis. . . . I have seriously and steadily looked Death in the face for long, long hours together when I have contemplated suicide! . . . Already—yes, already—are you advancing at a headlong pace towards the precipice which must swallow up your virtue. . . . You have work now—just for the moment, but how wretchedly is it paid! . . . You think yourself wretched now: but believe me when I tell you that your condition may become ten thousand times worse. . . . [T]hese wages are better than starving virtue—and human nature is too frail to hesitate long between the alternatives. Let those who blame me, act justly and blame the system of society. I am one of its victims—not one of its modellers. . . . [T]he gorgeous robe and elegant dress of every high-born lady is stained by the life-blood and infected by the pollution of the poor seamstresses who made them all!" (227–28)

Such passages show the influence of the firsthand testimonies gathered by Mayhew for the *Morning Chronicle.* The passages not only excite readers' indignation and sympathy over the conditions faced by needlewomen, but they add to Virginia's saintliness when she resists the sexual advances of an employer who was "well aware of the appalling fact nine-tenths of the females who worked for him were morally ruined by the system . . . [and] looked upon virtue in a seamstress as a phenomenon amounting almost to an impossibility" (356).

In both *Ellen Linn* and *Alton Locke* prostitution among seamstresses is alluded to rather than shown, but, in both cases, it is extreme poverty and starvation that prompt the allusions. In *Ellen Linn,* Ellen cannot find work and in a moment of desperation stretches out her hand to a passing lady and asks her to give something. The lady passes unheeding, but at the same moment a voice whispers, "'It is a pity that such a fine-looking girl as you should be begging.' She turned quickly round, not understanding the purport of the words; and at the same moment a gentleman (at least he had the dress of one) whispered something in her ear" (468). Ellen rejects the offer but is unable to find any other means of support. The portrait of the prostitute in *Alton Locke* resembles that of Nelly in *Lucy Dean,* one girl prostituting herself to feed another who is so sick she cannot work:

"I cannot see her starve, and I cannot starve myself. When she first fell sick she kept on as long as she could, doing what she could, and then between us we only earned three shillings-a-week, and there was ever so much to take off for fire, and twopence for thread, and fivepence for candles; and then we were always getting fined, because they never gave us out the work till too late on purpose, and then they lowered prices again; and now Ellen can't work at all, and there's four of us with the old lady, to keep off two's work that couldn't keep themselves alone." (91–92)

Thus the desire to create an understanding of the conditions faced by needlewomen, and explain why the women became the prostitutes Mayhew interviewed for his series, was an important factor to later writers. And it was this desire to place slopworkers among the "deserving poor," and therefore worthy of interest and aid, that inspired writers and illustrators to emphasize the martyrdom of young women to social abstractions such as economic theory or a heartless aristocracy. The sense of seamstress as martyr is constructed through the saintly behavior of the women in either resisting temptation or in aiding others, the redemption they achieve through emigration, and the suggestion of the inevitable destruction they face if they remain in England.

While visual artists did much to further the image of the seamstress as a secular saint, emigration itself offered little opportunity for visual representation of the seamstress. The established iconology—including the attic room, the candle, the flower, and the shirt—was impractical in pictures of emigration. Furthermore, artists who portrayed emigration during this period established a separate iconology, primarily centering around the image of the family—an image that automatically excluded the Victorian construct of the needlewoman, except as part of a contrasting diptych such as "The Needlewoman at Home and Abroad." Finally, Mayhew's reports, which facilitated much of the interest in emigration as a solution to the seamstress's plight, accentuated many of the things most artists only hinted at or actually ignored in their work: the filth associated with extreme poverty; the crowded conditions often forced on the women because of lack of funds; and the physical devastation caused by long hours, poor nutrition, and lack of heat and ventilation. Few artists presented these conditions with any realism, and when they did they were subject to criticism. In *Blackwood's Magazine,* John Eagles contests the value of such work: "I cannot conceive a greater mistake than to make 'familiar life' as it is called, doleful, uncheerful subjects that are out of the rule of love and pity, very easily run into the class of terror, the subject of art" (185). And when Redgrave first exhibited *Fashion's Slaves* (1847) the *Athenaeum* forcibly observed that art's purpose is not to serve as a reminder of the unpleasantness of life: "Praiseworthy as may be the motive which makes the language of his Art picture the injustice that 'patient merit from the unworthy takes,' the taste for dwelling on such matters is, yet, not a sound one. Mr. Redgrave has employed himself on these for some years; but we doubt the policy of doing so for the reputation of his pencil. The end of Art is pleasure; and to dwell habitually on the dark side of humanity is to miss that end" (552). It is hardly surprising, then, that the majority of artists chose to enhance their subjects, suggesting hardship symbolically through setting, shirt, and isolation, rather than portraying the physical effects of such suffering on the figure itself. As Edelstein explains, Victorian art functions most effectively when "social documents become more complex because what they omit assumes as great an importance as what they portray" ("'But who,'" 8). Indeed, only a few works rival Redgrave's *The Sempstress* for realistic portrayal of the seamstress herself, and one of the most graphic, George Frederic Watts's *The Seamstress,* was never finished and was exhibited only after the artist's death. While artists tempered their portrayals, perhaps stirring more pity than reformist zeal, they were, nevertheless, part of the interventionist spirit of the reform movement and their works did, according to Edelstein, "perform a dual purpose, serving as an anodyne at the same time that they advocate reform" ("But who," 12). Yet because of the restrictions of the system, suggestions for reform play little part in the artwork surrounding the seamstress; such possibilities remained the sole province of writers.

Drawn together by their concern for the seamstress, and by emigration as a possible resolution of her problems, the literary works of 1850 reflect the influence of earlier narratives through their choice of audience. The works of Stone and Tonna had been directed toward upper-class women, while those of later writers—Dickens, Toulmin, Rowcroft, and Gaskell— were aimed at both men and women. The works of 1850 represent both stances, with one work directed chiefly at men. *David Copperfield, The Seamstress,* and *Alton Locke* are influenced by their immediate predecessors and address both men and women, although Kingsley leans more toward addressing his male readers. In contrast *Lucy Dean* and *Lettice Arnold* return to the audience of earlier novels and address the question of what women can do to help other women, but include working-class as well as upper-class women and self-help. *Ellen Linn,* however, breaks from tradition, addressing male readers about a "woman's question": not only is the reader addressed as "he," but the only person who can aid Ellen is Mr. Fishlock, who is also the subject of the moral lesson contained in the tale. Thus, while the narratives of 1850 reflect the issues of the time, they are, in general, linked to their predecessors both in the form of their presentation and in the selection of their intended audiences.

Acculturation

In using these works as social documents we must remain aware that they create their own reality, a reality that can reflect a larger sphere, but not a one to one correspondence, it is an artistic reality.

—T. J. Edelstein, "'But who shall paint the griefs of those oppress'd?'"

Despite the articles and stories praising various emigration schemes, to many Victorians it had soon become obvious that emigration was not going to be the salvation for working women that many had hoped. As A. James Hammerton reveals in *Emigrant Gentlewomen,* even Sidney Herbert's Fund for Promoting Female Emigration, whose original aim had been to finance the emigration of distressed London needlewomen, was ineffective: "No total figures for the entire duration of the scheme survived, but various reports indicated that needleworkers were never in a majority. The first report classified only 167 out of its 409 emigrants in 1850 as needleworkers or dressmakers of various kinds" (107). Perhaps earlier reformers had been too successful in equating the seamstress with workers generally, allowing workers and philanthropists to read the articles advocating emigration for needlewomen as supporting the emigration of all workers; or perhaps it was the realization that most women emigrating to Australia would need farming skills, and there would be little employment for women in luxury-service occupations such as needlework.

Interestingly, Dickens, who is often seen as a barometer of Victorian thought, continued to advocate emigration, particularly for single women, well into the 1850s.[1] As late as April 1853, he published in *Household Words* a lengthy article praising a "Home for the reclamation and emigration of women," whose residents were predominantly needleworkers. Of the eight case studies presented, three are of seamstresses, and all the stories stress the dire poverty faced by women trying to earn a living sewing ("Home," 169–75). Of all the articles concerning emigration published in *Household Words,* only one, "A Digger's Diary," published 3 September 1853, sounded a warning to women considering emigration. The article concludes: "Certainly no respectable or even decent lodgings [are available abroad] for ladies, who want them immediately, and have no resident friends" (11). That the article ends on this warning note only emphasizes its negative connotations.

Dickens's reluctant admission that emigration might not be the solution to the problems facing needlewomen is finally made with the publication of "The Iron Seamstress" in *Household Words* on 11 February 1854. Although the article is primarily a description of a sewing machine, it opens with an overview of past and present conditions faced by seamstresses. In looking at the immediate past, the article praises the formation of needlewomen's benevolent societies, by which "some few poor women were snatched from death ... and hundreds of seamstresses were helped to shops that would carry them to comfortable homes." But as it continues, the article calls attention to the state of needlewomen remaining in England: "Here, the seamstresses are fewer, and have, of late, commanded higher wages. Still at the present moment, their prospects and experience are not of the brightest. Still the day's hard work brings only the coarsest food and coldest home" (575). Nevertheless the article is a positive one, holding out the hope that the "Iron Seamstress," the sewing machine, will "drive the seamstresses of (not much) flesh and blood to more remunerative employments" (576), and suggesting that the sufferings of needlewomen may soon be a thing of the past, without the women's resorting to extremes such as emigration.

Although a number of articles and editorials concerning seamstresses were published during the 1850s and early 1860s, and there was a continual increase in the number of paintings, only a few novel-length fictional works featuring needlewomen appeared. The sheer number of stories published in 1850 partially accounts for the lack of interest in needleworkers on the part of fiction writers a year or more later. And an impression of helplessness had been created, since emigration had done little to alleviate, let alone solve, the problems faced by seamstresses, despite much praise in both fictional and nonfictional presentations. In addition, as more time passed, new events and issues such as the Great Exhibition of 1851 and the Crimean War (1854–1856) became popular topics for fiction. Finally, the 1864 *Report to the Children's Employment Commission* solidified the impression that the plight of the seamstress had not improved despite two decades of reformist fiction, exposés, and charitable work.

Whether a response to the failure of various calls for reform, or merely a weary reaction to didacticism, there was yet another shift in the use of the seamstress in fiction.[2] A major factor was probably the change in attitudes about the working classes generally. Britain had been practicing free trade since 1846, and the end of the Great Famine moved England from the "Hungry '40s" to the "Fabulous '50s." The Chartist movement had been in retreat since 1848 and the Young Ireland movement had failed. And, finally, the peace and orderliness of the Great Exhibition—no demonstrations, strikes, or violence—convinced many Victorians that things had changed and that the country was entering a time of prosperity, confidence, and social peace. In fact, Thomas Macaulay asserted that 1851 would "long be remembered as a singularly happy year of peace, plenty, good feeling, innocent pleasure, national glory of the best and purist sort" (206). Thus there was little need for a nonthreatening representative of the working classes; for most Victorians the violence associated with worker reform appeared to be a thing of the past, and conditions seemed to be improving daily. It is not surprising, then, that during the 1850s few works focused on the plight of the seamstress. Many authors avoided dealing with the seamstress as an issue but, instead, used her as a vehicle for character studies of larger groups, often only tangentially associated with working-class issues: in *Ruth* (1853) Gaskell studies the "fallen" woman who is good, while in *Out of the Depths* (1859) Henry Jebb investigates the redemption of a woman who "falls" because of vanity. Dickens deals with the impact of financial failure on the middle class in *Little Dorrit* (1855–1857), while Julia Kavanagh's *Rachel Gray* (1856) studies the anonymity and fiscal instability of the lower-middle class.

I

In the first four chapters of *Ruth,* Gaskell presents the seamstress and her conditions much as they appeared a decade before. Ruth is an orphan from the country who was apprenticed by her guardian to a millinery shop at age fifteen. The novel opens at two o'clock in the morning with the dressmakers working to finish orders for a ball, orders placed only the day before. The seamstress suffering from consumption, the lack of adequate rest following the late nights, and the fear of competition among millinery houses all appear in the first pages of the novel. But Gaskell's emphasis on the character of Ruth, rather than the suffering of needlewomen in general, begins in the midst of the familiar recital. The women take a half-hour break, with the narrator moving from girl to girl showing the variety of reactions to the late night:

> It was curious to watch the young girls as they instantaneously availed themselves of Mrs. Mason's absence. One . . . laid her head on folded arms and was asleep in a moment; refusing to be awakened for her share in the frugal supper, but springing up with a frightened look at the sound of Mrs. Mason's returning footstep. . . . Two or three others huddled over the scanty fireplace. . . . [S]ome employed their time in eating their bread and cheese, with as measured and incessant motion of the jaws . . . as you may see in cows ruminating in the first field you happen to pass.
>
> Some held up admiringly the beautiful ball-dress in progress, while others examined the effect, backing from the object in the true artistic manner. Others stretched themselves into all sorts of postures to relieve the weary muscles, one or two gave vent to all the yawns, coughs, and sneezes that had been pent up so long in the presence of Mrs. Mason. But Ruth Hilton sprang up to the large window, and pressed against it as a bird presses against the bars of its cage. (4)

Despite the variety and detail given, Ruth stands out from her fellow workers. Gaskell accomplishes this in a number of ways. First, the conjunction *but* implies contradiction or exception, singling Ruth out from the others; second, and most obvious, Ruth is the only seamstress mentioned by name; and third, with the verb *sprang* Ruth is shown as more active, more lively, and therefore more interesting than her coworkers. And while the use of animal imagery is not unique, the analogy with a caged bird contributes to the reader's interest and, recalling the familiar city/country dichotomy associated with the seamstress, begins creating the sense of pathos that will mark Ruth's character later in the novel.

The time period of the opening chapter is a January night "many years ago" (3), reminding readers of the works of the early 1840s. Indeed, much of the material in Gaskell's early chapters seems to have been taken from these earlier works. When Ruth gazes out the window she sees "a little distance off, the feathery branches of a larch waved softly to and fro in the scarcely perceptible night-breeze," and she is reminded of home (5). Readers familiar with *A London Dressmaker's Diary* would have been reminded of the young seamstress portrayed there and her longing to be able to watch the branches of the tree just outside the shop. Similarly Mrs. Mason's carelessness about how her apprentices spend their Sundays recalls Tonna's *The Wrongs of Woman* and Ann's concern for how her sister spent her Sundays. Also Gaskell's incorporation of evidence from the October letters of Mayhew's series in the *Morning Chronicle* parallels earlier incorporations of parliamentary reports. For example, in letter LXXV (20 October 1850), Mayhew provides typical backgrounds of seamstresses—"daughters of clergymen, of military and naval officers, and of surgeons, farmers, and tradesmen . . . fully three-fourths of them have been reared in the country." He then supplements these figures with statistics for London shops: using figures from the 1841 census he informs readers that there were 20,780 dressmakers and milliners, of whom 3,480 were under twenty years of age.[3] He concludes the letter by describing "a first-rate establishment in the West-end." The description of the large workroom, with a fireplace at each end and long tables running down the middle filled with young girls working industriously, is both reminiscent of earlier descriptions and analogous to the shop Gaskell creates in *Ruth*. Gaskell relies on both Mayhew's physical descriptions of the young women and his recounting of their actions; however, she does not cite her sources, as did earlier writers such as Tonna.

In addition, Ruth's despair at the length of her apprenticeship and the conditions under which she must work are also typical of the earlier works— "'Oh! how shall I get through five years of these terrible nights! In that close room! and in that oppressive stillness! which lets every sound of the thread be heard as it goes eternally backwards and forwards,' sobbed out Ruth, as she threw herself on her bed, without even undressing herself" (8). And while Ruth herself does not suffer from consumption, her closest friend does. Although the girl does not die, she is forced to leave and forfeit the remainder of her apprenticeship since her "illness it was understood, although its severity was mitigated, was likely to be long and tedious" (28). Combined, these scenes form a pattern recalling the established semiotic system of seamstress fiction, which is immediately recognizable and allows the writer to cover the plight of the seamstress with minimal detail. Gaskell uses this codification to move from the issue of the sufferings of a particular group of young women to a larger social issue. As J. M. Ludlow, the reviewer for the *North British Review*, explains:

> In "Ruth," the occasional element occupies the very smallest possible space. The milliner's workshop,—the country ball and the milliner's apprentices looking upon the luxury and the pleasures from which they are excluded,—are the merest introduction to what follows; the rest of the story lies far from all class-feelings, from all the subjects for blue-books and commissions of inquiry.... [T]he writer takes no trouble to conduct us to the warehouse, to shew us the needlewomen waiting for orders, and the foreman bullying or fining them. She knows well that such scenes would but distract us *here* from her main purpose, the growth of holiness in the heart of the fallen woman, of the much-tried penitent. (163–64)

The reviewer's awareness of what has been omitted demonstrates that readers would have noticed the signs of abuse associated with the seamstress, recognized the iconology of suffering, and filled in any existing gaps in her portrayal.

Gaskell also uses circumstances and situations developed in earlier works. The constant references to Ruth's "remarkable beauty" and her meeting with a young gentleman while working at a ball would have reminded readers of Trollope's *Jessie Phillips*. Similarly Jenny's reluctance to write her family about her illness would have reminded readers of Alice Wilson's unwillingness to return home in Gaskell's earlier work *Mary Barton*. When illness tempts Jenny to write, she remembers "the premium her father had struggled hard to pay, and the large family, younger than herself, that had to be cared for" and she trusts that "when the warm weather came, both the pain and the cough would go away" (9). For Jenny, as for Alice, returning home would mean adding to the economic hardship of her parents.

For those readers familiar with *Jessie Phillips*, the gentleman's seduction of Ruth, the virtuous indignation expressed by his mother and the callousness with which Ruth is dismissed come as no surprise. Similarly, readers familiar with works such as Reynolds's *The Seamstress* would have quickly noticed references to saintliness, such as the wallpaper with "white lilies, sacred to the Virgin" that Ruth studies while working (6), and the statement by an old woman that "God watches over orphans" (26). By using material familiar to her readers, Gaskell is able to move quickly from the comfortable stereotype of the seamstress to a topic to which her readers would have been less receptive: the possible value of both the woman who has been seduced and her offspring.

The use of the seamstress to speak out against the fragile hold women, especially working women, had on respectability is a recurring theme in the works appearing during this period. Although Gaskell's *Ruth* was the first English novel to fully and realistically portray the social rehabilitation of the fallen woman, the idea that the sheltered lives led by many middle-class girls left them unfit to fend for themselves and unprepared for the temptations they would then face is found in popular journals as well. The plot of Mrs. White's "The Struggles of a Needlewoman," beginning in the 3 January 1852 issue of the *Home Circle*, is built around the destruction of a young woman's life when it is discovered that she has apparently had a child out of wedlock. In this serialized story, virtually the entire first installment is spent developing the young woman's character: she is shown as commanding admiration and respect from her employer and her fellow workers, as being charitable when encountering those less fortunate (giving a begging mother the piece of bread that was to be her only meal that day), and as voicing concern over the moral welfare of the young women under her charge. The installment ends with the revelation that she has hired a woman to care for her infant "at three shillings a-week, while she went about looking as modest as you please, and holding up her head like an honest woman!" (4). Having a child out of wedlock leaves the young woman vulnerable to sexual harassment by her employer's son, results in the loss of her job, and eventually culminates in her death. As the circumstances of her past are gradually revealed, the reader is again presented with the story of a young woman victimized by a society that values strict adherence to sexual rules of conduct and appearances more than the lives of young women who have innocently violated societal norms. Although much more conventional than Gaskell in her portrayal of the repercussions of the loss of chastity, White also emphasizes that it is the loss of reputation, more than chastity, that destroys her protagonist. Thus, like Gaskell, she wishes "to make readers think about their unexamined assumption that a woman who lost her chastity had to be totally cut off from society so that she would not contaminate decent people" (Mitchell, 33).

A year later G. M. Viner's *Aunt Eliza's Garret* (1854) returns to this theme. After demonstrating through the lives, and deaths, of various characters that needlewomen had three choices—a slow death through overwork and starvation, prison for pawning materials to be made up, or prostitution—Viner ends his novel with the marriage of the heroine's brother, George, and her closest friend, Susan, who had become a prostitute to survive. With George's return from Australia, both Amelia—the heroine—and Susan are rescued from the horrors of destitution, but because Amelia refused to supplement her income through prostitution, her health is ruined and she dies of consumption. For Susan, despite the fact that she prostituted herself out of need and often helped support Amelia with her extra funds, her brief time on the streets leaves "in her heart a secret source of unhappiness and reproach to herself" (190). But for the reader, one of the most telling scenes occurs a page later when, on her deathbed, Amelia encourages her brother to consider marrying Susan despite her past. Throughout the novel Amelia has been the character who has been able to look beneath the surface, both with people and situations, and see the true motivations and implications—her brother and aunt comment numerous times on her insight. Thus the reader is compelled to consider seriously her unconventional attitude when she tells George,

> ". . . and though her whole life may not be without a blemish—and whose is?—remember, dear, that the fallen, yet repentant woman, was not rejected by our blessed Saviour; and if, my dear, you . . . should feel inclined to wed—and when I'm gone you will be lonely, very lonely, perhaps—who so able to cheer you, and to make the hours of sorrow less sorrowful, as that kind soul who saved me from a wicked death, and gave me time to seek my God? Her love alone would prompt her to do so; give her then the right." (191)

Not only does George marry Susan, but we are told that "their sorrows and their sins had been to them as a purifying furnace" (192), signifying that they are actually better people for their experiences.

The suggestion that the fallen woman could marry would have been startling to many middle- and upper-class Victorians. For them, women served as the moral center of the home, the "angel in the house," creating a shelter from the chaos and moral corruption of the business world. This sanctuary protected men from being sucked into the confusion of the world at large. Yet, this very premise was constructed on a paradox: women are physically inferior to men and therefore are to be submissive, supervised, and protected; women are spiritually superior to men and therefore are to provide leadership, guidance, and protection. Thus for an ex-prostitute to serve as the moral and spiritual guide to a family would have been a disturbing concept for Victorian readers, for she would be weak in the very area in which she was supposed to be superior. Viner's showing the fallen woman to be not only a victim of society, but also a person whose inner spirit remains uncorrupted, who is thus eligible for marriage, was a significant message for Victorians.

Much as does Gaskell, Henry Jebb takes issue with society's unwillingness to accept that fallen women could be rehabilitated, and he uses the occupation of seamstress to provide a background to the story of a woman's moral fall. But Jebb's female protagonist, Mary Smith, is not like Ruth—a naive young woman seduced by a heartless rake. In a first-person narrative, taking the form of a memoir, Mary recounts her life always taking responsibility for actions. The daughter of a head gardener on an estate, Mary becomes engaged to an Oxford student staying at the house. And even here, Mary makes it clear that, at least in moralistic retrospect, she was a participant, not a victim. She falls because of vanity:

> I chose to believe myself of a finer nature than my born equals, and I determined to rise out of that class if I could, and never mix with them more. One thing confirmed me in this presumptuous opinion; and this was that among the few young women I knew, not one of them had the same thoughts or aspirations as I had; they read, some of them, the same books, but did not extract the same ideas from them, and I considered that they were low and common in comparison with me. (29)

When the young man learns she is pregnant he sends for her, but dies of a fever before she arrives. The baby is stillborn; and while her family does not turn her out, she feels uncomfortable in the village, where everyone knows her, and frustrated by her more limited employment opportunities. She goes to Oxford to work with two young dressmakers, who are friendly and generous—and prostitutes. Mary adopts their life, not because she is starving or has no choice, but for pleasure, for extra finery, and for the sense of power it gives her. Associating with wealthy, educated men initially increases her sense of self-worth and provides her with opportunities to better herself mentally. But while reading the Bible for a dying prostitute, she experiences a conversion. Despite her initial experiences as a dressmaker, her return to needlework is cut short when her recent past is revealed. At this point she turns to a clergyman for help. He helps her secure a teaching position and encourages her to accept the marriage proposal of a young widower with children who, despite knowing of her past, wishes to marry her. However, despite his belief in prostitute reclamation, like Gaskell, Jebb cannot take his tale that far; Mary dies of a fever before the wedding. Nevertheless he makes it clear that marriage should have been an acceptable outcome. As the clergyman assures Mary:

> "If you were still as before—if you were not a truly repentant woman—what you have just said [that for her marriage would defile the word *wife*] would be most proper and correct—but you are changed;... why should you thrust from you what seems to me to be of His especial sending, to remove you, perhaps, out of all temptation, and to graft you again fully into that society which you once feel away from?... If God has wiped away your soul's sins, shall no man erase the memory of your body's sins? Surely he should, and you should give him the opportunity." (338–39)

Thus for both Gaskell and Jebb, the established figure of the seamstress functions as a device to introduce characters and quickly establish situations preparing for a discussion of a larger issue—magdalen reform.

Yet despite the common equation of needlework and prostitution, especially following Mayhew's letters in the *Morning Chronicle,* it was essential that a seamstress maintain an image of respectability. This was especially important for dressmakers, since they not only encountered female clients in the shop, but were often sent into the clients' homes for fittings. For example, in Dickens's *Little Dorrit,* to maintain an air of respectability Amy Dorrit finds it "necessary to conceal where she lives and to come and go as secretly as she could," for if her life at Marshalsea Prison became known she would be unable to find work (75). Little Dorrit's need for secrecy piques the interest of the wealthy gentleman in the story, and his interest in her brings him in contact with her family and thus integrates the two threads of the narrative. Since needlework was one of the few occupations in Victorian England that allowed the working poor to enter the homes of the wealthy and have contact with them, the seamstress is an obvious choice when creating a novel intertwining the lives of destitute characters with those of wealthy ones.

Dickens's use of the seamstress in *Little Dorrit* assumes knowledge on the part of the reader, to an even greater extent than Gaskell's work. Since Dickens's story centers around the family of a gentleman imprisoned for debt, the traditional association of the seamstress with impoverished gentility makes her the perfect female protagonist in his novel. Dickens does not bother to explain seamstresses' conditions, work hours, or wages to his readers, relying on such details being firmly entrenched from previous stories about the occupation and trusting the reader to recall them when given subtle reminders. When telling the reader that Little Dorrit is a seamstress, the narrator reminds the reader of the poor wages with a brief parenthetical phrase: "Little Dorrit let herself out to do needlework. At so much a day—or at so little—from eight to eight" (51). Similarly the discussion between Little Dorrit and a milliner in the prison recalls the physical hardships of the occupation, while reinforcing the poor monetary gains:

> She watched and waited months for a seamstress. In the fullness of time a milliner came in, and to her she repaired on her own behalf. . . . "If you please I want to learn needlework."
>
> "Why should you do that," returned the milliner, "with me before you? It has not done me much good. . . . I am afraid you are so weak, you see," the milliner objected. . . . "And you are so very, very little, you see," the milliner objected. (70)

The repetition of structure and phrasing in the milliner's protest calls attention to the warnings about health, reinforcing the reminder of the hardships faced by needlewomen.

Dickens's decision to use a seamstress may also have been influenced by the pressures of serial publication. For, although she was the title character, Amy Dorrit did not appear in the first installment of the novel. In fact, there was much speculation as to the significance of the title, as illustrated by the *Athenaeum*'s response to Amy Dorrit's belated appearance: "Let us say at once, that 'Little Dorrit' is not a broom, not a village, not a ship,—as has been variously surmised at various tea-tables,—where the book in the green cover is as eagerly expected as the news of the last battle,—but a live flesh and blood little girl." Thus when Amy Dorrit did appear, Dickens needed to establish her character very quickly. By placing her in a profession with which his readers were familiar, Dickens could present small pieces of information, such as reminders of wages and hours, as an iconographic shorthand, establishing his character with minimal effort or delay. Once the character was established, like Gaskell and Jebb, Dickens had no need to dwell on the well-known images associated with needlewomen; hence the lack of detail concerning Little Dorrit's profession after the initial presentation.

Similarly, in *Aurora Leigh,* Elizabeth Barrett Browning is able to quickly establish Marian Erle's character both as a representative of the working classes and as a hard-working character worthy of interest, as well as the care and protection of Romney Leigh and the love of Aurora Leigh. Born of working-class parents, Marian flees when her mother attempts to sell her to a local squire. Hospitalized in the aftermath of exposure, Marian comes to the attention of Romney Leigh, who secures her a place in a London millinery house. The working conditions Marian encounters there are so familiar that Browning is able to evoke them in less than a verse:

> ... through the days and through the nights
> She sewed and sewed and sewed. She drooped sometimes,
> And wondered, while, along the tawny light
> She struck the new thread into her needle's eye,
> How people, without mothers on the hills,
> Could chose the town to live in!—then she drew
> The stitch, and mused how Romney's face would look
> and if 'twere likely he'd remember hers
> When they two had their meeting after death. (ll. 3.1234–42)

Thus, as she ends the third book, Browning evokes much of the standard iconography: the long nights, the weariness, the city/country dichotomy, and the sense of doom associated with the occupation.

Browning then opens book four with a slight twist; rather than succumbing to fatal illness herself, Marian leaves her employment to nurse a young friend who is dying and whose mother is unable to care for her. Because of the familiarity of the reader with the situation, Browning can present the girl's story in fewer than thirty lines. Nor would the reader have been surprised when the narrator reveals that in leaving to nurse the girl, Marian

> ... knew, by such an act,
> All place and grace were forfeit in the house,
> Whose mistress would supply the missing hand
> With necessary, not inhuman haste,
> And take no blame. (ll. 4.32–36)

In his work among the poor, Romney Leigh again finds Marian and, recognizing her sacrifice and her character, asks her to marry him, though it is clear that the match will be primarily a culmination of philosophy rather than of love:

> "'Twixt class and class, opposing rich to poor,—
> Shall *we* keep parted? Not so. Let us lean
> And strain together rather, each to each,
> Compress the red lips of this gaping wound,
> As far as two souls can,—ay, lean and league,
> I from my superabundance,—from your want,
> You,—joining in a protest 'gainst the wrong
> On both sides!" (ll. 4.124–31)

The blurring of class demarcations in earlier portrayals of needlewomen and the establishment of the seamstress as a figure of suffering and sacrifice make Romney Leigh's proposal effective symbolically and minimally feasible.

Browning then uses the somewhat stereotypical portrayal of the unthinking client to foreshadow Marian's downfall. After describing "used out" nights followed by days "worn . . . into shreds" (ll. 4.243–44) and thoughtless comments from clients, Marian notes that "they forget to look behind [their reflection] / And mark how pale we've grown, we pitiful / Remainders of the world" (ll. 4.258–60). The indirect reference is to Lady Waldemar, who tells Aurora Leigh of the engagement in the hopes that she will pressure Romney to break it off. When Aurora instead gives her blessing to the match, Lady Waldemar schemes to remove Marian by deceit, giving little thought to the possible consequences. Thus the established tropes surrounding the seamstress allowed Browning to establish Marian's character with a minimum of explication, and to foreshadow motivations and plot lines without distracting the reader or undermining necessary points of uncertainty (as when Marian fails to appear for the wedding ceremony).

Not all authors relied on the established codes in their portrayals of needlewomen, however. The publication of Julia Kavanagh's *Rachel Gray* is significant for its departure from earlier fictional portrayals of the seamstress. Unlike her predecessors, Rachel Gray is a millinery shop owner and is able to get sufficient work. George Eliot marked the novel's departure from the norm when she reviewed it for the *Leader:*

> *Rachel Gray* is not a story of a fine lady's sorrows wept into embroidered pocket-handkerchiefs, or of genius thrust into the

background by toad-eating stupidity. It does not harrow us with the sufferings and temptations of a destitute needlewoman, or abash us with refined sentiments and heroic deeds of navvies and rat-catchers. It tells the trials of a dressmaker who *could* get work, and of a small grocer, very vulgar, and not at all heroic, whose business was gradually swallowed up by the large shop over the way. Thus far *Rachel Gray* is commendable: it occupies ground which is very far from being exhausted, and it undertakes to impress us with the every-day sorrows of our commonplace fellow-men, and so to widen our sympathies. . . . [H]ere is really a new sphere for a great artist who can paint from close observation, and who is neither a caricaturist nor a rose-coloured sentimentalist. (19)

Thus, as in Gaskell's *Ruth,* the figure of the seamstress is being used as a vehicle for a character study. In *Rachel Gray* Kavanagh is studying a specific social group: the middle-class entrepreneur who is barely able to maintain her place in society. Kavanagh, however, does not focus on the working existence of her character, but rather on her relationships with those around her: her impatient stepmother, her unloving father, and her distressed neighbor. Kavanagh recounts a story as bland as the protagonist's name, Gray, thus matching the presentation to the subject, nonsuccess and social anonymity. The introduction of Rachel presents the most detailed description of her life as a seamstress, but at the same time the motifs of monotony, observation, and characterization through relationships with others are also introduced:

It was but a little room . . . The furniture though poor and old-fashioned, was scrupulously clean . . . A few discoloured prints in black frames hung against the walls; two or three broken china ornaments adorned the wooden mantel-shelf . . . Near the window, two apprentices sewed, under the superintendence of Rachel Gray. . . . She sewed on, serious and still, and the calm gravity of her aspect harmonized with the silence of the little parlour which nothing disturbed, save the ticking of an old clock behind the door, the occasional rustling of Mrs. Gray's newspaper, and the continuous and monotonous sound of stitching. . . . She sewed on, as we have said, abstracted and serious, when gradually, for even in observation she was slow, the crocuses attracted her attention. She looked at them meditatively, and watched them closing, with the decline of day. And, at length, as if she had not understood, until then, what was going on before her, she smiled and admiringly exclaimed:

"Now do look at the creatures, mother!"

Mrs. Gray glanced up from her newspaper, and snuffled rather disdainfully.

"Lawk, Rachel!" she said, "you don't mean to call crocuses creatures—do you?" (5–7)

The simplicity and cleanliness of the room, the monotony of the work, and the reference to the flowers outside the window might recall earlier narratives. But the knickknacks scattered about the room, the sense of serenity despite monotony, Rachel's role as shop owner rather than apprentice, and the number of people—neither a roomful nor the lone needleworker—all mark Kavanagh's narrative as different from its antecedents.

Rachel Gray is not completely removed from its predecessors, however. Reminiscent of *Mary Barton*, the protagonist for whom the text is named is a distanced observer rather than the main focus of the narrative. Much as the security of Mary Barton's position at a millinery house isolates her from the working-class community around her, making her an observer rather than a participant in its troubles, so Rachel Gray's occupation places her in the position of observer, isolated from the uncertainties faced by most middle-class businesspeople. From her seat at the shop window, Rachel watches the neighborhood surrounding her. She notes with interest the opening of new businesses, and with sorrow the gradual destruction of Richard Jones's store. Yet her curiosity and worry are for them; she has no need to be concerned about her own business failing.

Nor is Kavanagh's work the first in which the seamstress's life is not one of active suffering, but one of prosaic duty. In November 1852, the *Working Man's Friend and Family Instructor* published a short story, "The Seamstress," that provides a moral lesson on duty to family and the dangers of gossip. At the center of the story is a seamstress whose suffering is caused not by her occupation but by idle gossip that prevents her lover's mother from giving her blessing to their marriage. Because the young woman will not let her lover violate his duty to his mother, they cannot be married until the two women have overcome the barrier created by another's spite. Thus, although most literature concerning needlewomen highlighted the continued abuses of the system, *Rachel Gray* is not a complete anomaly in its presentation.

Moreover, the novel's subtitle, *A Tale Founded on Fact,* and the explanatory preface recall earlier writers, Tonna in particular, in both tone and content:

> This tale, as the title-page implies, is founded on fact. Its truth is its chief merit, and the Author claims no other share in it, than that of telling it to the best of her power.
>
> I do not mean to aver that every word is a positive and literal truth, that every incident occurred exactly as I have related it, and in no other fashion, but this I mean to say: that I have invented nothing in the character of Rachel Gray, and that the sorrows of Richard Jones are not imaginary sorrows.... I wished to show the intellectual, the educated, the fortunate, the minds which they are apt to slight as narrow, that lives which they pity as moving in the straight and gloomy paths of mediocrity, are often blessed and graced beyond the usual lot, with those lovely aspirations towards better deeds and immortal things, without which life is indeed a thing of little worth; cold and dull as a sunless day. (iii–v)

In many ways *Rachel Gray* represents the culmination of the seamstress novel. Like *Ruth, Rachel Gray* is set in a millinery shop rather than in the home of a slopworker, indicating the influence of earlier narratives as well as documented reports, in this case Mayhew's. But in Kavanagh's novel the return to the middle-class seamstress is also for the purpose of eliciting reader response. For as the authors of the early 1840s used the middle-class status of the seamstress to show her worthy of sympathy, Kavanagh uses middle-class status to ensure that readers find Rachel's character worthy of a detailed study, again relying on a sense of thankfulness and awareness that they could easily find themselves living the events portrayed in the study. The novel also marks a shift in emphasis from the sufferings of an individual or group to an interest in the workings of society as a whole, parallel to the focal shift that occurred in the later 1840s. In the use of the seamstress as a vehicle for a character sketch and in the emphasis on the monotony of Rachel Gray's existence, where "the story of one day was the story of the next" (42), Kavanagh brings the Victorian seamstress full circle from her first appearance in John Galt's 1833 short story, "The Seamstress."

II

Many of the stories published during the 1850s and 1860s use the semiotic codes established a decade earlier with little or no variation. Thomas Mills's "The Seamstress," published in the 1 February 1851 issue of the *Penny Illustrated News,* is almost a list of seamstress motifs: it opens at night around Christmas and moves to a poorly furnished, unheated attic room lighted by a single candle. There a young woman, worn by grief and work, plies her needle as the tolling of St. Paul's indicates that it is midnight. As she continues to work, we find that she is an orphan, from the country, unable to earn more than two pence to four pence a day. The short story presents four scenes from a two-year period. The day after the introduction, the young woman is threatened with homelessness. When she begs her landlady for more time to pay the rent, she is told that she is a bad risk—the last seamstress to live there had to pawn some of her clothes in order to pay the rent. That night, we are told, she falls. Yet Mills makes it clear that she is a victim of circumstance: "The remuneration for her labour was so small, so utterly insignificant, that she found it to be impossible for her to live, as she had hitherto done, in innocence and virtue ... Blame her not then if in an evil hour she fell; blame her not, if, when suffering under an accumulated load of sorrow and misery—poverty before her, and starvation and death staring her in the face—she succumbs to the power of the seducer" (35). Approximately a year later we find she has become the mistress of an affluent young man and they have a child, but he is leaving her to marry a woman his father has chosen. The story dramatically ends with her walking to her old home in the country and dying draped over the graves of her parents. Her story thus encompasses the range of images associated with the seamstress: the attic room, the long nights, the poor pay, the seduction, the betrayal, the inevitable death, and all framed by the city/country dichotomy.

A similar story, more fully detailed, is found in the second section of Ernest Jones's *Woman's Wrongs* (1852). Jones, a Chartist leader and publisher, often focused on the need for workers to establish a political power base in order to install themselves in socially and politically effective positions. In *Woman's Wrongs,* published serially in Jones's *Notes to the People,* he focuses on Victorian society's least powerful sector: women. Using a structure as reminiscent of Tonna's *The Wrongs of Woman* as his title, Jones divides his story into four sections—"The Working-man's Wife," "The Young Milliner," "The Tradesman's Daughter," and "The Lady of the

Title." He focuses on women in four different socio-economic groups—
lower-working class, upper-working class, petite bourgeois, and aristocracy. By examining the lives of women across the socio-economic spectrum,
Jones equates the corruption of power with that of poverty, and shows
that lack of power inevitably leads to seduction (literal or figurative) and
destruction. In "The Young Milliner," Jones depicts the gradual decline of
a needleworker's fortunes, as she is unable to find work and is forced to
compromise herself: first by borrowing money, then by becoming the mistress of a young medical student. The young woman's life continues its
downward spiral as her lover grows tired of her and, mistakenly assuming
she has been paid off, abandons her. The section ends with her death in a
teaching hospital and the use of her corpse in her lover's anatomy class.
Throughout the section, it is the woman who is the victim, and as such she
is expiated of her sin:

> Do not imagine that our object is to extenuate sin, or to gloze [*sic*]
> over vice with sentimental sophistry—but we do say this,—broadly,
> boldly in the face of society and all its prejudice, its ignorance, its
> cruelty, do we fling down the assertion: that young girl was better,
> more virtuous, more good—aye! more *pure*—than ninety-nine out
> of every hundred of the sanctimonious tyrants who, in their self-
> righteous morality, would trample that appealing spirit down into
> the street! (690)

The macabre irony of the final scene simply underscores Jones's moral
about the corrupting influences of both poverty and capital.

Stories of abuse with melodramatic conclusions were so well established
that they became the food for sensational literature, such as Edwin F.
Roberts's *Bertha Gray, the Parish Apprentice-Girl; or, Six Illustrations of
Cruelty*. Running in *Reynolds's Miscellany* during 1851, *Bertha Gray* used
the seamstress's established semiotic code in telling a highly imaginative
tale of greed, sadism, and corruption indicting both the needlework and
workhouse systems. In this novel, the common image of the innocent young
dressmaker suffering at the hands of an abusive, morally lax shop owner
becomes the story of an innocent young girl purposefully placed in the
shop of a sadist who literally whips her apprentices to death. Similarly, the
image of the well-intentioned but thoughtless magistrate becomes that of a
bumbling fool who carelessly leaves everything to his corrupt servant and
credits unlikely explanations of suspicious circumstances, such as screams

from within the shop. Typically, sensational literature adds melodramatic detail to conventional characters and situations. Although removed from the mainstream of reformist literature, Roberts's story is nevertheless interesting for what it demonstrates about the establishment of the iconography of suffering surrounding the seamstress, and for the way in which it alludes to familiar scenes, descriptions, and concepts, yet twists them to fit within the genre of the sensational.

Using as a base the publicity following the convictions of several shop owners for the deaths of apprentices through "ill-usage" as well as murder "out of hand," the narrative opens with a mix of factual information and editorialism familiar to readers of seamstress literature. The setting is a humble room in which a parent, in this case the father, is dying while attended by his dutiful young daughter. His dying speech makes it clear that he had been of the middle or upper classes but had fallen on hard times and will leave his child a penniless orphan. However, the illustration that heads the opening leaves no doubt as to the sensational nature of the text: in the etching a young woman, stripped to the waist, is suspended from the ceiling by her wrists while a dissipated woman draws back a whip and a man raises a cane as if to strike her. The contrast between the opening written material and the lead illustration carries the implication that the sufferings of needlewomen, long documented through government reports and various stories and artwork, were metaphorically equivalent to the beating portrayed in the illustration. Although the pictured beating occurs later in the story, it has, by that time, been established as an outgrowth of the depraved nature of a woman who would destroy the lives of young women out of greed—a standard portrayal of uncaring shop owners. The story closes with generalizations concerning cruelty and the representative nature of the scenes portrayed: Bertha, remembering her life since her father's death, "pictured herself . . . and she pictured others, young homeless, innocent of evil, yet punished like criminals, walking the cold streets, shivering, starving—scorned and insulted . . ." (171). Generally "there was much talk of neglect, and harshness, and cruelty on the part of the guardians of the workhouse; and how they were held up to public censure . . . and how it was of little use" (172). Finally she reflects, "CRUELTY is prolific, and invariably engenders its own punishment without forgetting the interest that long debt always incurs" (172). Thus the story, like many of its predecessors, deals with the sufferings of needlewomen and with the poor generally, although in a much more lurid manner. Ending with the execution of the shop owner and her son, as well as the imprisonment of the workhouse supervisor who purposefully sent Bertha to them, the novel contains a warning to all members of society who overlook the abuse of the innocent, represented by the seamstress, as well as to those who actually abuse them.

Three narratives that follow established paradigms with little variation are Mary Guigard's *The Unprotected* (1851), G. M. Viner's *Aunt Eliza's Garret; or, Scenes in the Life of a Needle-Woman* (1854), and Gabriel Alexander's *Lilias, the Milliner's Apprentice* (1854).[4] From the moment readers open the cover of *The Unprotected*, they are confronted with declarations of authenticity: the title page not only declares in the subtitle that the work constitutes "the facts in dressmaking life," but also identifies the author only as "A Dressmaker." The work is dedicated to the Earl of Shaftesbury, known for his interest in alleviating the hardships of needlewomen. The introduction of *The Unprotected* also opens with familiar affirmations of veracity: "The following pages were written by one who was not long ago a young girl in the workroom of a London dressmaker. She herself has passed through the ordeal of which she gives so graphic a description. Her volume was written in the intervals she was able to snatch from the labours of the same calling; for she is still a dressmaker, though now the head and chief worker in her small establishment" (iii). Claiming that "he" has met the author and can vouch for "the modest quietness of her manners and the unpretending good sense of her remarks" (iv), the narrator claims to have done "little more" than revise the portions "which betrayed the pen of an unpracticed writer" (v). He then attempts to substantiate her story in two ways, through other, similar stories and through parliamentary testimony. First he recalls two stories of women of his acquaintance to establish that the problems recounted are common ones. The first concerns two sisters, daughters of a "farmer of high standing" whose death necessitates that they work. They are apprenticed to a London dressmaker. Because they have an uncle with whom they can spend their Sundays, "they [are] thus saved from the dangers of the young unprotected dressmaker's assistant on that day intended to be a boon of blessed rest and refreshment to all the children of God" (v–vi). The second story, set not in London but in a "large provincial town," illustrates that the breakdown of health from exhaustion is also a common problem. The narrator then reminds readers of the earlier works of Charlotte Elizabeth Tonna and Anne Marsh, demonstrating that the issues are of long standing and ignorance is no excuse. Finally, he asserts that the accounts are "fully confirmed" by "published evidence" taken by the House of Lords in 1855, and includes more than thirty excerpts on topics such as age, hours, and clients (vii–xii). The introduction ends with the acknowledgment "legislation might do," but asserts that "even the most stringent legislation would be powerless" unless supported by millinery shops' customers; "the remedy," he insists, "is in the hands of our English ladies" (xiv).

Given the evangelical nature of Guigard's novel, it is not surprising that the problems surrounding Sundays receive much attention. Not only does the work address the turning out of workers and lack of meals, but, in presenting the late Saturday work nights and the women's resulting exhaustion on Sundays, Guigard also confronts the issue of hypocrisy and false charity. When a wealthy, aristocratic customer stops late Saturday and leaves two dresses to be altered for an event on Monday, three apprentices must stay up Saturday night working. That a customer could be unaware of the impact of such work seems unlikely, given the public attention dressmakers had received; in the story the thoughtlessness is compounded by the fact that the woman is a known reform advocate:

> "I say," said one of the girls when they reached their room, "it is now nearly one o'clock. Her grace is a leading character in the early-closing movement, or rather that portion of it connected with ourselves—'the overworked milliners and dressmakers.' I wonder what she will say when she finds her dresses going home on Sunday morning. . . .
>
> "It amounts to a mockery to make all this to-do about us, and yet let our employers execute orders in a space of time so short as to render it impossible that they could have been done without carrying out the very thing they are professedly opposing." (203–4)

Guigard goes on to argue that when seamstresses are confronted with such hypocrisy, and worked to the point of exhaustion, it is not surprising that few of them attend church on Sundays. That many of the dressmakers, forced to leave their rooms mid-morning, choose to walk in the parks rather than attend church becomes an outgrowth of the cynicism brought on by the moral blindness of those who claim to advocate reform. Thus *The Unprotected* focuses as much on the moral responsibilities of those who patronize dressmaking and millinery establishments as those who own them.

From the title page of *Aunt Eliza's Garret* on, Viner also follows established models: opening with lines from Hood's "The Song of the Shirt," he moves to a preface in which he declares that he has "not drawn on the imagination, but related facts that have occurred." The beginning of the novel establishes the orphan status of the title character's niece, Amelia, and nephew, George, and the widowing of Aunt Eliza, which results in their economic fall. The novel then follows the predictable pattern of relating the horrors of the workroom, the gradual economic decline finally resulting in an inability to make ends meet, and the deaths of the needlewomen by overwork and consumption. Other elements derived from the seamstress iconography, but used here to add touches of melodrama, are the evil landlady, plotting the seduction of the impoverished women who board at her house; Amelia's attempted suicide following the death of Eliza's infant son, who had been entrusted to her care; and the return of the male relative, Amelia's brother, who temporarily rescues the seamstress, but too late to save her from her illness. A unique characteristic, however, is the way Viner includes the various levels of needlework. As their economic situation slowly declines, we watch Eliza and Amelia work in a variety of positions: from forewoman at a dress shop doing embroidery, to an apprentice in a dress shop, to a worker making bonnets, to a pieceworker, and finally a shirtmaker. We find that needlework covers making embroidery, dresses, waistcoats, shirts, bonnet casings, silk fringes, and baby linen, all described with careful enumeration of the low wages and abuse by shop owners and middlemen. As in earlier works, much of the information is conveyed to the reader as an experienced worker explains the system to Eliza or Amelia.

Like other fictional works of the 1850s, *Aunt Eliza's Garret* is scathing in its denunciation of false charity, but specifically that of evangelicals and tract societies that minister among the poor. Particularly condemnatory is the scene in which Susan Green, a book stitcher, explains why she cannot earn a living working for a local society that distributes Bibles and tracts to the poor. Noting that the five to eight shillings she makes a week are not sufficient "'to keep one from the streets,'" Susan questions, "'If giving bibles away can do so much good, I wonder we, who prepare them, are not better off; and if it's good to give them away, it must be better action in the giver if he paid a proper price for the labour which produced them'" (42). When Amelia accuses her of being harsh toward religion, Susan denies it, arguing:

"No one can be religious, who will unmercifully grind you down, just to humour a whim of going about giving books away, and talking largely of religion, without one feeling of reality. They have come to me and wished to read and pray with me; they have even offered me the very book I've stitched, and bade me have *faith*. Let them find the means to give us all work at a fair price first, and then we may possibly be brought to understand what *faith* is. It's hard, indeed, for a starving person to have faith in that being who is said to feed the sparrows, and yet who allows us to feel the gnawing gripes of hunger." (42–43)

At another point, when Amelia tries to take in sewing at home while she cares for her nephew, a "class leader of the Wesleyan persuasion . . . condesend[s] to patronize" her but is willing to pay only a shilling for the work. The woman explains, "'I want all my money for charitable societies that I belong to, or I might offer you more. I can't afford it, indeed I can't. You seem to be very poor, I should fancy it would be a charity to you to do it at any price.'" As the woman lists the various charities to which she contributes, Amelia wonders, "'whether it were also honest to endeavour to get work done at less than one-half the proper price for the sake of appearing liberal and charitable'" (117). While the issue is a common one during the period, few works are as vehement in their condemnation of false charity as Viner's novel.

Although its overview of the wide variety of needleworkers makes *Aunt Eliza's Garret* unique, Viner does use some set patterns when portraying the women at work, especially at home. Such patterns draw in readers through the reassurance of the familiar. Thus it is not surprising that when Eliza is shown slowly dying through overwork, Viner closes the chapter by alluding three times to Hood's "The Song of the Shirt," and uses the refrain "stitch, stitch, stitch," in the concluding paragraph (119). And much as Hood and other early reformers tied the seamstress to the mothers, sisters, and wives of the middle class, Viner asks his readers: "Who is there, that having once spent an hour in such society, and having any love for a sister, would look unmoved at that sister's living and breathing in the same atmosphere with those poorly paid needle girls?" (67). Compounding any feelings of dread he may have evoked, Viner then expounds on needlework as inevitably being the "high road to prostitution," a horrific picture for any Victorian reader to contemplate in general, let alone for his or her sister.

But the work that draws most strongly on previous works is Alexander's *Lilias, the Milliner's Apprentice*. Published in penny weekly numbers and six-penny monthly parts, Alexander's novel is about a convoluted love triangle involving an orphaned milliner's apprentice, a young aristocrat, and a curate's daughter. Mixing melodramatic romance with social protest, the novel reiterates much of the material presented in earlier works. As in many novels that equate the seamstress with saintliness or martyrdom, the heroine, Lilias, is spoken of as having an "angel-face" and "fearless innocence"; she is an "angel" and "the bird of Paradise." Like Reynolds, Alexander uses his novel to indict young, male aristocrats for the careless seduction of young women, an act considered "safe and fair when practised upon the humbly born, the unprotected, the 'nobodies,' . . . the poor, the parentless, and the helpless of the tender sex" (42). Early in the work, in a chapter entitled "The Needle-Girl's Peril," Alexander carefully lays before the reader the moral danger facing needlewomen. As one jaded, young aristocrat explains to another, more naive gentleman:

> "[T]he dress-making sister hood are the most legitimate game of the sort. They are very generally creatures that have some pretensions to good looks, and also to genteel breeding. Many of them come fresh from the country to mighty London, . . . they have neither friends nor relations that care a rush about them after coming up to the metropolis; mere simple, credulous, country creatures, whom a practical gentleman of my sort, for example, knows how to waylay, to tempt, cheat, and ensnare in less than a week." (43)

Later chapters, with titles such as "The Dressmaker's Destiny" and "The Martyr-Sisterhood," present readers with an overview of the 1843 *Second Report of the Children's Employment Commission,* then discuss the conditions of the house where Lilias is working as a first hand, implying that little has changed. Alexander details the wages, the hours, the sleeping arrangements, the food, the lack of mental stimulation, and the problems with Sundays. So that readers are reminded of the universality of the problems, Alexander has Lilias visit three friends who work at a millinery house where the conditions are even worse than the one at which she is employed. In fact two of her friends are dying, a "waste of flesh and blood . . . emaciated . . . in that killing millinery establishment" (140). In a scene rife with the language of martyrdom, the young women die and with their deaths convert the shop owner to more humane business practices. Unevenly mixing reform doctrine with melodrama (multiple kidnappings, seductions, suicide attempts, attempted murders), Alexander declares his aim is "to teach, by the force of example, the necessity of self-control to all who wish to be good, happy, and eminent; to exhibit the results of senseless and pernicious training in youth; and to inculcate the advantages to be reaped from cherishing pure and lofty aspirations" (155). Thus he uses an established figure of both innocence and suffering to create a moralistic tale about the danger of those who would try and corrupt others.

Later in the decade, Wilkie Collins combined many of the common-places associated with pieceworkers with the increasingly negative reports about emigration and created his first murder mystery, "The Diary of Anne Rodway," published in *Household Words* on 19 and 26 July 1856. As Richard Altick has noted, "Collins saw the commercial value of combining a contemporary realistic setting with a social theme that lent itself to melo-dramatic treatment" (57). In this case, he uses a young pieceworker who nurses a friend who has been fatally injured while walking between work and home, all the while anxiously awaiting word from her sweetheart, whose business in America is not doing well. Collins relies on many of the stereotypes surrounding needlewomen: both the women are fallen middle class; the narrator is morally strong, while her friend's virtue is more ques-tionable; the women work hard, but are underpaid and physically weak. Not only does Collins use these factors to establish character, but they are central to the mystery: the police initially rule out foul play when investi-gating the friend's death because the woman fainted at work and was sent home without sustenance or escort. Anne Rodway wonders if her death might have been the result of a lover's quarrel and investigates from that perspective. In the end, the mystery returns to the corrupt business partner of the woman's father. Even the diary format, which was to become one of Collins's most important techniques, is reminiscent of earlier seamstress narratives. But he doesn't detail the breakdown of the seamstress. Instead, readers witness how Anne uses the mystery surrounding the death of her friend to counter her concern over her fiancé. Thus Collins twists the stan-dard details to create a new type of story, exploiting the commonly accepted horrors to create a new sense of drama.

About the time of the reissue of *The Unprotected*, Augustus Mayhew also wrote a novel incorporating the established iconology of the seam-stress, *Paved with Gold; or, the Romance and Reality of London Streets* (1858).[5] And in this case, the seamstress's use as a narrative device rather than as the topic of study is much more overt. Mayhew envisioned his novel as a response to the romanticized poverty of Dickens's *Oliver Twist*. Never-theless, the family history of his foundling hero, born in a workhouse, but with aristocratic bloodlines, incorporates one of the conventions of seam-stress fiction: the aristocratic young woman, cut off from her family for mar-rying beneath her, forced to earn a living sewing after she is deserted by her husband. When she is unable to earn a living and becomes homeless, she wanders the streets for over thirty hours and contemplates suicide. Finally she breaks a window so she might be arrested; however, her physical condition has been so strained by hard work, lack of nourishment, and pregnancy that she dies in jail that night while giving birth to a son. Although merely introductory material and not the focus of his novel, the iconology of suffering and death, often as a result of an economic fall, associated with the seamstress quickly establishes the context Mayhew needed for his story.

III

Like much of the earlier fiction, many of the periodical stories relied on "testimony" and investigative reports for details, particularly Mayhew's letters in the *Morning Chronicle*. Describing millinery shop workrooms little changed from those of the 1843 *Second Report*, his 24 October 1850 letter (LXXV) reports:

> [The seamstresses] are so thin and pale-looking that their appearance is not very prepossessing. . . . After tea they go up to work again until ten o'clock, when they go down to supper . . . They then go up to work again, and work probably until four the next morning. Perhaps one of them may faint, and ask if she may leave off and go to bed, as she feels too ill to continue working. The first hand says that it is quite impossible, as, if she did allow her to go to bed, the work could not be done. So the poor creature sits down to work again. At four in the morning they leave off, and retire to rest. . . . There are eight beds in it, and two sleep in each bed. At half past seven the young ladies are obliged to assemble to breakfast.

Echoes of Mayhew's descriptions abound. For example, the description of the workrooms in Mrs. White's "The Struggles of a Needlewoman," published in the 3 January 1852 issue of the *Home Circle*, draws directly from his accounts:

> Mrs. Bush's workrooms were situated at the top of the house . . . [in] a front attic, [there] sat fourteen to fifteen young women, varying from fifteen to twenty years of age, all occupied in the different departments of mantle making. . . .
> But of the entire number, there was not one that did not exhibit

the worn expression of the face, the marks of premature anxiety, and overworn strength—with sometimes signs of worse significance—signs, to which the drawn-up shoulders, the sunken chest, the frequent cough, the glittering eyes, and hollow cheeks of a few, more hopeful ones—for in these, the reckless laugh, the bold tone, the defiant air told of the decay more sad and terrible than that of the consumptives which late hours, bad air, close work, and famishment had made. (2)

Thus the periodical literature returned to familiar scenes of poor young women wasting away in upper rooms, women whose seemingly inevitable death by consumption can be forestalled only by an even worse fate, a moral fall.

The issue most reformers focused on was the dire poverty forced on needlewomen by otherwise generous people in search of a bargain. For example, in its first issue of the year, the *Lady's Newspaper* ran an article on the "Distressed Needlewomen of the Metropolis." The article echoed earlier accusations that, while competition was a factor in the hardships faced by seamstresses, "this distress is mainly occasioned by that craving desire for *cheapness* unhappily so prevalent in the present day—a desire which, it would appear, must be gratified, irrespective of all consequences either to the employer or the employed." Equally clear about the suffering that can result from misguided economy are two articles in the *Working Man's Friend and Family Instructor*. The first, "The Oppressed Needlewoman. A Sketch from Life," appeared 5 April 1851, and makes its point in the opening paragraph: Some people seem to think that they pay too much for everything, and that it is a positive duty to employ those who will work the *cheapest*; they are never satisfied with anything that is not a bargain, and although the money saved is very often but of little importance to them, they rejoice in these little acts of parsimony as commendable domestic economy, disregarding the privations of those whom they compel to labour for reduced wages. (14) The article then presents the story of a young woman who bargains down a poor seamstress and her daughters to save enough money to by an elegant fan. She brushes aside issues such as the seamstress's rent being due as minor inconveniences: "'Pshaw, rent is nothing; make your landlord trust you'" (15). Her unthinking attitude and the contrast of the seamstress's destitution, despite her labor, with young woman's glee over saving a few shillings for an extravagance presents a strong moral lesson for the middle-class reader.

Approximately eighteen months later, in November 1852, the journal published a story by Harriet Beecher Stowe. A more developed story than the earlier tale, "The Sempstress" presents readers with three different types of customer, all unintentionally cruel to a widow and her daughter trying to support themselves through needlework. The story begins by carefully establishing that, although poor, the two women keep their room spotless and as pleasant as possible, with a few "relics of better days" scattered around, placing them in the established categories of fallen middle class and "deserving poor." After detailing the long hours and hard work of the two women, the story illustrates that much of the needlewomen's suffering is the result of thoughtless clients, another established motif. The first customer dickers over the price of shirts, finally paying the younger seamstress an amount that is "not half the price of one of the handkerchiefs" her daughter has just purchased. After the seamstress leaves, we are told, "Mrs. Elmore never accused herself of want of charity for the poor, but she had never considered that the best class of the poor are those who never ask charity. She did not consider that by paying liberally those who were honestly and independently struggling for themselves, she was really doing a greater charity than by giving indiscriminately to a dozen applicants" (116). Another customer insists that the seamstresses remake items for which she sent the wrong pattern, not paying for the extra time. And, finally, the third customer neglects to pay the seamstresses until they have billed her three times, simply because she "was so used to large sums of money, that she did not realise how great an affair a single dollar might seem to other persons" (117). In their focus on unnecessary suffering though others' carelessness, these stories support the attitude that times have changed and it is the responsibility of the middle and upper classes to pay workers adequately and on time so that all may enjoy the new prosperity. Throughout the decade much of the needlewoman's suffering is laid at the feet of the client, with most authors specifying that it is the unreasonable desire to drive a bargain that is at fault.

Also typical of the articles appearing after 1850 is "On the Best Means of Relieving the Needlewomen," published on 19 July 1851 in *Eliza Cook's Journal*. Perhaps influenced by Henry Mayhew's 1849 and 1850 letters in the *Morning Chronicle,* reformist articles such as this turned once again from the slopworker to the dressmaker. The article first alludes to the number of stories about the seamstress that had been recounted, and through the use of rhetorical questions indicates that conditions had not changed. Two stories of needleworkers with families, forced into begging in order to avoid starvation, are recounted, followed by a statement of verisimilitude reminiscent of that in Stone's *The Young Milliner:*

> These are no fanciful pictures; they are true stories, real scenes which have taken place within the last year! And their origin is not idleness, not drunkenness, not extravagance. No. . . . The poor needlewoman, about whose condition much has been written, said, and doubtless thought, is injured and reduced to misery by the disgraceful monopolies existing by the patronage awarded to shopkeepers, milliners, dressmakers, tailors because they live in large houses. . . . (190)

As in earlier articles and stories, effort is made to place the needlewomen and their families among the "deserving poor," those who remain poor not through vice or moral weakness and in spite of industry and frugality, who thus deserve help. For this writer, the issue is not too many women competing for a limited amount of work, but, rather, a hierarchical system that, by its very nature, exploits those at the bottom—the seamstresses.

The solution advocated by *Eliza Cook's Journal,* suggestive of Stone and other early writers, emphasizes women's helping women by recognizing which houses abuse their workers and making such activity unprofitable. But the article also demonstrates knowledge gained from later writers in its advocacy of eliminating middlewomen and dealing directly with the seamstress:

> It remains in the hands of our countrywomen to do away with such bitter facts. . . . [L]et them abandon the shops until they pay properly for labour, and seek out the workwomen themselves. By this means the shopkeepers will be compelled to *pay* their needlewomen and milliners, instead of extorting life with labour and rewarding it with a remuneration they would even themselves blush to own were they called upon to do so! (191)

Thus women were admonished to take an active part in reform, if for no other reason than that millinery houses that abused women while charging exorbitant prices were deceiving and cheating their customers, making the issue one of self-respect.

Such stories are variations on the established iconography of the pampered client and the wretched seamstress—the image established visually by works such as the *Pictorial Times*'s "Slaves of the Needle," Redgrave's

Fashion's Slaves, Cruikshank's "Tremendous Sacrifice," and Leech's "Pin Money/Needle Money." Many artists helped develop the iconographic pattern in which comparative views of needlewomen and their clients are presented. Some illustrations, such as "Tremendous Sacrifice" and "The Belgravian Venus Attired by the Graces" (1853), build on a frequently implied but less commonly stated motif: that there is a seemingly unending supply of young women in need of work who constantly replenish the supply of those destroyed through abuse. Others, such as "Pin Money/Needle Money" and "The Maker/The Wearer" (1864) are straightforward comparisons of the industrious, poverty-stricken young woman and her idle, pampered client; however, where Leech's "Needle Money" gives some indication of the toll needlework takes, R. S. E. Gallon's "Maker" is little more than a simply attired Keepsake beauty. The point of the contrast is indicated through dress and manner: the "Maker" is conservatively attired in a plain, dark dress, her hair pulled back with no hat, her eyes modestly downcast, and her profession indicated by the fabric she holds in her hand; the "Wearer" is richly dressed in an ornate, off-the-shoulder gown, her hair down with a frilly cap, her eyes boldly meeting those of the viewer, and in her hands a bouquet of flowers.

Other comparative sets, such as *The Women of England in the Nineteenth Century* (1852), "The Belgravian Venus Attired by the Graces," and "The Haunted Lady, or 'The Ghost' in the Looking Glass" (1863), paint a more macabre picture of the cost of the night's pleasure. Interestingly, Mrs. Hurlstone's work, *The Women of England in the Nineteenth Century,* exhibited at the Royal Academy, was viewed by the *Art Journal* as "a satire on the charity of the time," rather than a commentary on the human cost of elaborate dress:

> The essay is in two chapters: an opera-box, with its *habitués,* and in the distance, Taglioni or Carlotta Grisi; the other part of the story tells of the most abject misery. We see a creature starved and in rags, drudging for bread which is served to her in crumbs. She seems to be making a shirt. The splendour on the one hand, and the squalor on the other, are brought into inevitable contrast. They are, indeed, not nearer to each other in the picture than in reality. ("The Society of British Artists," 137)

Reliant on two common iconologies associated with needlewomen (the crowded social event and the seamstress working on a shirt), the painting would seem to cross genders if read as typical: earlier comparisons, such as the illustration for the *Pictorial Times*'s "Slaves of the Needle" and Aneley's opening illustration to *The Seamstress*, had focused on women clients in social settings and the needlewomen who worked to make their gowns; yet the shirt in Hurlstone's work shifts the focus to a male client. Perhaps it was the mixing of icons that led to the *Art Journal*'s reading of the painting.

In *Punch*'s "The Belgravian Venus Attired by the Graces," both the poem and the cartoon contrast "Beauty and Youth at a Ball" with the "Grim Graces" who have created their clothes (figure 5.1). The scene in the upper-left corner, based on illustrations from the 1840s, would have been familiar to readers and need little detail or development beyond the lines:

> . . . —in a Garret close, reeking, and hot . . .
> From dawn till past midnight the needle they ply,
> Oft till the next morning's twilight appears in the sky. (151)

The rolled curtain and the winding rose quickly lead the eye to the sleeping beauty and the contrast of her slumber and solitude with the crowded working conditions of the seamstresses. Nevertheless, the line of grieving needlewomen that seems to flow from the drapery to the young woman dancing at the bottom of the drawing, "Hov'ring round her . . . their spirits attend[ing] her wherever she goes," reminds readers of the individual sufferers of earlier works. And, finally, the ghostly figure in the bottom-right corner, whose dress has transformed into the shapelessness of a ghost, makes clear the message of the poem: women are responsible for the working conditions and thus the lives of those employed by shops they frequent: "should Venus disrelish such haunted attire, / Ere she fix on her milliner— let her enquire" (151). Ignorance of the human toll is no longer an excuse.

The idea of a client "haunted" by the spirit of the young women responsible for her dress also occurs in John Tenniel's "The Haunted Lady, or 'The Ghost' in the Looking-Glass" (1863), probably inspired, in part, by the death of Mary Anne Walkley (figure 5.2). Walkley, a dressmaker employed by Madam Elise of Regent Street, died of apoplexy at the age of twenty. Her death was brought to public attention through a letter to the *Times*. Capturing public sympathy, the story was soon sensationalized and taken up as a public rallying cry for reform.[6] Tenniel's subject is the unthinking or uncaring use of millinery shops that abuse workers, and the responsibility of women to check the conditions of the workers and to be reasonable in their demands. Indeed, in this case it is the latter that is emphasized,

FIGURE 5.1 "The Belgravian Venus Attired by the Graces," *Punch* 24 (16 April 1853): 151.

with the caption: "Madame La Modiste. 'We would not have disappointed your ladyship, at any sacrifice, and the robe is finished *a merveille.*'" The angle of the mirror ensures the viewer is aware of the sacrifice that the demands of the affluent, thoughtless customer have necessitated, with the figures of the customer and needlewoman at opposite and opposing angles. The suddenly aware customer is bent at the waist, leaning forward toward the right side of the drawing, while the unconscious seamstress slumps backwards in her chair, her upper body angling to the left of the picture, with the intersection forming the focal point.

A variation on the unthinking client is the presentation of the economically displaced woman struggling to support herself—and often her children—faced with an uncaring male businessman in paintings such as Thomas Brooks's *Relenting* (1855) and Edward Hughes's *Ruinous Prices* (1861).[7]

FIGURE 5.2   "The Haunted Lady, or 'The Ghost' in the Looking-Glass," John Tenniel, *Punch* 45 (4 July 1863): 5.

A classic "problem picture," Brooks's work challenges the cult of romanticized widowhood promoted by Queen Victoria. The accompanying quotation is from Shakespeare's *The Winter's Tale*: "The silence often of pure innocence persuades, where speaking fails." The quotation establishes a parallel between Shakespeare's helpless Perdita—separated from her mother, Queen Hermione, and about to be denounced by her father, King Leontes—and the poor widow separated from society about to be evicted by her landlord. Various details in the painting attest to both the past gentility and the moral character of the widow: the oriental rug and empty birdcage suggest better days, while the Bible on the windowsill and the attempt to retain various mementos of her husband testify to virtuousness and depth of feeling. The sparsely furnished room, curtainless windows, and empty watchstand on the mantle testify to the family's poverty; the widow's apparent unwillingness to pawn or sell her husband's sword or portrait, while touching, implies a certain unbending pride and, perhaps, unwillingness to face reality. That she and her eldest daughter are apparently trying to support the family through needlework is in keeping with this image, for even in the latter half of the century, as Harriet Martineau observed, "tutor, the tailor and the hatter" continued to be "the only occupations that the gently-bred" might pursue with propriety (*Deerbrook*, 68).

And in this painting admonishing the patriarchal Victorian world for abandoning its helpless dependents, Brooks incorporates many of the familiar icons of the seamstress to establish the family's suffering and indicate the possible future toll. The widow stands in the center of the painting, leaning with one arm on the table and her hand in the middle of a shirt. A window with a cityscape surrounds her head and shoulders, with the birdcage in the upper-right corner balanced by the Bible and a pot of flowers in the lower-left corner. Behind her, the eldest daughter is sewing, but is propped up in her chair with a pillow, the indications of her illness furthered by the medicine bottles on the mantle under the mementos of her father and his military service. All the details serve to underline the message of sacrifice to society and personal loss. But most telling in reading the picture is the way light divides the picture: to the left is the male world of stern, practical business, with the clerk noting the family's possessions in a ledger and the dour landlord, finely dressed in top hat and spats, darkly shadowed with only the barest reflection of light shining on his profile. On the right are the widow and her children. The brightest light falls on the children, with the sunlit pillow behind the girl suggestive of a halo and the infant in the cradle lit so brightly that the young child attending it seems almost to be lit by reflection. Standing between light and dark is the widow, clad in black and supported by the white shirt. The pathos of the picture and its title make its implicit moral clear: society must no longer ignore its ethical responsibilities to those who cannot help themselves.

Showing a poor shirtmaker, accompanied by her child, bringing her work to her employer, who seems displeased with the work, while a woman customer views the scene with apparent sympathy, Hughes's *Ruinous Prices* focuses on the inadequate pay a seamstress received for her work. The downcast eyes of the seamstress and her daughter indicate their modesty, their lower economic status, and the sense of futility in asking for adequate renumeration. While the female client appears sympathetic, the indifference to the scene of the clerk and the passing crowd suggests that the situation is a common one. While the *Art Journal* viewed the painting as a "great moral teacher" (170), the lack of any overt interference on the part of the client makes any inspiration to reform unlikely.

IV

In contrast to the limited number of novels, there was a flurry of short articles and stories in periodical publications during the early 1850s and in 1863 following the death of Mary Anne Walkley. The amount of artwork continued to build, with over a dozen paintings and illustrations being exhibited or published during the 1850s and early 1860s. There is also a strong contrast in the use of the seamstress in literature and art during this period: in the novels, the seamstress is used primarily to represent a larger group or cause; in the periodical literature and the visual arts, the focus is the seamstress herself.

In 1854, *Punch* published an ironic "Market and Trade Report" stating that the large number of emigrants had "caused an unparalleled rise in wages . . . to as much as a farthing per dozen on 'gents' dress' [shirts]." But at issue, more than the low wages, was the number of hours seamstresses were still being required to work. Reporting the rumor of a strike by the United Distressed Needlewomen over working conditions, *Punch* relates that the women wanted their hours reduced to "twenty-one hours of a day, with three intervals of two minutes each for meals, except during the busy season which comprises only about eleven months in the year" (42). The satire plays on frequently recounted stories of abuse, but suggests that as seamstresses began to emigrate, conditions in English millinery houses actually worsened rather than improved.

Another variation on the iconography occurs in Charles Rossiter's *Sad Memories* (1854). Incorporating much of the standard iconography—the lone shirtmaker, the bare attic room, and the window—Rossiter uses a letter rather than a plant to signal the longing for home and the past. The significance of the letter, underscored by the painting's title, was not lost on viewers, as the *Athenaeum* review indicates: "Mr. C. Rossiter's *Sad Memories* . . . represents a London needlewoman, who has just received a letter from the country, and is looking musingly and regretfully out of [the] window into the blue sky, which is all that her new home has in common with her old. The subject could not be simpler, but it is delicately painted, and the face fully conveys the sentiment expressed" (627). Thus the establishment of series of symbols working together allows for variation, substitution, and displacement of any one element with little or no loss of connotation for the whole.

In order to present the poverty and physical devastation wrought by needlework, visual artists used compensating factors that made the paintings and illustrations more palatable to the viewer. Building on Redgrave's *The Sempstress,* during the 1850s and 1860s artists quickly developed a unique iconographic system through repetition and association, building on realistic detail and transforming it to the symbolic. Some of the images tie the seamstress to established religious iconography and continue the themes of martyrdom and saintliness established primarily in the literature. T. J. Edelstein clarifies the process in "'But who shall paint the griefs of those oppress'd?'": "In order to be effective with their audience these artists mitigate the disturbing aspects of the iconography, develop a recognizable vocabulary of symbols, and maintain a traditional attitude towards the moral efficacy of beauty. The power of these images is that they treat contemporary, topical issues but do so in a language that is universal" (304). Thus the upturned gaze of the shirtmaker in Redgrave's *The Sempstress* can be connected with the pious saints who turn their eyes toward heaven in the popular works of seicento painters such as Carlo Dolci and Guido Reni (Edelstein, "They Sang," 190). The upturned face is picked up by painters such as J. T. Peele and Anna Blunden, but it is in Blunden's *"For only one short hour"*[8] that the upturned face is linked to other images with religious connotations, clarifying the semiotic system. Blunden's figure clasps her hands, as if in prayer, while looking up and out a window at the dawn sky, as if directing her prayers toward heaven. Whether she is a saintly figure praying for strength or, as Deborah Cherry argues, a Magdalene praying for forgiveness, within the narrative structures established by preceding visual and written texts the young woman's fate is presumed to be suffering and death.[9] In the series of rooftops visible through the window is a church spire, insinuating either forgiveness through faith or a condemnation of the Christians who brought her to this place or failed to relieve the woman's sufferings. The church steeple glimpsed through the window was quickly adopted by the artists who followed: although it is viewed through the darkness, rather than the dawn, a church tower can also be spied through the window of C. W. Cope's *Home Dreams* (1869). Even more emphatic, a steeple dominates the view from the window of Charles Rossiter's shirtmaker in both his engraving for a collection of Hood's poems (1858) and his composition for the Royal Academy, *"Work! work! work!"* (1859).

Some iconography carried multiple references, both secular and religious. For example, in most of the paintings there is a plant in the windowsill. In earlier works, the plant, usually spindly and occasionally even dead, indicates the rural existence the young woman has left behind and foreshadows the cost of her profession and the urban world on the seamstress. A few works reference specific flowers, and it is at this point that the multiple referencing becomes overt. In "The Song of the Shirt" Hood specifically mentions the primrose, a common English wildflower but also one associated with temptation, the "primrose path." Several writers and artists followed Hood's lead but a few diverged, choosing different but equally symbolic flowers. In many ways George Hicks's *Snowdrops* (1858) uses typical seamstress iconography: a young woman sits alone at a table with a shirt in her lap. A harsh, white, vertical streak in the upper-left quarter, created by the widow casement, indicates the slanted roof of an attic room, and the teapot and cup and saucer signify the meager food and the need for stimulants. But on the table is also a plant, not wilted but blooming. And while much of the symbolism recalls the suffering and poverty typical of earlier images, Hicks's shirtmaker is not gaunt, nor does she look ill. The light from the window highlights the face of the young woman, the shirt in her lap, and her hand as she strokes the plant's blossoms, linking them to her and giving them significance. The flower specified in the title, the snowdrop, is the first flower to appear in the spring and, as such, has religious connotations. The *Home Circle* poem "The Snowdrop" elucidates the symbolism and illustrates why the flower would have been an effective symbol for the seamstress:

But when all my prouder kindred,
   Frightened, hide them in the earth;
I am heard amidst the whirlwind,
   And the storm of winter's wrath.

Pale and downcast, timid, trembling,
   Rudely cradled, roughly nurse'd;
I, of every flower, am chosen
   To proclaim His glory first. (418)

The first stanza sets up the image of suffering and fear; the second echoes both physical descriptions of needlewomen and the now familiar saint/ martyr imagery. Thus by specifying this flower Hicks adds a layer of symbolism: spiritual hope. Whether interpreted as hope for the afterlife or hope of a better future in the present life, it is a more positive presentation than that of many previous works.

The use of light also carries religious implications in many paintings. Working until dawn associates the seamstress with Christ's endurance of the trials and temptations in the garden. And, besides being dramatic, the use of a single, often sputtering, candle suggests a symbolic significance— especially through repetition. The fate of the candle holds parallels with that of the seamstress: it accentuates her isolation and her poverty; it also car- ries the suggestion that as the candle sputters and eventually goes out so, too, will the needleworker's life.[10] Displacement of the candle, as in Peele's *The Seamstress* (1847), accentuates the symbolic quality since, standing on the top of a cupboard, it cannot light the woman's work.[11] Edelstein even suggests that in compositions where there are two light sources, moonlight or sunrise as well as the candle, as the candle representing the seamstress's life flickers out, "the promise of her reward is symbolized by the other light source" ("They Sang," 202). Thus it is not surprising that virtually every portrait of a seamstress—visual or verbal—includes the image of a woman plying her needle by candlelight. The goal of such symbolism is to high- light the concept that these young women suffer and die needlessly, that they are martyrs to society. And when combined with the religious semiol- ogy, such as a church spire, the iconology depicts them as saints sacrificed to the secular world of Victorian society. The significance of such symbol- ism should not be discounted. As Christopher Wood explains in *Victorian Panorama,* Victorian genre paintings, such as those of the seamstress, "form a remarkable iconography of the preoccupations of Victorian society, its aspirations and failures, its hopes and fears, its likes and dislikes, its prejudices and paradoxes. Some of the pictures may not be great art, but they are often very good social history" (9). Thus, even if we find the presentations melodramatic or the technique a little weak, the repetition of the figure, the religious symbolism, and the urban setting (often accented with a lone indicator of a rural past such as a plant or a bird) all combine to present a comment on how Victorian society viewed the sufferings of the working poor, particularly women, and even more specifically needlewomen.

The iconology carries over to into the literature of the period as well. An explicit instance is found in the *Leisure Hour*'s "The Little Candle" (1857), a poem that incorporates many of the associations between the candle and the seamstress: hope, diligence, life, death, and Christian suffering. As the young seamstress cheerfully works throughout the night she is held up as a role model, both for her perseverance and for her suffering, ending with the inducement:

> But let us ne'er in darken'd hours
> Forget what Christ has done;
> But patient, in the sweet hope, await
> The glorious *Rising Sun*! (559)

However, the religious typology, although clear, is often problematic. For while the seamstress figure is often seen as a victim, after Mayhew's 1849 and 1850 series her virtue would always be questionable. The seeming paradox between typology and reality was a tension fiction writers also found useful, although they often exploited it for larger representations than the sufferings of needlewomen alone. For Gaskell, the seamstress presented an ideal character for a novel intended to show that the "fallen" woman was often a person of great potential whose value to society was lost through prejudice. Earlier narratives had established the character of the seamstress as a naive young woman thrust into a harsh environment and frequently subjected to compromise and temptation. As Sally Mitchell illustrates, in these stories the woman succumbs to outside pressure that "destroys the woman's life, but not her soul. She has lost her ability to sin; as a victim she is guiltless before God." She is "a social problem rather than a religious one" (13). Nevertheless, as Mitchell goes on to explain, social dictum still necessitates that the victim be punished by death, although she has committed no crime. In these works the seduced woman, because she is a woman, is powerless—she is acted upon rather than active (13).

But as the sufferings of needlewomen and the problems with reform began to seem insurmountable, painters and illustrators worked to establish the seamstress as a more general representative of the suffering that resulted from the abuses inherent in urban industrialization. Many of the symbols present in earlier works, where they represented issues that were specifically tied to the plight of needlewomen, shift from the specific to the universal, the realistic to the metaphorical. One hazard of needlework that left young women particularly vulnerable to both temptation and scandal was the lack of visible male protection. Not only did milliners frequently have to walk around the city unescorted, they also lacked the economic and social benefits of male protection. The image of the needlewoman as unprotected, and thus vulnerable to temptation, was also one that engaged many visual artists. Many illustrators portrayed the image primarily in terms of impoverishment and need, as in Millais's "Virtue and Vice," but many painters sought instead to focus on some of the societal issues. In paintings such as E. C. Barnes's *The Seducer* (c. 1857–1860) and Charles Hunt's *A Coffee Stall in Westminster* (c. 1860) the focus is on the man, as seducer and betrayer, and the woman as victim.[12] That the women portrayed are millinery workers is incidental to the larger issue, the vulnerability of women forced by economic circumstances to move from the private to the public sphere. And the appearance of these works in public venues provided a sense of institutional legitimization to the signified messages, since the finished works would have been vetted by either the editors of periodicals or the board of the Royal Academy.

Barnes's painting, that of a young milliner resisting the attentions of a well-dressed gentleman, is particularly interesting because of the various supporting symbols of temptation and resistance in the picture. First, the setting is urban and barren, with a rough brick wall and broken paving stones. The very isolation of the two figures suggests the woman's vulnerability, and would have reminded viewers of numerous reports and stories in which the delivery of goods to a client left a milliner or dressmaker vulnerable to unwanted advances. Emphasizing this reading of the scene are the posters on the wall: an announcement of "A Lecture on Conscience by Rev. A. Mursell," a playbill for *La Traviata,* and a third poster whose heading reads "Lost." The first two represent the two options facing the young woman, while the third indicates the probable outcome. Also significant is the presentation of the seducer: he immediately draws the viewer's attention both from his central placement and from the way the light accents his hat and face, yet creates a shadow hiding his eyes, creating a sense of sinister anonymity. His body position furthers the sense of threat he presents: significantly taller than the woman, he is also leaning in and his outer leg is forward, in effect caging the woman against the brick wall. In his left hand is a cane with a serpent coiling around the handle and stock, suggesting the role of tempter, while the result of succumbing to temptation is insinuated by his tiepin, which is in the form of skull. Ironically, his lapel flower is a lily of the valley, which traditionally represents a return of hope and happiness. In contrast, the milliner's plain, dark dress, coupled with her stance (head turned away, eyes modestly lowered, one hand raised as if to stop him, the other placing the hatbox between them) implies virtuous modesty, which, because of the appropriate passive feminine behavior, makes her vulnerable to such encounters. Despite the woman's attempt to repulse him, Barnes's male protagonist boldly attempts to take the woman's hand or her box. Such familiarity, particularly in public, would have been quite improper unless he was a relative or close family friend. That the man continues to wear his hat, rather than remove it in deference to her femininity, reinforces the implied lack of respect and predatory encroachment.

A similar scene is found in Hunt's *A Coffee Stall in Westminster* (figure 5.3). Although depicting a crowded city corner rather than an isolated alley, Hunt nevertheless focuses the viewer's attention on two figures set to the right of the canvas, a richly dressed "swell" and a young milliner. The seducer, in his dark cloak, checked pants, and top hat, creates a strong vertical line separating the milliner from the rest of the people around the coffee stall. Furthermore, in a canvas crowded with figures, the gentleman and the milliner occupy approximately a third of the canvas. And finally the eyes of virtually every figure on the canvas are turned toward the two figures, some in seeming disapproval, others in gossiping speculation. Hunt, like Barnes, pictures his seducer towering over his victim, although standing upright rather than leaning in, with his hat on, increasing his height, thus both increasing the threat and the disrespect for the woman. The young woman's eyes are modestly downcast, but she obviously is the focus of his attention and, unlike Barnes's milliner, she does not offer any physical signs of resistance; in fact, she does not even turn away from his gaze. Although Hunt does not incorporate the iconology of Barnes's work, the message that gentlemen often considered milliners easy prey is still relatively obvious.

On 1 February 1859, Arthur J. Munby expressed in his diary the typical Victorian attitude toward the vulnerability of milliners:

My impression is that the morality of the milliner class is lower than that of any other: they have all the temptations and none of the safeguards of the classes above and below them ... with the men of their own class it would be indelicate to associate as friends ... there remains then, only men of the class above her—gentlemen. Here lies the danger, and their responsibility: all the better parts of her nature, as well as some of the worse, are attracted towards their higher education and manners, and if they are unworthy of her confidence, the end is what we know. (19)

For Victorians, the seamstress was vulnerable both because she often had to travel across the city alone, fitting and delivering gowns, and because she lived either alone or in the company of other young women rather than with her family. As Lynda Nead reveals, "it was the women who were alone, outside the protection of home, family and religion, and who were therefore flouting the ideal, proscribed sphere and role of woman ...

FIGURE 5.3   *A Coffee Stall in Westminster,* Charles Hunt, c. 1860. Courtesy Museum of London.

who risked seduction" (318). For these women simply working for a living made them morally vulnerable in the minds of middle- and upper-class Victorians, yet any actual question concerning her respectability could cost a needlewoman her home and her job. Thus needlewomen were forced into the position of assumed transgression, with the resulting liberties men assumed they could take and the knowledge that any indication of actual transgression could result in their dismissal and even the loss of their living quarters.

V

During the 1860s the figure of the suffering seamstress continued to appear in newspaper articles and magazines. On 17 June 1863 the *Times* published a letter presenting conditions in a millinery house little changed from those portrayed by novelists two decades earlier:

> Sir, I am a dressmaker, living in a large West-end house of business. I work in a crowded room with 23 others. This morning one of my companions was found dead in her bed, and we all of us think that long hours and close confinement have had a great deal to do with her end. We are called in the morning at half-past 6, and in ordinary times we work until 11 at night, but occasionally our hours are much longer; on the Friday before the last Drawing Room, we worked all night and did not leave off until 9 o'clock on Saturday morning.
>
> At night we retire to rest in a room divided into little cells, each just large enough to contain two beds. There are two of us in each bed. There is no ventilation; I could scarcely breathe in them when I first came from the country. The doctor who came this morning said they were not fit for dogs to sleep in.
>
> This poor girl was taken ill on Friday. We are often ill, so that not much notice is taken of that; she was worse on Sunday. Some of us sat up with her until she went to sleep. In the morning her bedfellow found her dead by her side.
>
> Of course we are all very much shocked, and although we do not complain of our house, which is better conducted than many, we should be so glad if some plan could be discovered by which we could get a little less work and a little more air. I remain, Sir,
>   *A Tired Dressmaker.*

A slew of articles followed. But while most invoked Walkley's name in their titles, few focused on her situation or on the issues surrounding her death. Many, such as "Our Legacy from Mary Ann Walkley" and "Point of the Needle," argue that the cause of needlewomen is hopeless. Pages are spent demonstrating that various benevolent societies and numerous exposés have had little effect and that, although legislation might seem to be the answer, the large labor pool makes enforcement of laws impossible since there will always be women desperate to work no matter the conditions. Other articles, such as "Death among the Dressmakers" used the occasion to pursue a related topic; in this case the association of dressmaking with prostitution and the need for women to choose millinery shops carefully. Walkley is not specifically mentioned until the penultimate paragraph, despite a sensational opening alluding to her death: "It is only another girl that has fallen a victim to the white slaver of the needlewoman's trade" (682). Regardless of the approach, however, it is evident that while Walkley's death occasioned many articles, there was no move to instigate reform.

And the following year, in 1864, the Children's Employment Commission published another report further demonstrating that, while conditions had improved somewhat since the 1843 *Second Report,* for many young women needlework was still a form of slavery. The toll dressmaking took on the health of women was expressed in the surprise of an examiner when he saw the effect of a brief holiday following the summer season: "I scarcely recognized her, and for the first time fully estimated the extent, to which her physical powers had been depressed by the work of the season, and, indeed, of the whole period since her previous vacation" (Lord, 188–89). Last-minute orders and the thoughtlessness of patrons continued to be a problem for millinery houses. One dressmaker presenting evidence recalled: "a dress ordered at 12, fitted on at 6 pm, finished the same night, and sent home first thing the next day. The lady who ordered it said, 'I suppose you work till 11, and begin at 6 in the morning.' She did not care how long we worked. We were very much hurt at the way in which it was said" (Lord, 105). And women were still subjected to dismissal on moral grounds, despite having nowhere to go or no way to earn a living once they were dismissed. As the superintendent of a home for young women employed in the dress trade told investigators: "I have unfortunately had to dismiss two or three; they were receiving notes from gentlemen, and making appointments to meet them. It might be all innocent, but for the sake of the rest we had to send them away. [They] were particularly pretty and well-mannered girls. I had great doubts what I ought to do, for to dismiss them was perhaps to take away their last chance . . ." (Pike, 183). Yet despite the similarity of the testimony, the 1864 *Report* did not elicit the same fictional response that the 1843 *Second Report* had. The reason for the lack of response was twofold: first, there was such a proliferation of seamstress literature following the 1843 *Second Report* and again after Mayhew's series in 1849 and 1850 that the seamstress was considered to be a hackneyed subject. Second, by the mid-1860s the social-protest novel itself was falling out of popularity.

Thus during the 1850s and 1860s the seamstress's power as a symbol waned. Frequently used in novels and paintings as a way to quickly delineate a particular type of character, she was rarely presented in detail, nor was she used to represent the working poor generally. As the century drew to a close, the trend continued. During the last quarter of the century the seamstress virtually disappeared from literature, occasionally appearing in periodical articles but rarely in novels. But as her presence disappeared from the verbal media it flourished in the visual arts, becoming a stock portrait in virtually every artist's portfolio. Yet here, too, there was a shift in the portrayal from representative to commonplace.

6

The Aesthetic Vision

The aesthetic act is itself ideological, and the production of aesthetic or narrative form is to be seen as an ideological act in its own right, with the function of inventing imaginary or formal "solutions" to unresolvable social contradictions.

— Fredric Jameson, *The Political Unconscious*

The last three decades of the nineteenth century are generally recognized as radically different socially, politically, and aesthetically from those of the mid-century, with many historians seeing 1866 as a turning point. That year for the fourth, and last, time in the nineteenth century there was a major cholera outbreak, which killed more than fifteen thousand people. It was followed by a harsh winter that drove the poor and unemployed onto the streets in protest, and made the destitute and homeless more visible. Earlier that year, discussion concerning the Second Reform Act had begun, and a meeting of the Reform League in Hyde Park grew heated enough to be labeled a riot. Although the clash was unusual, discussion concerning the act tended to be heated, since its passage in August 1867 added large numbers of urban laborers to the electorate. Establishing the principle, though not the practice, of universal manhood suffrage, the act was viewed as "a leap in the dark," with the widespread conviction that political power was shifting from a responsible few to what Walter Bagehot described, in his introduction to the second edition of *The English Constitution* (1872), as an "ignorant multitude."[1]

Another event, early in 1866, changed the way journalists investigated questions concerning the poor, and the way the stories about the poor were told. Dressing himself in shabby clothes, James Greenwood spent a night in the casual ward of a London workhouse. His account of his evening first appeared in the *Pall Mall Gazette,* then was reprinted in the *Times,* and finally was published as a pamphlet, *A Night in a Workhouse.* Not only did Greenwood's exposé initiate a standard for investigative reporting of conditions among the urban poor, but the stark reporting established a tone picked up by working-class writers such as Arthur Morrison later in the century. Catherine Gallagher insists that the reshaping of social realism in the 1860s resulted from "stressing the necessary discontinuity between facts and values." Often described as "somber or disillusioned," these later works of social realism lack "a certain optimism and naiveté" typical of earlier social protest literature (Gallagher, 266). Such realism also affected periodical publications. While *Punch* had moved away from its early radical stance, in December 1869 W. L. Thomas founded the *Graphic,* a journal that soon became known for its social realism, especially in its engravings. Using a single full-scale engraving, such as Luke Fides's "Houseless and Hungry" (1869) or Hubert von Herkomer's "Christmas in a Workhouse" (1876), the *Graphic* "captured the complex social and artistic mood" of the period with "stunning accuracy" (Keating, 129).

But at the same time a very different mood was sweeping much of the literary and artistic world; 1866 was also the year in which Algernon Charles Swinburne published, with a dedication to Edward Burne-Jones, and then withdrew his first series of *Poems and Ballads.* Advocating the artistic principle of "art for art's sake," Swinburne's volume, despite its withdrawal, marks the shift in art circles toward aestheticism. The 1873 publication of Walter Pater's *Studies in the History of the Renaissance* and the first annual exhibition in 1877 of the Grosvenor Gallery, an alternative venue for artists unhappy with the more conservative Royal Academy, further established the aesthetic movement in the late-Victorian art world. And just as the work of writers such as Greenwood and publications such as the *Graphic* can be seen as expressions of Victorian society's curiosity about and fear of those now being granted, at least in theory, political power, the rise of the aesthetic movement can also be seen as reflective of the late-Victorian social and political climate. For in 1874 the Liberal Party, under William Ewart Gladstone, was defeated, ending twenty-eight years of Whig-Liberal dominance. Thus it is not surprising that while images of the "Great Unwashed" remained a constant feature of Victorian art, the majority of Royal

Academy and Grosvenor Gallery exhibitors avoided disturbing viewers, sanitizing their characters and portraying the poor as suffering but surviving. And it was only practical that the most pointed illustrations of poverty occurred in the popular periodical press rather than on the walls of public exhibitions; not only were the situations and solutions pointedly critical of the middle class, but also a magazine or book can always be closed if an image becomes too disturbing, while a painting confronts its owner daily. Yet, as Julian Treuherz concludes, "paradoxically, it was the successful introduction of 'difficult' subjects in a journalistic context which prepared public taste to accept them in works of art" (11). And by their appearance, the works constituted institutional legitimization, whether granted by the editors of the periodicals or the board of the Royal Academy. So, while social realism found its strongest foothold in periodicals such as the *Graphic*, it also appeared, albeit in a more acceptable form, on gallery walls, despite the dominance of the aesthetic movement.

I

During this period the seamstress virtually disappears from Victorian literature, surfacing occasionally as an acceptable female occupation in works such as Thomas Hardy's *Return of the Native* (1887), but one mentioned in passing and not discussed. Instead, the few novels that incorporate needlework do so as a plot or thematic device rather than as an issue for reform or as a metaphor for the working poor generally. In Walter Besant's *All Sorts and Conditions of Men* (1882), when a young brewery heiress decides to discover her roots and do something useful for the working classes, she pretends to be a dressmaker who has come into some money and sets up a cooperative association, complete with gymnasium and tennis court. Within the context of this story, the profession can account for her education and upper-class mannerisms while allowing her access to the working classes to determine their character and needs. Part of Besant's moral is that the differences between rich and poor have more to do with outside factors, such as education and opportunity, than with inner qualities. And thus many of the assumptions made by the upper classes about the lives and morals of the working poor are incorrect. But unlike in previous presentations, there is little attempt to document working conditions or to stimulate reader intercession; needlework is a plot device, not a social problem.

Rosa Nouchette Carey also utilizes upper-class women who become dressmakers in *Not Like Other Girls* (1884), a novel in which three genteel daughters must support themselves and their mother after what little money the family has is lost to bad investments. "More natural, more industrious, more courageous, more religious" (207), the Challoners are not like other girls because they are willing to commit "moral suicide" (213) by earning their living as dressmakers in order to stay together. Her best-received work, *Not Like Other Girls* features the flawless heroines typical of Carey's work. Denouncing the social standard that insists that earning one's living means removal from polite society, especially in an unstable economy, Carey emphasizes the conflict between social and moral worth. As Phyllis explains to her mother, "'Work can not degrade us. Though we are dressmakers, we are still Challoners. Nothing can make us lose our dignity and self-respect as gentlewomen'" (87). Interestingly, her mother replies in language reflecting the foreignness, the otherness, of the working classes to the upper classes: "'You will lose caste. No one will visit you. Among your equals you will be treated as inferiors'" (87). The same terminology appears later when a wealthy woman remonstrates with one of the girls: "'but when one sees you things like you about to forfeit caste and build up a barrier between yourselves and your equals that the bravest will fear to pass, it seems as though one must lift up one's voice in protest'" (163–64). Although the work is hard and shown to take a toll on the young women, it is not extreme; they are pale and fatigued rather than blind or dying. Much more debilitating is the emotional cost resulting from the loss of friends and lovers after the women begin working. In fact, there is little discussion of the profession itself, just the social repercussions.

A similar utilization appears in the two-part story "The Dressmakers," published in the evangelical magazine *Good Words* (1871). In the story dressmaking is shown to be a respectable and profitable way for two sisters to help support their family. The work, while demanding, is not shown to be harmful. In fact much of the plot turns on the idea that the declining health of one sister is assumed to be caused by the stress of overwork rather than her overly emotional nature. The only negative thing said about dressmaking as an occupation is that it provides too much opportunity for young women to think too much or to dwell on their emotions if they are so inclined. Even the illustrations reflect the change in focus and the influence of visual aestheticism: the first installment shows the two sisters sitting in a glade; they are beautiful young women, neatly dressed, and neither shows signs of malnutrition, exhaustion, or illness. One, however, melancholically stares into space while the other industriously plies her needle. A male figure stands in the distant background, but does not threaten. The overall sense is one more of serenity than of suffering. And even the deathbed scene in the second installment reflects a change in perspective. Rather than working despite her illness, the young woman is resting on a sofa with pillows and blankets; nor does her sister work, but rather hovers to offer aid as the sister's fiancé solicitously tucks the blanket around her. The sofa, carpet, and pictures on the wall, as well as the sisters' dress, all suggest middle-class status rather than poverty. And even the features of the dying woman reflect extreme melancholia rather than starvation or consumption. Thus in fiction the seamstress no longer functions as a metaphor for the sufferings of the working poor, nor as a singular occupation for study. And since the needleworker is no longer an object of study, her working and living conditions receive little attention; familiarity has rendered the details unnecessary. The life of the dressmaker is acknowledged to be hard, but the occupation is now used because it is well established and convenient: either because the occupation is one that can bridge the gap between classes or because it carries a degree of acceptability for those who find themselves suddenly impoverished.

At least one exception does exist, however, *A Manchester Shirtmaker* (1890) by John Law [Margaret Elise Harkness]. But as in much of the period's visual social realism, the thrust of the presentation is the dispiriting message that the plight of the seamstress has not improved. Law's novel, like many of the illustrations and journal articles of the time, stresses two points in particular: 1) the introduction of the sewing machine did little to improve wages, since greater productivity lowered the price paid per garment; and 2) the granting of government contracts for sewing to the workhouses undercut competition and further reduced prices.

Although earlier periodical articles such as Dickens's "Iron Seamstress" and *Punch*'s "A Seamstress that Won't Starve" hailed the sewing machine as a partial solution to the seamstress's plight—she would be able to make garments faster and therefore earn more—Law's novel and the social realism paintings at the close of the century demonstrate that such reasoning had failed to account for the economic principle of supply and demand, leaving many needlewomen earning even less. In the novel, a young widow with an infant tries to support herself by making dresses but finds she must pawn furniture to make ends meet and is slowly reduced to living in a Manchester slum. Once there she can no longer obtain dress work and, seeing an advertisement for shirtmakers, inquires about making shirts. Another shirtmaker informs her of the difficulties in making a living as a shirtmaker: "'Tenpence a dozen for men's shirts, eightpence, and sixpence a dozen for boys' shirts. . . . It used to be a penny each to make and finish. But now they have old women in the warehouses finishing. I dare say you've seen 'em. Things never was so bad as they is now in the shirt trade'" (42). The novel details the hard work, poor pay, and lack of respect that accompanied shirtmaking despite technical improvements, such as the sewing machine, and numerous programs for social reform.

The Women's Industrial Council, formed in 1889, conducted a series of investigations of the London home industries. Their second report, presented in 1906, reveals that conditions were brutal, marked by harsh competition and unremitting toil. And far from improving conditions, "sewing machines speeded up production for the ready-made and made-to-measure markets; women worked longer hours, under greater pressure, and their work was increasingly deskilled" (Beckett and Cherry, 78). Social realists therefore made the sewing machine a part of their iconography in the closing decades of the nineteenth century. In the visual arts, works such as Thomas B. Kennington's *Adversity* (1890) and John Collier's *Trouble* (1898) use many standard motifs indicating the suffering and despair of needlewomen, despite the incorporation of a sewing machine. Kennington presents two dressmakers whose bare room and simple dress testify to their poverty (figure 6.1). One figure is seated, holding a gown while clasping the hand of the other figure, who is standing and looking across the canvas at a window. Prominently displayed under the window is a sewing machine. In *Trouble* two women are shown in a cramped room with a sewing machine and a white shirt on the table between them (figure 6.2); one of the women is sitting with her head in her arms on the table, apparently exhausted or weeping, while the other stands, apparently just risen from her chair behind the machine, bracing herself and looking to the left as if she hears something ominous. The walls behind the women are bare, and there is nothing on the table but the sewing machine, shirt, and lamp, all indications of their poverty, as are their plain dress and the haggard countenance of the standing figure. Thus Collier and Kennington drew on elements from the established iconography and reshaped them to show that mechanization made little economic impact in the lives of slopworkers.

But rather than focus on the working conditions of slopworkers or dressmakers, the few late-century fictional works that feature the working-class needlewoman more typically utilize her occupation to quickly delineate her character. For example, an earlier Law novel, *A City Girl* (1887), tells the story of a young working-class woman who machines trousers. But rather than concentrating on the sweating system—unregulated premises characterized by overcrowding, unsanitary conditions, and workers who receive low wages despite long hours of monotonous work—Law looks at a number of issues that all work against the young woman: religious dogmatism on the part of the priest serving her community, tenement owners interested in profit rather than safety, and particular sweaters who abuse their workers. One of the foremost issues is the middle and upper classes' misconceptions about the moral integrity of the working classes. Law uses the heroine's occupation, her hard work, and her generosity to establish that she is of better character than her mother and brother, who live off of her earnings. Law then has the heroine, Nelly, meet a man who works among the poor—as an accountant at an East End hospital and a lecturer at a socialist club—but who has little respect for or understanding of the people involved. Bored with his marriage and family, he seduces Nelly and then drops her when he goes on vacation with his family. Pregnant, Nelly loses her position with the sweater, and her brother forces her out of their

FIGURE 6.1 *Adversity,* Thomas Benjamin Kennington, *The Graphic,* 27 June 1891.

home because she is no longer bringing in money. When she tells her working-class admirer what has happened, he finds her a place with the Salvation Army. Later, despite her attempts to care for it, Nelly's baby dies and she once again encounters her seducer as she leaves the hospital. Amazed at what has happened, since "he had thought that 'hands' took babies as a matter of course; he had imagined that babies made very little difference to East End sweethearts" (177), he reevaluates his conceptions about the working poor and tries to aid Nelly financially as she attempts to rebuild her life. Although defuse in its presentation, the novel's stark depiction of working-class life—at work, play, and as a society—is note-worthy. After reading the novel, Friedrich Engles wrote Harkness praising its "realistic truth" (763), and establishing a definition of realism that became a measuring stick for many who followed: "Realism ... implies, besides truth of detail, the truthful reproduction of typical characters under

FIGURE 6.2 *Trouble,* John Collier, 1898. The FORBES Magazine Collection, New York ©All rights reserved.

typical circumstances" (764). Thus, for many in the nineteenth century, social realism was not so much the particular detail as the representation of a particular type. And needlewomen, because of their familiarity, provided a rapid way to delineate one element in the working classes.

One of the least likable characters in *A City Girl* is that of the sweater's wife, who is cruel and abusive to the needlewomen who work for her and her husband. Not only does she verbally abuse her workers and refuse to pay Nelly when she is dismissed because she is pregnant, but also we are told repeatedly that the wife uses a cudgel on workers she considers slow or when she is in a foul mood. Three years later, in *A Manchester Shirt-maker*, Law again censures the sweating system when the book's young widow finds that the advertisement for "one-hundred shirt hands wanted" is a sham to suggest to customers that the company is extremely popular. When she tries to apply for work, the shopkeeper laughs at her naïveté and sends her to a sweater to obtain work. When first entering the shop, she is taken aback by the number of women she sees working at sewing machines: "in a long, low room, that held at least two hundred women. There was a deafening noise of machinery, for each woman sat before a sewing machine. Two hundred heads were bent over the machines and four hundred hands were working, when she came in. The noise made her quite bewildered" (56). Because she wishes to work at home, she speaks to the sweater about slopwork. Arguing that he does not know her, the sweater demands she leave her rent money as security for the cloth to make the shirts. Although she is a skilled needlewoman and has done a careful job on the shirts, the sweater insists that they are not done correctly and not only refuses to pay her but also refuses to return her security. The implication in the novel is that this was a regular practice and just one more way needlewomen were abused.

Throughout the final decades of the Victorian age and the beginning of the Edwardian era, reformers attempted to bring the problems of sweated workers before the public. One of the primary ways became exhibitions viewed by the public as sites of information and education, entertainment and pleasure. International exhibitions in Glasgow (1901), Bradford (1904), and the Palace of Women's Work at the Franco-British Exhibition in London (1908) all featured displays on women's work and women workers (Beckett and Cherry, 72). On 1 May 1906, the *Daily News* Sweated Industries Exhibition opened at the Queen's Hall, Langham Place, London. Among the occupations presented was that of needleworkers, and as Jane Beckett and Deborah Cherry note, conditions were still incredibly harsh:

The Royal Commission of 1890 defined "sweating" as low pay, excessive hours of work and insanitary conditions: a life of unremitting toil for a pittance. The Commission recognized that these characteristics applied not only to "sweat shops" and home workers, but "in the main to unskilled or partially skilled workers." The *Daily News* Sweated Industries Exhibition sought to draw public attention to the conditions of working class women throughout Britain and to increase demands for state legislation to govern their working conditions. (71)

That same year, however, the victory of the Liberal Party led to the formation of the Anti-Sweating League. A parliamentary commission, established in 1907, also helped secure the passage of the Trades Board Act of 1909, instituting "a minimum wage for chain-making, box-making, lace-making and finishing, and the making of ready-made clothes" (73). Nevertheless, evidence suggests that these reforms were not implemented or had little effect on the industry.

"The Workroom" from the *Penny Illustrated Paper* (4 March 1865) and Claude Calthrop's *"It's not linen you're wearing out, / But human creatures' lives"* (1891) both illustrate the toll taken by the long hours and harsh conditions needlewomen encountered in sweaters' workrooms. Reminiscent of earlier works such as the *Pictorial Times*'s "The Milliners" (1843) and the *Illuminated Magazine*'s opening illustration for Toulmin's *The Orphan Milliners* (1844), "The Workroom" presents several women gathered round a table working on a gown. Under the harsh light, the women are bent over working except for the center figure, who sits as if pausing for a moment with her hand to her forehead in fatigue. To the left one young woman looks at a painting, perhaps a rural landscape reminding her of her past, as she either ties her bonnet in preparation for leaving or unties it so that she may join the others. To the far right one woman, directly under the clock indicating the late hour, midnight, reclines in her chair with her head against the wall in an exhausted sleep. Another figure wearily stands close by, gazing at the clock. Thus the illustration incorporates much of the established iconography; yet there is a notable change—the figures themselves. Although shown in attitudes reflecting fatigue, the faces of the women are rounder and less shadowed, and the figures and apparel do not suggest ill health or extreme poverty. The features of the young women show the influence of aestheticism and the overall impression suggests hard work rather than suffering.

Calthrop's work is less traditional in its presentation. At the back of the painting a bank of windows provide a lighted backdrop against which four dark-gowned figures sit around a table sewing. The plain, light background provides a stark contrast to the women in their dark gowns and white aprons, heightening the drama of the scene. With the figures brought toward the front, almost frozen in place, and sharply contrasted through the use of light and dark, the work reflects the influence of neoclassicists such as Albert Moore and Lawrence Alma-Tadema in its relief-like arrangement. The right half of the painting holds three of the four workers: two are set back, at the end of the table, diligently working; the third, seated in front and quarter-turned toward the viewer, stares across the room at another woman who has just entered the back of the workroom with a fresh bundle of work. The fourth woman, also in front and facing the other three, bends over sobbing, hands and head resting on the table. Because of the figures' placement, they appear divided into two groups, the three working women on the right and the sobbing woman on the left. Such an arrangement highlights the despair of the one figure and suggests an equation between the work of the three figures on the right and the suffering of the woman on the left. Despite the conventional subject matter, only the title and the light-colored garment allude to earlier works; thus Calthrop's work relies on pathos more than established iconography to convey his meaning and reflects the influence of aestheticism in its design and presentation.

II

In terms of artwork, the last three decades of the nineteenth century saw an unprecedented interest in the image of the seamstress. During the 1840s reformers had emphasized the seamstress's link to the home as a way of overcoming the stigma of the factories. For social problem painters in the last quarter of the century part of the seamstress's appeal was again her tie to the home. For many, the rise of the "New Woman" created a sense of nostalgia for a time when women worked only out of economic necessity and then chose occupations associated with domesticity.[2] And from the beginning, Victorians had embraced the seamstress as a distinctly English character—a fact that increased her appeal as rising immigration rates and a working class increasingly identified as non-English spurred developing xenophobia. For both reasons, the image of needlewomen as coming from a rural English home, with a tradition of hard work, piousness, and moral innocence, made them immensely appealing as the era drew to a close. The suffering and hard work associated with the seamstress lent her an old-fashioned nobility. And while the artwork reflects the two broad tendencies that had come to divide the art world by the 1870s—the "engagement with the times and retreat from them" (Warner, 39)—the latter, aesthetic, tendency was by far the dominant one. The chief icon of aestheticism was the beautiful female face shown virtually without expression, "a monument of isolation—hinting of sadness" as Whistler terms it (155). The seamstress, long associated with suffering and sadness and typically shown alone in her attic room, became a staple of aestheticism.

Much more reflective of the dreamy lassitude typical of Albert Moore or John Leighton, the seamstress in Charles W. Cope's *Home Dreams* (1869) seems to have little in common with earlier sufferers portrayed by Redgrave and Watts. Her well-fed appearance and neat dress, including earrings, do little to suggest hardship. Nevertheless, Cope's incorporation of virtually all the standard iconography—an attic room indicated by the city view, potted plants blooming on the windowsill, bare cupboards, sewing basket, and shirt—would have triggered immediate recognition in Victorian viewers, allowing Cope to evoke a sense of melancholy or gentle regret. The appearance of the woman is somewhat awkward: her head tilts to the side rather than forward or back and the body is stiff, especially the right arm, which is rolled outward with the hand open in her lap. And there is a strange impassivity about the figure; her features express neither the pleasure nor the regret one might expect from the title—the implied fond remembrance of a rural home while living an impoverished urban existence. Such impassivity distanced viewers, allowing them to respond to the works on what came to be viewed as "the proper high level of suggestiveness, not too literally, as if they were actual people one might know" (Warner, 29). For artists such as Cope, the purpose was no longer reform—too much exposure for too long had made such a response unlikely. Rather the artwork became a gentle reminder of a continuing social issue that affected amorphous others.

To many artists the seamstress appealed precisely because the strongly established iconography allowed them to tap into the entire history and all the accompanying responses with a single reference. Thus a work such as John Everett Millais's *Stitch! Stitch! Stitch!* (1876) could create a sense of pathos even though the title is the only indication of distress (figure 6.3). In the painting a woman sits at a window sewing. Positioned somewhat awkwardly, at a quarter turn, so that she is viewed primarily from the back, she nevertheless clearly sews a shirt. She looks healthy, if pensive, and is

FIGURE 6.3   *Stitch! Stitch! Stitch!* John Everett Millais, 1876. Courtesy Johannesburg Art Gallery.

dressed neatly and even has a bit of lace at her neck. The positioning effectively blocks everything but her face and the shirt from view, focusing the viewer's gaze on both. Although her face has almost no expression, because she is awake and viewed in profile, it does not have the masklike somnolence of many aesthetic portraits.[3] It is only the title—which immediately suggests the next line of Hood's poem, "In poverty, hunger, and dirt"—that creates in the mind of the viewer a touch of sadness or distress in her expression; the symbols of suffering—the attic room, bare walls, broken furniture, burnt-out candle, and spindly plant—have become unnecessary. The seamstress has moved from social problem to aesthetic image; and in so doing, has become even more entrenched in the Victorian social identity. As Carol Christ and John Jordan explain, "The Victorians were interested in the conflict, even the competition, between objective and subject paradigms for perception." The seamstress presented as an aesthetic image would have been intriguing because she engaged Victorians' imagination by "simultaneously accommodat[ing] a uniquely subjective point of view and an objective model of how perception occurs" (xxiii). The apparent contradiction between the beauty of the figure and the known suffering of the worker creates a tension that would have stimulated thought and thus interest.

T. H. Schäfer's *Needle and Thread* (1902) also uses the title to create ambiguity and suggest complexities in a work that in itself appears relatively simple. Presenting a woman, seated in profile, sewing next to a table holding her supplies and a large, healthy plant, the picture contains nothing to suggest poverty or suffering; in fact, the lace at her collar and sleeves and the Japanese appearance of the plant suggest the woman is of the middle class. Nevertheless, the iconologic tradition is strong enough to create ambiguity.[4] A similar ambiguity exists in Louise Jopling's *"Hark! Hark! The Lark at Heaven's Gate Sings"* (1903): the woman's dress designates her as working class, while the harsh shadow thrown on the wall as she stretches indicates the late hour; nevertheless, she looks healthy, not haggard or gaunt, and there are no clocks to indicate the hour, nor is the candle burnt low. If not for the title one might assume it is early evening rather than dawn. Such illustrations demonstrate that, for the Victorians, acculturation moved the seamstress from a symbol of working-class reform to a reminder of a more genteel past, in which industry was associated with the home and workers were unmistakably English. And even works more overt in their presentation of class rely more on aesthetic techniques than on the harsh presentations of earlier years.

For aesthetes the seamstress was attractive because by the last quarter of the century she was considered a distinctly English subject. Earlier portrayals had established a particularly English history: a rural upbringing combined with strong domestic ties. An iconographic tradition incorporating loss of family, purity despite temptation, and eventual death easily moved the figure into the realm of pathos through mere suggestion, such as a title. The seamstress, with her established iconography, adds emotional depth to an art form marked by beautiful women with particularly expressionless faces. Thus the figure gives a sense of depth, even if only sentimental, to otherwise empty portraits.

III

Social realism, the other major artistic movement of the age, tended to focus on the economically dispossessed, the homeless and outcast, although a few artists did include the seamstress in their works of social realism. But for these artists the seamstress was not the focus of the work; rather, she functioned either as a trope or as part of the setting. For example, the focus of Hubert von Herkomer's *Eventide* (1878) is the abuse of the elderly in workhouses, but to illustrate the principle he presents elderly slopworkers; Collier's *Trouble* is a narrative painting that uses the established assumptions surrounding needlewomen—that they are hardworking, honest, poor, and often abused—as a shorthand to establish the characters and the situation of the two women in the painting. A common theme in the work of Thomas B. Kennington is the strength and stoicism of working-class women in the face of hardship. Since decades of literature and artwork had established the image of the slopworker as a martyr to society, it is logical that Kennington chose to include images of slopworkers in his works. But when analyzing paintings such as *Widowed and Fatherless* (1888) and *Adversity* (1890) one realizes that the issue is not the suffering that results from women's trying to earn a living by sewing, but rather that the sewing is merely part of the trappings of suffering within a larger set of circumstances.

Much of the momentum behind the realist movement came from the developments in illustrated periodicals, which began commissioning artists to provide their illustrations. In 1871, G. J. Pinwell's "The Sisters" appeared in the *Graphic* (figure 6.4). "That drawing," according to Vincent van Gogh, "represents two women in black, in a dark room; one has just come home and is hanging her coat on the rack. The other is smelling a primrose on the table while picking up some white sewing. . . . He [Pinwell] was such a

FIGURE 6.4   "The Sisters," G. J. Pinwell, *The Graphic* (6 May 1871): 415.

poet that he saw the sublime in the most ordinary commonplace things" (*Letters,* 334). More suggestive of shabby gentility than working-class poverty, the etching relies on the established iconology to establish the situation and to create a sense of pathos. The pot of primroses in the center of the table represents the sisters' rural roots, while the portrait in the upper-right corner suggests past gentility. Although the dire poverty of earlier works is missing, the scraps and partially finished garment indicate ongoing work, and the shadows under the eyes of the central figure testify to the weariness of labor. Increasing the emotionalism is the action of the central figure: she has paused in the midst of her work to smell a primrose, suggesting reminiscence. For van Gogh, the sentiment of this engraving is comparable to "the full warble of the nightingale on a spring night" (*Letters,* 334). The picture evokes a sense of melancholy and, perhaps, nostalgia, but not the shock of dire poverty, suffering, and probable death suggested in earlier works.

Also playing on Victorian viewers' sense of the pathetic, von Herkomer's *Graphic* engraving "Old Age—A Study of the Westminster Union" (1877) deals with the issue of women and employment in the workhouse (figure 6.5). Designed to motivate the poor to become productive and independent, workhouses offered monotonous work, poor food, and uncomfortable surroundings. The perspective of von Herkomer's illustration, from one end of the long room, gives the impression of an observer who has just stepped in the door (heightened by the seeming glance from a figure to the right of the etching), while the absorption of most of the figures in their tasks or their thoughts creates a distance, a sense of objectification. Combining the frequently depicted subject of the charitable institution with easily identified images associated with the seamstress, von Herkomer's double-page wood engraving presents viewers with the sense of loss and hopelessness facing poor, elderly, working-class women. The gloom of the hall; the gaunt, despondent face of the center figure; and the struggle of the woman immediately below to see her needle and thread create a bleakness deepened by the knowledge that these are women who have been failed by Victorian society. Either unmarried with no family to turn to or separated from their families by workhouse rules, the women have been reduced by poverty to statistics. An additional irony is that the work done here will undercut the prices of those outside, and force more women into the institution.

Like many *Graphic* illustrators, von Herkomer created paintings based on his illustrations. In 1878, he exhibited *Eventide: Westminster Union* at the Royal Academy. There are a few changes—a sleeping figure in the center of the etching now has a book in her lap, while her neighbor is no longer sewing but, rather, gazing vacantly toward the viewer; the figures along the back wall are more indistinct, their white caps no longer forming a vertical line in the gloom; and the standing figure to the right of the etching is now seated reading, with the horizontal break now provided by a young woman pointing to a paper pattern. But the painting is obviously a slightly modified version of the etching. A touch of humor is added by the figure in the right forefront: looking at the viewer, she drinks her tea from her saucer. But her face is gnarled with age and infirmity, adding pathos as well. More disturbing is the "24" stitched on the cap of the woman trying to thread her needle, indicating that these women have been reduced to numbers. Both the etching and the painting illustrate the general conditions, with the cavernous room and the backless chairs, but the painting mutes the presentation a little since the color palate softens the features of the women, making them less cadaverous. Further lightening the presentation is the addition of some comforts such as a bouquet of flowers on the table, paintings on the far wall, and a teapot and cup and saucer in the foreground. Von Herkomer believed that "truth in art should be enhanced

FIGURE 6.5   "Old Age—A Study in Westminster Union," Hubert von Herkomer, *The Graphic* (7 April 1878): 324–25.

by sentiment" (qtd. in Maas, 237). His addition of a young assistant in *Eventide* not only provides a sharp contrast to the age of the other women, but also lightens the emotional gloom through her interaction with the women; no longer do they seem completely abandoned by society. For the Victorians the sentimentalization that accompanied aestheticism was not mawkish, self-indulgent, or excessively emotional; rather, it was a moving quality resulting from the artist's sympathetic insight into what he was depicting.

In part, artists responded to a public that wanted to be touched rather than to be pained. Much like realist writers, the realist painters at the end of the century were asking viewers to see their art as "information about the way real people behave in a real place." As Robert Scholes contends, "The real context is always present; the fictional one does not efface it but brings some aspects of it into a particular focus for our scrutiny" (33), especially with a familiar figure such as the seamstress. The original attention to physical detail—the attic windows, the medicine, the candle, the shirt—established an iconology, but part of the semiotic process is the modification of presentation revealing shifts in power, at times indicating the achievement of the dominated groups, at times the achievement of the dominant group. Thus as social interest shifted, or concerns about needlewomen shifted, so did the representation. Charles Booth's comments on the late Victorian perception of the "unending struggle" of the poor may explain some of the changes:

> The lives of the poor lay hidden from view behind a curtain on which were painted terrible pictures: starving children, suffering women, overworked men; horrors of drunkenness and vice, monsters and demons of humanity; giants of disease and despair. Did these pictures truly represent what lay behind, or did they bear to the facts a relation similar to that which the pictures outside a booth at some county fair bear to the performance or show within? (1:172)

Paintings by their very nature objectify; the object portrayed is transformed from the actual to an image allowing viewers to distance themselves mentally and emotionally from the horrors portrayed. But the gaze is not simply an act of vision; it is an ideological arena that encloses and dramatizes power relationships, both of class and of gender. Thus it becomes significant that the majority of patrons viewing such works would have been middle- and upper-class men. In terms of class, the working poor were conceived of as foreign beings whose lives were curiously different, and paintings whose settings or implied narratives demonstrated the abject poverty of the working classes reinforced the sense of otherness. In terms of gender, the gaze becomes representative of male dominance, as Laura Mulvey terms it, scopophilic: finding "pleasure in looking at another person as an erotic object," and containing a strong element of male voyeurism, emphasizing a "woman's to-be-looked-at-ness" (Mulvey, 61, 63). In terms of both class and gender the gaze is patriarchal, reflecting the power relations of the culture.

In Edward Radford's *Weary* (c. 1873), for example, the center of the canvas is dominated by a female figure exhaustedly reclining in a chair after working through the night stitching the shirt that lies in her lap.[5] A genre painter who specialized in highly detailed interiors, Radford incorporates most of the seamstress iconography—the slanting attic ceiling, the window with a plant, the cracked dishes, and the guttered candle. Radford adds to the narrative by placing a wooden child's toy prominently in the right foreground, and the child's head barely perceptible in the bedclothes on the right. Critics noted the visual symbols of both the seamstress's toil and her devotion to her child, but as the *Art Journal* noted, the overall interpretation still remained open: "Artists who design compositions of this kind, having in themselves no definite meaning—one, that is which admits of varied reading or interpretation—certainly give the spectator an opportunity of putting his own construction upon it" ("Weary," 68). For male viewers the presence of the child, without evidence of a husband, combined with the recumbent pose and the slightly disheveled clothing, creates a sexual awareness and helplessness. The man's shirt in the woman's lap is emphasized not only by its central placement, but also by its whiteness in a canvas otherwise colored in browns and yellows. Further, it is painted with a detailed, hard-edged realism that differs from the slightly softened edges and shadows of the rest of the painting. Thus the view's gaze is pulled from the central figure to the symbol of male domination, both financial and sexual.

Frank Holl's *The Song of the Shirt* (1875) provides viewers with an interesting blend of realism and aestheticism. The drab interior with a single print over the fireplace and a few flowers on the mantle, the rough floor with a scrap of rug for warmth, and three young women sewing align Holl's work with that of other social realists. Also typical is the placement of the figures: two working industriously on the right, one threading a needle and the other stitching intently, while the third sits listlessly, head down and eyes apparently shut, on the left. At first glance the woman on the left suggests the lassitude typical of aesthetic portraits, but there is an ambiguity in the details of her position: while her right arm rests limply in her lap, she nevertheless holds a pair of scissors in her right hand; her left hand lies on the table, but the elbow is at a sharp right angle and the wrist is unsupported, a position impossible to maintain in sleep, while the thumb and forefinger curl as if fingering or picking up a needle or pin. On the floor beside her chair is a black garment with white trim. Is she resting a moment after finishing the garment, or has she fallen into an exhausted sleep? Holl also employs an interesting mixture of garments—a blue gown, mourning, and a shirt—bringing together the iconography of dressmaker and slopworker and giving his portrayal a universality. But the portrayal lacks the drama of most social realism; there is no obvious despair, no attentive look signaling concern. Instead, the painting can be seen as a metaphoric portrayal of the gradual decline of needlewomen: on the right, the youngest woman diligently works on a shirt, while next to her a slightly older woman works on a ball dress, and the young woman on the left, who has been working on mourning, seems to be the eldest of the three. The presentation suggests a gradual decline as needlewomen work their way through the various strata of needlework. The slight foregrounding of the figure on the left, along with the contrast of the white tablecloth and lighting, emphasizes that the end result of living by the needle is physical and mental decline. Further, the drabness of the room and the black-and-white coloration of the seamstresses' dresses and the rest of the sewing create a sense of gentle melancholy. Indeed, the only color in the painting comes from the blue dress sewn by the center figure, indicating that relief from monotony exists only for the affluent.

One of the few artists during the 1880s and 1890s who painted numerous works of overt social realism, as compared to those who represented the sufferings of the underclasses only occasionally or incidentally, was Thomas B. Kennington (Treuherz, 115). But an examination of four Kennington paintings demonstrates some of the shifts in representation that can occur as social factors change. For example, the setting and the seamstress in *Widowed and Fatherless* are familiar, but added to the scene are two daughters, increasing the pathos—especially since one is obviously ill. Many of the details signify the family's impoverished state, and also recall earlier presentations of needlewomen: the attic room indicated by the sloping roof; the patched coverlet on the bed and the broken chair, with a board replacing its missing seat, at right; the rough floorboards with a scrap of carpeting to provide a little warmth during the long nights spent sewing; the burnt-out candle; and the lack of wall decorations, only a shelf with the family's plates and cups and a print next to the bed containing the ill child. And the print, showing a leaping animal, increases the sense of pathos through the contrast of the healthy, vibrant animal and the ailing, languid child. A cup rests on the board across the chair and the sister kneels with her body resting against the bed, indicating that she has endeavored to comfort her sister; nevertheless, the ill child's attempt to reassure her sister, indicated by her hand's covering her sister's, and her mother's obvious concerned attention project a sense of foreboding, as does the shroudlike garment the mother is sewing. Kennington furthers the sense of dull pessimism through his coloration: despite a pinkish cast, the coloring is drab, suggesting the unsensational, everyday dreariness of the lives of the working poor. In this respect Kennington is typical of the social realists of the end of the century, who conveyed hardship and suffering more through a muted tonal palate and sparse background than with the display of emaciated beings.

Two years later, Kennington returned to the subject with *Adversity*. But where the earlier canvas strove for poignancy and pathos, the second one endeavors to present stoicism. Shortly after the painting was exhibited at the Royal Institute of Painters in Oil, an engraving was published in the *Graphic* (27 June 1891) with the accompanying caption:

> The two sisters, who have evidently seen better days, have been forced by the loss of their parents to try and gain a precarious living by dressmaking. The little room is bare and sordid and littered with fripperies of dressmaking, while the black dresses of the sisters make a sad contrast with the gay ball-dress which the elder one is making, and which lies in all its unfinished splendour across her lap. The melancholy of their surroundings has plainly come upon the younger with full force, and she is appealing to her sister for comfort and consolation in her misery. Outside the withered stump of some sickly plant stretches forlorn arms against the window-pane, and a garish light is reflected from the plastered wall of the dull courtyard into which the sisters' room looks. There is much quiet pathos in the drawing, and the appearance of the girls but emphasises the squalor of their surroundings, and points the freshness of their loss.

Thus Kennington again incorporates many of the standard symbols—the plant, the window, the bare room—but varies the canvas slightly—a dress, a sewing machine, and two women—increasing the originality and the realism. But Kennington's canvas underscores the feelings of many Victorians: despite nearly a half century of protest and reform, the situation of needlewomen, particularly slopworkers, was bleak.

After the turn of the century, however, Kennington exhibited two images displaying a very different view of needleworkers, *The Work-Room* (1907) and *Relaxation* (1908). Both paintings are set in large workrooms. The first shows a millinery establishment where the women appear healthy, contented, and industrious (figure 6.6). The women are well dressed; the room is clean and not crowded. In the second picture, also set in a workroom, the dressmakers are taking a break or perhaps finishing for the day, since two women are donning hats. Of those remaining, one reads aloud from a book or letter while the others listen. Again all are well dressed and well fed, while the room appears well lighted and clean, although a little messy. The work is similar to Stanhope A. Forbes's *A Village Industry,* exhibited at the Royal Academy that year. In Forbes's painting three young apprentices are in a workshop with an older man who is drawing or explaining a design; all are well dressed and well fed, with the workshop relatively clean, creating an impression of intelligence and industry. Although there were no overtly reformist works in the Royal Academy catalogs from either year, these works by Forbes and Kennington may have been more about a hope for the future than a denial of the present. The victory of the Liberal government in 1906 and the establishment of a parliamentary commission in 1907 to oversee the sweated trades, combined with the 1906 *Daily News* Sweated Industries Exhibition, may have suggested that the Edwardian age would bring remediation and a new respect for workers. Yet even as the *Daily News* exhibition opened, the photos in its catalog, showing neat, orderly interiors and clean, industrious workers, were labeled as "realistic, lying photographs" by reviewers for other papers (Suthers, 5). Perhaps realizing that the representation of the working classes had been transformed from an educational opportunity into a "social function" (Gavin-Duffy, 744), a pleasurable spectacle rather than an informative documentation of working-class labor, the editor of the *Daily News* lamented that for many viewers the exhibition was little more than "a painful interlude between a visit to the shops in the morning and a visit to the theatre in the evening" (Gardiner, xv). Decades of exposure, in illustrations and fiction and art, had blurred the lines demarking reality and fiction to the extent that even real workers, when represented in works exhibited for public view, seemed to be little more than players on a stage, their labor reduced to entertainment.

IV

For more traditional illustrators, the social realist movement led to a renewed interest in comparative images of client and seamstress. For example, Gustave Doré's illustration of Thomas Hood's poem "The Lady's Dream" (1844) for the 1870 Moxon Folio edition of Hood's works incorporates this motif.[6] An early example of the dream vision, Hood's poem expands on the theme of suffering and exploitation presented in "The Song of the Shirt." But, typical of many later works, "The Lady's Dream" replaces the sufferings of the shirtmaker with the miseries of the working poor generally. In the poem, a wealthy, pampered woman dreams that she is haunted by the ghosts of

> . . . those maidens young
>   Who wrought in that dreary room,
> With figures drooping and spectres thin,

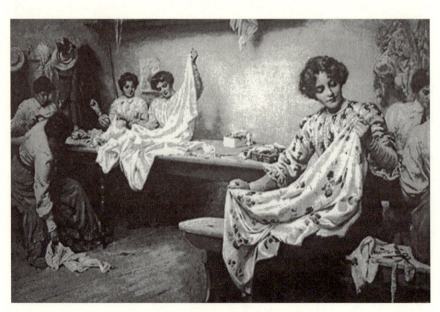

FIGURE 6.6   "The Work-Room," Kennington, 1907. *RAP.*

And cheeks without a bloom;—
And the Voice that cried, "For the pomp of pride,
We haste to an early tomb!" (ll. 25–30)

In Doré's illustration, the lady partially rises from her bed, confusedly scratching her head, while starving women and children occupy the chamber, surrounding her richly hung bed. In the center of the drawing a woman and child clamor for the lady's attention, but she gazes out toward the viewer with a puzzled frown. Isolated by the white bedclothes, in the right corner is a needlewoman. One of the few figures given an occupation, she is clearly highlighted, thus providing viewers with a familiar referent.

A quarter of a century after publishing "The Belgravian Venus Attired by the Graces," *Punch* returned to the classical allusion with "The Modern Venus Attired by the Three Dis-Graces" (1888). The detailed and carefully shaded central figure, proudly standing, hand on hip, is in stark contrast with the outlined, colorless figures who dress her. Furthering the contrast is the old-fashioned plainness of the dresses of the "graces" as compared to the stylish layering of the dresses of the "Venus," their hollow cheeks and simple hairstyles as compared to her well-fed features and elaborate coiffure, as well as the industry of the needlewomen as compared to the leisure represented by the stance and walking stick of the client.

Two years later a more common diptych theme appeared in *Ariel, or the London Puck,* in "So Tired: The Close of the Season" (1890). Featuring back-to-back illustrations of client and seamstress, the half-page illustration utilizes many traditional referents while incorporating a few modern touches, such as a sewing machine. On the left, the client reclines, eyes closed, relaxed, a pillow behind her head, in an overstuffed chair. A decanter and glass sit on a table, a lamp and a large mirror or picture serve to lighten the picture and, along with the fine dress and elaborate footwear, demonstrate the woman's affluence. On the right, the haggard seamstress also reclines in her chair. But in contrast to the elaborately tufted chair belonging to the client, the seamstress's chair is a plain, straight-backed, wooden one. The garment in her right hand indicates that she has fallen into an exhausted sleep, head resting on the windowsill, in front of her sewing machine. And rather than a lamp and mirror, the seamstress's room features a guttered, smoking candle, and curtainless windows. The seamstress's plain dress, the hole in the wall close to her head, the bare wall facing the viewer, and the medicine and loaf on the mantle next to the candle further suggest the woman's poverty. But most telling are the faces of the two women: both are profiled, with the client facing slightly away from the viewer and the seamstress facing slightly toward the viewer. The client's face is lighted, unwrinkled, and serene, while the seamstress's face is in the shadow, lined seemingly by poverty and weariness. These illustrations are not subtle in contrasting the abstractions of sacrifice, cost, and responsibility. There is a comparative element in the illustrations, but it is between thoughtlessness and consequence rather than a direct contrast of the people involved.

7

Conclusion

SLAVES OF THE NEEDLE

Every literary description is a *view*. It would be said that the speaker, before describing, stands at the window, not so much to see, but to establish what he sees by its very frame: the window frame creates the scene. To describe is thus to place the empty frame which the realistic author always carries with him (more important than his easel) before a collection or continuum of objects which cannot be put into words without this obsessive operation (which could be laughable as a "gag"); in order to speak about it, the writer, through this initial rite, first transforms the "real" into a depicted (framed) object; having done this, he can take down this object, *remove* it from his picture: in short: de-depict it (to depict is to unroll the carpet of the codes, to refer not from a language to a referent but from one code to another). Thus, realism (badly named, at any rate often badly interpreted) consists not in copying the real but in copying a (depicted) copy of the real.

—Roland Barthes, *S/Z*

The seamstress appeared in literature, periodicals, and artwork throughout the Victorian age. Following the publication of Hood's "The Song of the Shirt," she rapidly became a recurrent element in fiction and the visual arts, creating a shared code, a recognizable set of interlocking tropes and similitudes. At every point writers and artists were building on previous material—whether it was earlier writers drawing on established assumptions about women or about the working poor, or later artists usurping established background details. What Barthes's frame analogy makes clear is that Victorians were always at one remove from even the most realistic portrayal, and from the beginning the image was just that, an image that was shaped and molded as needed.

And like all created characters, the seamstress cannot be said to point to any "real" worker; inevitably each portrait is created from a synthesis of social knowledge, social desires, documentary material, and literary and aesthetic convention. The character becomes "significant as it is imagined in relation to other characters representing class configurations, as an indicator of the writer's [or artist's] model of social order and government"

(Bodenheimer, 6–7). Thus the trajectory of the symbol—its early form, representative development, acculturation, and disintegration into an accepted commonplace—presents a revealing account of a public problem. It sketches a series of possible responses within the confines of a given social milieu, and creates a series of fantasies about the manner and possibilities of social reform over time. That the seamstress became an identifiable icon during the Victorian age is not surprising. According to Hodge and Kress, potential social agents are powerful in terms of three specific criteria: age, gender, and social status (72). The seamstress, as reformers portrayed her, fits all three categories in such a way as to elicit a maximum response: she is young, female, and displaced middle class. Her age and gender make her non-threatening and in need of protection; her middle-class status makes her worthy of interest. At the same time the displacement distances her enough that her situation is not threatening but, rather, pathetic.

Indeed, her social status may be why Victorians focused so strongly on the seamstress. According to Rosemarie Bodenheimer, one of the major solidifying aspects of social-problem novels, and by association social-problem paintings, is that "they display conflict about the nature and diversity of a newly empowered and newly fragmented middle class as they attempt to reimagine the roles it should play in the maintenance of social order" (5). As someone who has fallen out of the middle class through no fault of her own, the seamstress would hold a special appeal: she is both of and not of the middle class and she is someone who can be assisted in a multitude of ways—through work, increased wages, legislation.

By examining the various representations of the seamstress, both visual and verbal, we learn several things about Victorian society. We gain insights into the lives of working women at both ends of working-class status, the dressmakers at the upper end and the slopworkers at the lower. Such representations also reveal much about the attitudes, both perceived and actual, of the middle and upper classes toward the working poor. We also discover Victorian attitudes toward social responsibility and reform. And finally, we gain insight into the uneasy balance between aesthetics and practicality, and how art might be used to present uncomfortable realities and instigate change.

I

On 20 May 1843, an explicit, shocking, and frequently indignant article exposing the working and living conditions of urban needlewomen appeared in the *Pictorial Times*. Primarily a recital of testimony taken from seam-stresses who appeared before the Children's Employment Commission in 1842, "Slaves of the Needle" marked a new adaptation of the metaphor established by radical spokesmen such as Richard Oastler for factory work-ers, the metaphor of worker as slave. What makes this usage notable is that the analogy is narrowed to deal with a specific group, needlewomen, rather than the working classes as a whole. It proved to be a comparison that so captured the Victorian imagination that it was repeated in a variety of forms in numerous articles, stories, and novels throughout the remainder of the century. Soon reformers had adopted a three-part analogy—more complex than Oastler's equation of worker and slave, using the emotional reaction engendered by the word *slave* combined with the helpless appeal of young needlewomen—to speak of the poverty and sufferings of the working classes in general. A close examination of the analogy's develop-ment reveals in microcosm the iconologic development of the seamstress for Victorian society.

As Catherine Gallagher has established, in the early decades of the nine-teenth century humanitarian reformers began to switch their attention from the sufferings of blacks in the West Indies slave trade to the sufferings of factory laborers in England.[1] This change in emphasis is not in itself remark-able, but the language and imagery used by factory reformers are surprising. Spokesmen for the slave trade had, from the beginning of the abolitionist movement, compared the two to the detriment of the English factory sys-tem. One of the most vehement and most successful critics of the Anti–Slave Trade movement was William Cobbett, who discarded the mild sar-casm of the eighteenth-century proslavery supporters for blunt accusations of "cant and hypocrisy" directed at supporters of Anti–Slave Trade legis-lation. In 1806 he told readers of his *Weekly Political Register* that "so often as they agitate this question, with all its cant, for the relief of 500,000 blacks; so often will I remind them of the 1,200,000 white paupers of Eng-land and Wales" (845).

However, by the 1830s the slave trade was no longer an issue in England and many reformers soon began to turn their attention to the local abuses that had been called to their attention by the debate surrounding the Anti-Slavery movement.[2] In writing and speaking about the factory system, these reformers used the rhetoric established by opponents of the Anti–Slave Trade movement, often equating factory workers and slaves in order to stress the oppression and suffering found in the factory system, an effective analogy since the slave-trade debate, with its discussions of the sufferings and indignities faced by blacks, was well established and the factory debate was relatively new. In a letter to the Leeds *Mercury,* dated 16 October 1830, Richard Oastler exposed the long hours and unhealthy working conditions suffered by children employed in the Bedford textile mills. Many historians view Oastler's letter, entitled "Yorkshire Slavery," as the beginning of the Ten Hours Movement, and it marks one of the first comparisons of West Indian slavery with industrial slavery aimed at eradicating the latter through association with the former:

> One shade alone obscured my pleasure, arising not from any difference in principle, but from the want of application of the general principle to the whole Empire. The pious and able champions of *Negro* liberty and *Colonial* rights should, if I mistake not, have gone further than they did, or perhaps, to speak more correctly, before they travelled so far as the West Indies, should at least for a few moments, have sojourned in our own immediate neighborhood, and have directed the attention of the meeting to scenes of misery, acts of oppression, and victims of Slavery, even on the threshold of our homes. (98–99)

The equation of factory worker and slave became more effective as parliamentary reports established that a majority of factory workers were women and children. The traditional image of women and children as helpless creatures in need of protection and guidance made the comparison between worker and slave appear a natural one. Adding to the effectiveness were the revelations of long hours, the use of corporal punishment by overseers, the lack of education and religious training, and the breakdown of accepted family roles. Finally, by focusing on women and children, reformers were able to avoid many of the Victorian fears of revolt and violence associated with the labor force in the early nineteenth century.

The Luddite uprisings in 1812, Manchester's Peterloo Massacre in 1819, and machine breakings in 1826 and 1828 created images of violent working-class mobs in the minds of many Victorians. The workers in these early strikes were inevitably pictured as male, and the image of the worker as an ignorant, violent animal out of control was a frighteningly believable one for many middle- and upper-class Victorians. Early fictional presentations of strikers, such as Harriet Martineau's *The Rioters* (1827), did little to reassure nervous Victorians. In this short novel (104 duodecimo pages) she portrays the strikers, lit in the glare of torches, as men whose "haggard and infuriated countenances . . . were, indeed, terrible enough to strike fear into any heart" (14). The strikers break machines and the commanding officer of the soldiers called out to quell the riot is unable to reason with the angry crowd: "he might as well have spoken to the raging sea; not a syllable could be heard, and brickbats flew in all directions" (52).

The fear of machines and the men who ran them was also fed by essayists such as Thomas Carlyle, whose warnings about the "Condition of England" played on growing fears of mechanization. In "Signs of the Times" (1829) he warns:

> Men are grown mechanical in head and in heart, as well as in hand. They have lost faith in individual endeavour, and in natural force of any kind. Not for internal perfection, but for external combinations and arrangements, for institutions, constitutions— for Mechanism of one sort or other, do they hope and struggle. Their whole efforts, attachments, opinions, turn on mechanism, and are of a mechanical character. (228–29)

To Victorian readers, Carlyle's mechanized worker was an industrial Frankenstein's monster, a mad, destructive creature too repulsive, too horrible to even gaze upon. But his image of the worker in "Chartism," a decade later, was even more fearful. In the essay, Carlyle first reminds people of past incidents of violence by workers involving burnings, machine breakings, and vitriol attacks, then warns that things are little improved, that "Chartism means the bitter discontent grown fierce and mad, the wrong condition therefore or the wrong disposition, of the Working Classes of England" (119). Elizabeth Gaskell makes the analogy between Chartists and Frankenstein's monster explicit nearly a decade later in *Mary Barton*. In chapter 15, in which she carefully charts the disappointments that lead to John Barton's turn to Chartism, and in which she explicitly states her thesis—"the employers and the employed must rise or fall together" (221)—she first explains:

> He [Barton] acted to the best of his judgement, but it was a widely-erring judgement.
> The actions of the uneducated seem to me typified in those of Frankenstein, that monster of many human qualities, ungifted with a soul, a knowledge of the difference between good and evil.
> The people rise up to life; they irritate us, they terrify us, and we become their enemies. Then in the sorrowful moment of our

triumphant power, their eyes gaze on us with a mute reproach. Why have we made them what they are; a powerful monster, yet without the inner means for peace and happiness? (219–20)

Gaskell's warning seems clear: the upper classes cannot afford to ignore the needs of the laboring classes whom they create through their materialistic consumption. It is both an economic necessity and a moral duty to educate and meet the physical needs of the working poor. It is little wonder that, after early parliamentary reports indicated large numbers of women and children involved in industry, reformers quickly moved to portray them as the most pitiable "slaves," as suffering innocents bound to cruel masters.

Although the image of suffering children had an immediate appeal as a symbol of the need for change—perhaps even factory legislation—to many industrial reformers, the plight of young female workers was more useful. Not only were girls generally assumed to be weaker, more helpless, and more passive than boys, and thus more likely to need protection, but the feminization of the factory worker also meant that reforms would need to be carried on throughout the system and would need to be permanent. To Victorians, women were helpless and in need of protection throughout their lives, not just during their childhood and youth. Male factory children soon became machine breakers, but female children became, in the eyes of middle-class Victorians, wives and mothers. Thus the "emancipating" of these "slaves" would be ennobling rather than dangerous.

But the image of the long-suffering, helpless female laborer soon received a setback. The Blackburn Chartist riots in May 1842 and the Plug Plots in August of that same year marked renewed violence among the working classes, and reports of female involvement effectively destroyed the women workers' image of helplessness. The Victorians' horror at the growing militancy of women workers is reflected in Lord Ashley's speech before the House of Commons on the Ten Hours Bill:

> What says Sir Charles Shaw, for some years the superintendent of police of Manchester—what is his opinion of the condition of females of that town, and the effects produced, by the system under which they live, on their conduct and character?—"Women," said he, "by being employed in a factory, lose the station ordained them by Providence, and become similar to female followers of an army, wearing the garb of women, but actuated by the worst passions of

men. The women are the leaders and exciters of the young men to violence in every riot and outbreak in the manufacturing districts, and the language they indulge in is of a horrid description. While they are themselves demoralized, they contaminate all that comes within their reach." (26)

It is significant that Lord Ashley concentrates on the effect factory labor has on women. The Ten Hours Act would restrict the labor of children as well as women, but it is on the necessity to restrict the labor of women that Ashley centers his attention. Physicians' reports of factory workers had revealed that many women required to perform heavy physical labor had developed large, muscular frames, the opposite of the frail, feminine form the Victorians associated with ideal womanhood. The robust image of the female factory worker can be seen in artwork such as Eyre Crowe's *The Dinner Hour—Wigan* (1874), in which the carriage and positions of the female operatives on the canvas give the impression of vitality and independence, while their strong jaws and the well-developed muscular arms revealed by their short-sleeved garments give the figures an androgynous, if not masculine, impression.

In light of the fears such "distortions" of the feminine role evoked in Victorians, it is not surprising that reformers tried to stress that independence was an aberration of the factory, a response to the demand for extreme servility in the workplace, and that release from industrial labor would soon return working-class women to their traditional roles. Thus Ashley did not begin his address with shock tactics about role reversals; he worked up to them by beginning with a more modest form of feminine labor, though one whose long hours and poor pay were already well documented. He began with the harsh labor of seamstresses and milliners:

> I confess that ten years of experience have taught me that avarice and cruelty are not the particular and inherent qualities of any one class or occupation;—they will ever be found where the means of profit are combined with great, and virtually irresponsible, power—they will be found wherever interest and selfishness have a purpose to serve, and a favorable opportunity.... Look at the frightful records of the London dress-makers—for whom do they wear out their lives in heart-breaking toil? Why, to supply the demands and meet the sudden and capricious tastes of people of condition! Here is neither farmer or manufacturer at fault; the scene is changed,

and the responsibility too: we must ascribe it entirely to the gentler sex, and among them, not a little to our own intimacies and connextions [sic]. (4)

Ashley does not attempt to draw close connections between seamstresses and factory workers. Instead he seems to drop the issue of needlewomen and proceeds to focus on women and children employed in factories, but soon narrows the focus to female factory workers. Yet one of the first points he makes harks back to his earlier subject: "Look again to the effects on domestic economy; out of thirteen married females taken at one mill, only one knows how to make her husband a shirt, and only four knew how to mend one. I have the evidence of several females, who declare their own ignorance of every domestic accomplishment ..." (22). In his citing of case studies that follows, Ashley repeatedly stresses that the young women interviewed cannot sew. The linking of sewing with domesticity, and thus traditional home and family life, combined with the tenuous linking of two types of paid female labor, needlework and factory work, provided a combination that social reformers were to pick up and exploit for over half a century: the seamstress as a symbol of the working poor.

II

Between 1840 and the close of the century the seamstress became a Victorian commonplace, appearing in virtually every periodical (conservative and radical, news and literary), in every writer's oeuvre (fiction and poetry), and every artist's portfolio (realist and aesthete). Her plight captured the attention of both men and women and became a cause célèbre among the social elite. The popularity of her cause across gender and class lines, and its duration, make her an important figure in the study of Victorian culture, but the seamstress is also of interest to those interested in semiology. An examination of her presentation and of the modifications that occur over time provides an opportunity to trace the life cycle of a symbol, beginning with a realistic presentation by reformers, followed by the addition of the metaphorical, and finally resulting in a familiarity that undercuts the symbol's effectiveness and reduces it to a stock artistic image.

The alignment of the seamstress with slavery was the first step in the symbolic process. It moved the discussion from the real to the metaphorical, since slavery was not a part of the English experience. For most, slavery was an abstraction debated in Parliament and associated with the colonies rather than England. For Victorians, equating a familiar image, and one with many English associations, with the foreign one would have been shocking, but also distancing because of the instinctive rejection of the image as unreal. Both aspects would be important to the seamstress's effectiveness as a symbol; for while the startling nature of the alignment would capture attention, the accompanying gap would challenge the observer to question both the real and the metaphorical aspects of the presentation.

Nevertheless the figure of the seamstress allowed social critics to portray workers in ways less offensive to middle- and upper-class Victorians, those in a position to instigate and participate in reform. Sewing, as Lord Ashley's speech indicates, was allied with images of domestic economy, with traditional female roles of wife and mother, with the home rather than the factory. It also removed the conditions of the working poor from the world of Chartist activities, for although female factory workers had been briefly linked to Chartist violence, politics were generally considered to be outside a woman's sphere, and the image of a woman employed in such a domestic activity as sewing made any link with Chartist politics seem ludicrous.

The problem for reformers, then, was to link, however tenuously, the hardships of needlewomen with those of the industrial poor. For many writers the easiest way was to take the analogy established a decade earlier, worker as slave, and modify it to seamstress as slave, letting the reader make a mental equation between the figure of the seamstress and workers in general. The idea was both popular and successful. In 1843, two articles using the slave image in their titles and describing the harsh conditions faced by needlewomen were published: "Slaves of the Needle" in the *Pictorial Times* and "The White Slaves of London" in the *Times*. In "Slaves of the Needle," composed primarily of testimony from the 1843 *Second Report of the Children's Employment Commission,* the opening paragraph uses the slave analogy to create a sense of situational irony: "In this wealthy and magnificent London—this city of churches and palaces, hospitals and asylums, where splendour walks hand-in-hand with charity ... in this wonderful abiding-place of riches and goodness, we have fifteen thousand girls and young women doomed to daily slavery, some to blindness, and some to early death, by the apathy, the arrogance, and the heartlessness of their takers" (145). The article ends with a comparison of the suffering needlewomen, working feverishly long into the night, with the women who wear the gowns, equally late but in settings of comfort and pleasure. Accompanying the article is a pair of etchings illustrating and emphasizing the comparison: on the left is a crowded room of women, heads bent, industriously sewing, the clock clearly showing three; on the right is a crowded ballroom with a number of well-dressed women sitting and standing, seemingly enjoying their evening. The tone of the *Times* article is less strident than that of the *Pictorial Times* article, and its comparisons between slavery and dressmaking are less explicit. It concentrates instead on presenting detailed figures of the long hours and poor pay experienced by seamstresses. The article ends with the story of a woman who has been brought to court because she pawned the garments she was working on to buy food.

A more forceful article, much more overt in its use of the slavery analogy, appeared in the *Times*. One of the most explicit comparisons between Negro slavery and needlework to appear in print, the article, on seamstress slavery, establishes the analogy between dressmaking and slavery with its opening sentence: "Granting that the negro gangs who are worked on the cotton grounds of the Southern States of North America, or in the sugar plantations of Brazil, are slaves, in what way should we speak of persons who are circumstanced in the manner we are about to relate?" The writer continues by exciting sympathy and acknowledging that the examples are to be extreme, but always returning to the comparison of Negro slavery:

> They are of a sex and age the least qualified to struggle with the hardships of their lot—young women, for the most part, between sixteen and thirty years of age. As we would not deal in exaggerations, we would promise that we take them at their busy season, just as writers upon American slavery are careful to select the season of cotton-picking and sugar-crushing as illustrations of their theories. The young female slaves, then, of whom we speak . . . (qtd. in Cobden, 178)

And like earlier industrial reformers, the author anticipates objections by pointing out that the freedom of choice to work at a set rate or starve is not really freedom: "The seamstresses may leave the mill, no doubt, but what awaits them on the other side of the door?—starvation, if they be honest; if not, in all probability, prostitution and its consequence. They would scarcely escape from slavery that way" (qtd. in Cobden, 179). Although these articles are effective in terms of equating seamstress and slave, they do little to connect the seamstress with the working poor in general.

It was not until a few months later, when James Malcolm Rymer published *The White Slave,* that the three-point analogy was established. In his novel, Rymer spends much time pointing out that the poor housing, low wages, and starvation experienced by needlewomen are common to all workers. For example, when Millicent, the protagonist, first begins to look for work, she is warned, "'I have no doubt but you will obtain some employment soon; but you must look forward to dreadful hard work, and very scanty remuneration; for all women's trades in London are brought down to so low a pitch, that those who are doomed to procure a living by them have been called by the appellation of white slaves'" (27). Rymer applies the term *slave* repeatedly when discussing the seamstresses, but occasionally when discussing other workers as well, reinforcing the complex analogy. And Rymer repeatedly asserts that needlewomen, and thus all workers, are not free agents because of choice limitations; they are free to work at the prices offered or starve. As an experienced needlewoman explains to a horrified newcomer:

> "They only want to ascertain how little a person can live upon, and . . . how much work can be got for the least amount of money. Well, then, you see, there's competition among the poor people; for if a thousand be employed and doing so much work each of them, there will be, perhaps, a thousand out of employment, and they will offer to do so much more for the same money, or to take less money for doing the same quantity, and then the old hands, in order to keep their employment, are compelled to give in, and adopt the new terms; and that's what keeps the work always down to starvation price. . . .
>
> "One shilling [less] leads to another, till the poor people can hardly exist at all; and that's what is called the manufacturing system, my dear, the country is told to be so proud of." (58)

At one point Rymer's heroine refuses to work at the price set and is turned away with orders not to return. Since the choice is work or starve, the seamstress is a slave to the system, an argument developed when the comparison between worker and slave was first used a decade earlier.

Not all writers used the slavery metaphor in their titles, but virtually all used it in their texts, even those writing nonfiction articles or novels that were little more than a fictionalization of parliamentary Blue Book reports. In 1845 Ralph Barnes Grindrod, a surgeon who had participated in the 1842 hearings before the Children's Employment Commission, published a penny tract in the "Popular Propaganda Socialist Pamphlet" series distributed by the Socialist Labour Press. In *The Slaves of the Needle; An Exposure,* Grindrod quotes extensively from commission testimony while employing the extreme rhetoric often associated with both antislavery and industrial reform tracts:

> Gross injustice and cruelty has long been, and is now being, exercised on a class of individuals, whose position in society, industry and unprotected condition, whether it regards their age—their sex—or their necessary separation from home and friends, entitles them to peculiar consideration. Well may the pious and humane reader peruse with shame and disgust the narration of cruelties mainly perpetrated in the metropolis of the Christian world—of slavery which exceeds in its refined atrocities, the abominations of the now happily-extinguished system of Negro bondage—of destitution and suffering which exists among a sex, who instinctively, look to man for protection, as a sacred deposit committed to his care by the Creator. (28)

Grindrod uses such rhetoric to appeal to his readers' sense of moral responsibility, their preconceptions concerning women's helplessness, and their fears about the breakdown of traditional family values. It allows him to attract his readers to a new cause, the suffering of needlewomen.

Despite the variety of purposes and portrayals, the body of fiction portraying needlewomen is held together by a number of common elements. In most of the works the protagonist is a young orphan from the country. A friend, relative, or acquaintance often "falls" into prostitution, but the heroine remains pure; however, under the harsh conditions of her employment her health is broken and she dies. The most constant literary element, though, is slave imagery—from the mention of coworkers as "fellow slaves" in *A London Dressmaker's Diary* and Tonna's call for "the liberation of thousands of slaves" in the nonfiction exposé *Perils of the Nation,* to the recurrent usage throughout novels such as *The Pageant* and *Fanny, the Little Milliner.* The imagery was also used in titles, from Rymer's *The White Slave* and Reynolds's series "The Slaves of England" and his chapters "The White Slave of England" and "The Close of the White Slave's Career" in *The Seamstress,* to articles and pamphlets such as the *Pictorial Times*'s "Slaves of the Needle" and John C. Cobden's *The White Slaves of England.* Even in works as late G. M. Viner's *Aunt Eliza's Garret,* the recurring image is still that of a slave. Viner's novel ends:

The churchyard where a neat stone, with the simple inscription:—
'God grant us peace!'—*Amelia*.
points out the spot where rests the body of an English slave ... (192)

Indeed, the association was so quick and so strong that as early as 1844 the phrase "white slave of England" was in such constant use in the newspapers and periodicals that Victorian readers could not escape equating it with the seamstress.

And the effectiveness of the metaphor is not surprising when one considers Clifford Geertz's contention that "the power of metaphor derives precisely from the interplay between the discordant meanings it symbolically coerces into a unitary conceptual framework and from the degree to which that coercion is successful in overcoming the psychic resistance such semantic tension inevitably generates in anyone in a position to perceive it" (211). In other words, a truly effective metaphor troubles the literally minded because it is "false," yet the metaphor is most effective when it is most false. In this case, especially in the early works that established the metaphor of the seamstress slave, the female needleworker is displaced from the middle class, not born into an underclass; quite the contrary, since the premium needed to obtain a position in a millinery house necessitates an income beyond that of the laboring classes but not of the impoverished middle class. Similarly the use of location, England, often specifically London, would be troublesome since slavery was an aspect of colonial life, not usually associated with life in England proper. Nor is the seamstress's employment an issue of race; again, the contrary is true, even emphasized through the adjective *white*. Her situation is, however, a matter of gender. Yet even here there would be a sense of falseness, since the perception of class and race would automatically suggest to the Victorian mind a need to pamper and protect rather than put to work. For many reformers, therefore, the seamstress/slave was a powerful metaphor. Yet as a symbol its usefulness was limited almost exclusively to the verbal. There was virtually no means of producing the same series of coercive, conceptual links through the visual arts. Indeed, the only attempt is Richard Redgrave's *Fashion's Slaves* (1847), and there the tension again depends, at least in part, on the verbal—the title.

III

Another common element in fiction, and the factor that ties the majority of visual renditions to the literature, is allusion to Hood's "The Song of the

Shirt." In the literature, Toulmin prefaces *The Orphan Milliners* with an epigraph from the poem, and Gaskell uses the line "Band, and gusset, and seam" when describing plain work in *Mary Barton,* while Reynolds uses the description of the seamstress's attic room to create the setting for *The Seamstress.* The flower Mary Austen gives Lucy, in *Lucy Dean, the Noble Needlewoman,* is a "primrose sweet," and one of the slopworkers in *Alton Locke* comments, "stitch, stitch, stitch.—Somebody's wrote a song about that" (93). In the artwork, allusions to Hood's poem appear in both titles and visual details. Richard Redgrave subtitled *The Sempstress* (both versions) with lines from the poem. And in the first version of the painting, the scrap of bread and the bare walls and floors are illustrative of the poem, while in the second version the dying plant and broken washbasin reflect images from the text. Many of the paintings that followed built on the images introduced by Hood and by Redgrave, establishing an iconographic vocabulary. For example, the majority of paintings portray a lone, seated figure, either at prayer—as in Anna Blunden's *"For only one short hour"*—or with head bowed in exhaustion—as in George Frederic Watts's *The Song of the Shirt.* In many of the works, either the needlewoman muses over a potted flower, as in George Elgar Hicks's *Snowdrops,* or a sickly plant sits in a windowsill, as in Thomas Benjamin Kennington's *Adversity,* recalling the lines:

> Oh! but to breathe the breath
> Of the cowslip and primrose sweet—
> With the sky above my head,
> And the grass beneath my feet;
> For only one short hour
> To feel as I used to feel.

Critics such as T. J. Edelstein argue that these flowers symbolize the seamstresses' "loneliness and isolation from their homes in the country" and emphasize the inhumanity of city life ("They Sang," 206). But most obvious of all the visual symbols is the shirt. Of all the garments made by needlewomen, a shirt is what virtually every painting shows a woman sewing, identifying the paintings with Hood's poem and with each other. One of the first overt acknowledgments of the power of the shirt as a visual symbol is the 1848 illustration in *Punch,* "'A Shroud as well as a Shirt.'" The caption, taken from the last line of the fourth stanza, the skulls, and the numerals 2½ leave little doubt that making the "twopenny-ha'penny shirt" is deadly. For later artists, the shirt is often a focal point, since the white color shows dramatically against the usual dark dress of the seamstress, making the allusion, often further emphasized through the work's title, clear.

In 1853, five years after printing "'A Shroud as well as a Shirt,'" *Punch* followed up with "A Startling Novelty in Shirts" (figure 7.1). The skeletons on the young man's shirt allude to the earlier sketch, but his proud demeanor and the shocked response of the housekeeper make the underlying message of the later cartoon more overt. "A Shroud" primarily called attention to the abominable rate of pay for shirtmakers, and the seemingly inevitable consequences of these wages; in contrast, "A Startling Novelty" comments on Victorian gentlemen who have neglected or ignored their duties as societal guardians and done nothing to alleviate the sufferings of needlewomen and, even worse, continue to purchase the cheaply made garments. Thus, the original functions as a commentary on the profession, while the latter comments on middle- and upper-class Victorian society. This intertextuality is an important factor in examining the artwork, both individually and in the larger context of Victorian culture, since an immediately identifiable symbol helps to create a predictable response.

IV

Initially, the visual depictions of the seamstress accompanied stories, novels, and articles. Such illustrations lent a new dimension to the verbal depictions, removing the portrait from the abstraction of language to the more concrete two-dimensional visual world. Yet it is only after the iconography is established, both through the verbal presentations and the early illustrations that accompanied them, that the formal visual artists take up the seamstress in a serious way. A possible reason for the difference in timing is the difference in artistic purpose. The Victorian writers who focused on the seamstress were part of the larger Condition-of-England movement that focused on several groups of the laboring poor, and that reached its pinnacle at mid-century. At that point, except for a few artists such as Redgrave and Watts, there was no complementary movement among the visual artists. For one thing, few people want to frequently confront images of suffering in their homes. However, the earlier establishment of an iconographic vocabulary allowed painters in the final quarter of the century to present the suffering in an abstract form. For example, Millais's *Stitch! Stitch! Stitch!* details nothing of the plight of the seamstress, but instead

A STARTLING NOVELTY IN SHIRTS.

FIGURE 7.1 "A Startling Novelty in Shirts," *Punch* 25 (23 July 1853): 31.

relies on allusion to incite a response from the viewer. Similarly, creators of narrative paintings, such as Collier's *Trouble,* rely on viewer familiarity with a multitude of tales so that a single frozen moment can elicit a predictable story line in the viewer's imagination. The familiarity of the story also made it a natural choice for beginning filmmaker D. W. Griffith (*The Song of the Shirt,* 1908). When he presents the story of two sisters earning their living by sewing, one eventually dying and the other falling into despair, audiences were able to immediately recognize situations and symbols, filling gaps in the story. Thus, although full cultural absorption necessitates both verbal and visual representations, the role and sequencing of the forms differ.

Early writers such as Tonna and Stone undertook serious research to authenticate their fictions and then sought to intertwine fact and fiction, convinced that "the novelist reached readers unaware of government publications" (Tillotson, 81). Women writers sought to raise issues and answer questions even though the majority of their readers were unenfranchised. The appeal was two pronged: women could subtly influence those who were enfranchised—husbands, brothers, sons—and as people without legal power women more easily empathized with other unenfranchised groups, such as the laboring poor. While most reformists believed, along with George Eliot, "how little the real characteristics of the working-classes are known to those who are outside them," early reformers also agreed that "social novels profess to represent the people as they are, and the unreality of their representations is a grave evil" (Eliot, *Essays,* 268, 270). To bring to life the findings of parliamentary investigations and to reassure Victorians of the verisimilitude of their presentations many early writers built directly from testimony and documented their presentations. Other writers, such as Trollope, Gaskell, and Dickens, used personal observation for their starting point. Periodical publications during this time tended to maintain a literal focus on needlewomen, focusing either on millinery establishments or on the tribulations of specific slopworkers. The visual image also flourished during this early period, appearing in periodical illustrations for magazines such as *Punch,* the *Pictorial Times,* and the *Illuminated Magazine.* And while Redgrave dramatized the figure and blurred issues such as class and actual living conditions, few painters took up Redgrave's imagery until after 1850. Thus during the 1840s the representation of the seamstress was primarily a literal one, based on government documents, testimony, and observation. But it is during this period that most of the iconography that marks seamstress literature and art were established: the clock, the dawn, the burnt-out candle, the attic room, and the shirt. The earlier tales, such as *A London Dressmaker's Diary*, *The Wrongs of Woman*, and *The Orphan Milliners*, concentrated on presenting facts concerning the hardships faced by seamstresses as documented in *The Second Report of the Children's Employment Commission* in 1843. Narratives published in the late 1840s, such as *Jessie Phillips* and *Mary Barton*, moved to the larger issue of the working class, using the seamstress as a symbol of suffering and bound by the common idea that "these two 'nations' are really parts of one" (Marcus, 233).

With the publication of Henry Mayhew's *London Labour and the London Poor* in 1849 and 1850, interest again focused on the seamstress herself and the possibility of relief through emigration, raising the literary figure to iconic stature. This development was quickly reciprocated in the fine arts with works such as Peele's *The Seamstress* and *Sewing Girls*, Blunden's *"For only one short hour,"* and Hicks's *Snowdrops*. Drawn both to the drama of emigration and the notion of a workable solution to the myriad problems surrounding needleworkers, periodicals quickly picked up the crusade using both texts and illustrations to promote various plans; however, the overwhelming number of works published during 1850 and the failure of emigration to deal with the problem of the seamstress made her a dead issue for later writers and illustrators. She was reduced to functioning as a vehicle for larger studies of the working poor or an efficient shorthand for establishing characters who are immediately recognized as hardworking and honest but poor. The number of fictional works and periodical articles focusing on needlewomen dwindled during the final decades of the era. Yet at the same time, as the force of her symbolic appeal waned, the seamstress became an increasingly popular topic for artists such as Cope, Doré, Holl, and Millais.

Despite the changes in focus some elements of the representation remained fairly constant. In the fiction, women employed in millinery houses were usually shown to be of impoverished gentility, a point emphasized both in the early 1840s and later during the 1850s as a means of capturing the sympathy and justifying the interest of middle- and upper-class readers, while working-class needlewomen were usually shown to be slopworkers. In the artwork, however, class representation was often more ambiguous, with details in the pictures often suggesting the slopworker had fallen out of the middle class. Repetition in early presentations quickly established a recognizable series of interlocking tropes: the attic room, a burnt-out candle, a spindly plant, and a clock indicating the hour. The iconography became so recognizable that writers, as well as illustrators, adopted it as a means of establishing a situation and character with a minimum number of details.

In the fiction, the central figure is usually a girl of high moral standards, ranging from the morally strong Ellen Cardan in *The Young Milliner* to the saintly Virginia of *The Seamstress,* whose integrity is emphasized by comparison with an acquaintance who succumbs to temptation and "falls" into prostitution. Often a novel closes with an air of pathos, as the seamstress dies of consumption resulting from the hardships associated with her occupation. And, finally, most writers of fiction dealing with milliners and dressmakers wrote for a feminine audience whom they encouraged to actively participate in some type of reform, from the boycotting advocated by Tonna and Stone to the involvement in emigration societies suggested by Rowcroft and Meteyard. Men were not totally excluded from the perceived audience, however. Tonna suggested that women inform their male relatives of millinery conditions and pressure them into bringing about legislative reform. And authors using the seamstress as a representative of the working classes often wrote for mixed audiences, suggesting women avoid shops known to abuse workers and support benevolent societies, while men might aid workers both through legislative reform and by financially aiding various relief organizations. The seamstress novel both called attention to the sufferings of a small class of working women and provided later writers with a heroine untainted by the factory.

Nevertheless, for Victorians the visual image predominated. During the era the image of the seamstress became so familiar that the Victorians themselves identified her as an image of their times. Her usurpation by social reformers may have been due to a recognition that the most potent forms of ideological expression occur when inscribed through spatial codes. As Hodge and Kress explain, "the role of verbal language is important but ancillary to the physical spatial codes" (64); to be a truly effective agent of change the seamstress had to be a concrete image, not just a verbal one. By blurring factors such as social class and incorporating religious typology, Victorian artists created not only a readily identifiable figure, but one that appealed to Victorian sensibilities. The appeal of the figure is crucial because a work cannot exist semiotically unless it has an audience, which will "set the text in some kind of social relationship, as well as attributing a relationship of text to world. The social relationship is crucial to the effectivity of the pointing. Without it, its ideological content will be inert" (Hodge and Kress, 60). Thus the visual arts reflect the viewer as well as subject, and as social concerns shifted so did the presentation of the seamstress. As events during the mid-1860s once again raised questions and concerns about the working classes, the seamstress again became a focal point, but in the visual rather than the verbal arts. Familiarity gave viewers a proprietary sense that, when coupled with associations of a pastoral past and domesticity, made the seamstress an ideal figure for dealing with the changes in ethnicity and gender affecting the social dynamic. But the art world had changed as well, and the overt typology of Redgrave and Blunden no longer appealed, nor, with the familiarity resulting from repeated presentations in periodicals and art shows, was it necessary. And while in many ways reformists' needs ran counter to aesthetics, the sentimentalized portrayal of needlewomen in later Victorian art affected Victorians on an emotional plane and kept the issue before them.

List of Seamstress Artwork

1837	"Madame Mantalini introduces Kate to Miss Knag," "Phiz" [H. K. Browne], *Nicholas Nickleby*
1842	(January) "The Milliner," *Punch* 2 (p. 10)
1843	(20 May) "The Milliners and the Dutchesses," *Pictorial Times* 1 (p. 145)
1843	Illustrations for *Story of a Feather*, John Leech, *Punch* 4–5
1844	(April) illustration for *The Orphan Milliners*, John Gilbert, *Illuminated Magazine* 2 (p. 279)
1844	(1 June) "Exhibition of the English in China—Case IV—A Sempstress," *Punch* 6 (p. 220)
1844	(June?) *The Sempstress*, Richard Redgrave [lost copy]
1844	Illustration for "The Seamstress," Mark Lemon, *Dick's Standard Plays*
1844	(October) "Death and the Drawing Room, or the Young Dressmakers of England," Kenny Meadows, *The Illuminated Magazine* 3 (p. 97)
1844	(And as book in 1846) illustration for *Fanny, the Little Milliner*, "Phiz"
1844	Illustrations for *The Chimes*, Leech
1846	*The Sempstress*, Redgrave
1846	"Tremendous Sacrifice," from *Our Own Times*, George Cruikshank
1846	*Throwing Off Her Weeds*, Redgrave
1847	*Fashion's Slaves*, Redgrave
1848	(19 August) "'A Shroud as well as a Shirt,'" *Punch* 15 (p. 76)
1849	*Song of the Shirt*, J. T. Peele [painted while in America; probably similar to 1852 *The Seamstress*]
1849	(22 December) "Pin Money/Needle Money," Leech, *Punch* 17 (pp. 240–41)
c. 1848–50	*The Song of the Shirt*, George Frederick Watts [unfinished, not shown until 1889]

1850	(5 January) "The Needle Women of London," *Penny Illustrated News* 1 (p. 156)
1850	(12 January) "The Needlewoman at Home and Abroad," Leech, *Punch* 18 (p. 15)
1850	(13 April) "Specimens from Mr. Punch's Industrial Exhibitions," Leech, *Punch* 18 (p. 145)
1850	(Begun 23 March, and as a book in 1850) illustrations for Reynolds's *The Seamstress*, Henry Anelay, *Reynolds's Miscellany* 4
1852	*The Seamstress*, Peele [exhibited with quotation from Hood: "Oh! But to breathe the breath / Of the cowslip and primrose sweet"]
1852	*The Women of England in the Nineteenth Century*, Mrs. Hurlstone
1853	(16 April) "The Belgravian Venus Attired by the Graces," *Punch* 24 (p. 151)
1853	(23 July) "A Startling Novelty in Shirts," *Punch* 25 (p. 31)
1853	"Virtue and Vice," John Everett Millais
1854	*Sad Memories*, Charles Rossiter
1854	*"For only one short hour,"* Anna Blunden (SBA) [also used as illustration to Hood obituary in *Penny Illustrated Paper*, 1862]
1854	*Sewing Girls*, Peele [exhibited with quotation from Hood: "Oh God! That bread be so dear, / and flesh and blood so cheap"]
1855	*Relenting*, Thomas Brooks (RA)
c. 1855–59	"Seated Seamstress with Male Companion," James McNeill Whistler [sketch]
1857	(1 January) cover illustration for *Roland Leigh; or, The Story of a City Arab*, G. P. Nichols, *The Leisure Hour* 6
1858	"The Song of the Shirt," *Passages from the Poems of Thomas Hood*, Rossiter
1858	*Snowdrops*, George Elgar Hicks (RA) [aka *Old Associations*]
1858	"Lucy in the Dressmaker's Workroom at the West-End of London" (illustration to magazine story), Anelay
c. 1857–60	*The Seducer*, E. C. Barnes
c. 1860	*A Coffee Stall*, Charles Hunt
1861	*Ruinous Prices*, Edward Hughes (RA) [also a version with updated fashions c. 1871]
1862	"Kate Nickleby," Thomas Faed
1863	(4 July) "The Haunted Lady, or 'The Ghost' in the Looking-Glass," John Tenniel, *Punch* 45 (p. 45)
1864	(15 January) "The Maker/The Wearer," R. S. E. Gallon [engravings]
1865	(4 March) "The Workroom," *Penny Illustrated Paper*
1866	*Tired Seamstress*, William Midwood
1869	*Home Dreams*, Charles W. Cope

1870	"The Song of the Shirt," Gustave Doré, illustration for *Poems of Thomas Hood*
1870	"The Lady's Dream," Doré, illustration for *Poems of Thomas Hood*
1871	(6 May) "The Sisters," G. J. Pinwell, *Graphic* 4 (p. 416)
1873	*Weary or 'The Song of the Shirt,'* Edward Radford
1875	*The Song of the Shirt*, Frank Holl
1876	*Stitch! Stitch! Stitch!* Millais
1877	(7 April) "Old Age—A Study of the Westminster Union," Hubert von Herkomer, *Graphic* 14 (pp. 324–25)
1878	*Eventide: Westminster Union*, von Herkomer [reworking of "Old Age"]
1888	*Widowed and Fatherless*, Thomas B. Kennington
1888	(16 June) "The Modern Venus Attired by the Three Dis-Graces," *Punch* 84
1890	*Adversity*, Kennington
1890	(16 August) "So Tired," George Hutchinson, *Ariel, or the London Puck* (p. 103)
1891	*"It is not linen you're wearing out, / But human creatures' lives,"* Claude Calthrop
1891	*The Milliner's Bill*, G. A. Story
1891	*Song of the Shirt*, Margaret Bird
1891	(27 June) "Adversity," Kennington, *Graphic* 45 (p. 733) [reproduction of 1890 painting]
1892	*Orphans*, Bird
1897	*A Mothers' Meeting in the Country*, Burgess
1898	*Trouble*, John Collier
1902	*Needle and Thread*, H. T. Schäfer [redone as etching, "Home"]
1903	*Hark! Hark! The lark at Heaven's Gate Sings*, Louise Jopling
1907	*The Work-Room*, Kennington
1908	*Relaxation*, Kennington

The following are examples of listed, but untraced and unreviewed, artwork (known by title only):

1845	*The Thread of Life*, Hon. Mrs. Arthur Dillon
1845	*The Poor Seamstress*, J. F. Martin [accompanied by Hood quotation: "Oh but to breathe the breath ... And the walk that costs a meal"]
1848	*Showing the Stitch*, D. Passmore
1848	*An Aged Seamstress*, J. Stanesby
1848	*The Dressmaker*, A. Melville [accompanied by quotation: "In contrast labour everyday / working for the rich and gay"]
1849	*The Little Seamstress*, Thomas Herbert Maguire
1852	*The Needlewoman*, H. Darvell [accompanied by Hood quotation]

1852	*The Seamstress*, Peele [see above, 1849 and 1852]
1853	*He Sang the Song of the Shirt*, R. C. Dudley [accompanied by Hood quotation]
1854	*Sewing Girls*, Peele [accompanied by Hood quotation]
1856	*The Poor Seamstress*, E. Fitzpatrick [accompanied by Hood quotation]
1856	*Long Stitches*, W. Bromley
1860	*The Little Seamstress*, T. Olding
1861	*The Last Stitches*, Miss Eliza Hunter
1864	*Threading My Needle*, Peele
1864	*The Poor Seamstress*, J. C. Horsley
1865	*The Sempstress*, Mrs. Curween Gray [accompanied by Hood quotation]
1870	*The Sempstress*, J. C. Playfair
1870	*Ruinous Prices*, E. Hughes [updating of 1861 picture]
1872	*The Poor Seamstress*, Hughes
1876	*Stitching*, H. King
1884	*The Seamstress*, Henry Vincent
1885	*Seamstress*, G. Bathgate

CHAPTER I

1. For a further discussion of gender and social protest fiction see Joseph Kestner's *Protest and Reform: The British Social Narrative by Women, 1827–1867* (Madison: University of Wisconsin Press, 1985).

2. Neff cites a variety of factors culminating in general economic instability: "After peace was declared [following the Napoleonic Wars], trade suffered the usual after-war deflation. England no longer enjoyed a monopoly of commerce with America. Her manufacturers had European competitors. Hundreds of firms failed. Factory hands had no work. Farmers went bankrupt with the drop in the price of corn. Rural labourers became paupers. The Corn Law passed in 1815 benefitted the landowners at the expense of the rest of England. . . . Young men on the brink of matrimony faltered. They could not afford to marry poor girls. They must marry wealth or remain bachelors. . . . Experienced men like Mr. Sedley went under. The unmarried daughters of a ruined father were thrown upon the labour market without warning, untrained and helpless" (12–13).

3. In 1832, five thousand people immigrated to Canada alone. Between 1840 and 1860, four million people emigrated from Great Britain, which had a population of approximately twenty-six million; thus, one in six left home, rarely to return.

4. Although technically a *dressmaker* made dresses and a *milliner* made headgear, most shops made entire outfits encompassing both, so that the terms became interchangeable. The shops were usually referred to as millinery establishments.

5. Chartism, a movement controlled by working men, was established in 1836 to achieve parliamentary democracy as a step toward social and economic reform. Believing that constitutional reform would improve the socio-economic conditions of the working classes, the Chartists brought their demands to Parliament three times: in 1839, 1842, and 1848. The Charter made six political demands: manhood suffrage, secret ballot, equal electorial districts, annual parliaments, no property qualifications for Parliament, and payment for members of Parliament.

6. The term *slopworker*, referring to women who worked out of their homes doing piece-work obtained through middlemen and -women, comes from the colloquial term for sailors' clothing, *slops*, which were made primarily by these women.

7. The 1841 census listed 20,780 dressmakers and milliners in London, and 106,801 people as employed in the dressmaking and millinery trades throughout England, of whom only 563 were men. The accuracy of these numbers is somewhat questionable since these statistics would not include slopworkers, whose irregular employment would have excluded them from notice, or married women whose husbands were listed as employed.

8. In response to Mayhew's reports on slopworkers, the *Times* printed a series of editorials (6–8 December 1849) arguing that needlework was *the* universal female employment and

that as such it could not be grouped as a class in need of assistance: "All women are needle-women. The competition embraces the whole sex. . . . It is not, then, so much a supposed class of needlewomen as the whole sex that is to be assisted" (7 December 1849, 4). Further, the editors argued that it was the ubiquitous nature of needlework that caused the competitive marketplace and depressed prices.

9. See Helen Rogers, "'The Good Are Not Always Powerful, Nor The Powerful Always Good': The Politics of Women's Needlework in Mid-Victorian London," *Victorian Studies* 40.4:589–623, for a discussion of reform and the loss of agency for needlewomen.

10. In 1841, the firm of Messrs. Silver and Co. employed twelve hundred to fourteen hundred women to do piecework. For a further discussion see R. D. Grainger, *Parliamentary Papers* 14 (1843): 833.

11. For a fuller discussion of Dickens's portrayals of needlewomen, see Lynn Alexander's "Following the Thread: Dickens and the Seamstress" in *The Victorian Newsletter* 80 (fall 1991): 1–7.

CHAPTER 2

1. As the three-volume *Autobiography of the Working Class: An Annotated Critical Bibliography* (edited by John Burnett, David Vincent, and David Mayall, New York University Press, 1984) demonstrates, female working-class autobiographies from the nineteenth century are relatively rare. Burnett, Vincent, and Mayall were able to locate twenty-three autobiographies that include references to women working as seamstresses. Approximately one-quarter of these are by men whose mothers worked as needlewomen. Of the remaining, most are short reminiscences in typescript, often less than ten thousand words, held in university libraries or in records offices. Virtually all are about turn-of-the-century experiences (women born after 1885) and were recorded in the mid-1900s. Most focus on family and domestic concerns, with only passing references to work. For example, Ellen Gill's "Diary" is a seventeen-page (about sixty-five-hundred-word) typescript at the Brunel University Library. Gill was born 12 January 1888 and the manuscript is dated 1965. The majority of her narrative concerns relatives and family, but the narrative also includes interesting comments on conditions of home and workplaces (tailoring shops and woollen mills) at the turn of the century.

2. Also see Joanne Shattock, ed., *The Victorian Periodical Press: Samplings and Soundings* (Toronto: University of Toronto Press, 1982) for fuller discussions of the importance of the periodical press in shaping Victorian culture.

3. Interestingly, within the novel itself virtually all parliamentary citations involve workers other than needlewomen. Paget, like the majority of male writers to follow, uses a portrayal of the more sympathetic worker, the seamstress, as a springboard to a discussion of the working poor in general.

4. See Robyn R. Warhol's *Gendered Interventions: Narrative Discourse in the Victorian Novel* (New Brunswick: Rutgers University Press, 1989) for a further discussion of the intersection of direct address, gender, and moral purpose.

5. In the introduction, as proof of the authenticity of his story, Paget quotes at length from a letter he received "from a lady, whose name, did he feel justified in mentioning it, would of itself give any statement a sufficient sanction" (x). The letter tells the story of a young girl apprenticed to a London milliner who suffers abuses much like those alluded to in the novel, then closes with the statement, "'All this you will say is shocking enough, but there is a Mrs. S— — who has eighty apprentices in her establishment in H— — S— —, and who treats them still worse than do Mr. and Mrs. G— —'" (xiv). It was this sentence that was the basis of the suit brought by Mr. Henry George Smith on behalf of his wife, the owner of a

millinery house in Hanover Square. Paget's defense rested on the grounds that he had received and used a letter that he had every reason to believe to be true and that he was totally ignorant of the name and existence of Mrs. Smith at the time the preface was written, and could not possibly have had any intention to injure her or her business.

And although Lord Ashley, later the Earl of Shaftesbury, paid for Paget's defense and offered to protect the young milliner who was supposedly the source of Paget's information, Paget refused to reveal her name for fear she would be turned out and unable to get work. It was a fear that was not as unreasonable as it may seem to twentieth-century readers: Grainger's 1843 parliamentary report, which makes up Paget's appendix A, includes testimony that three seamstresses were, "at a moment's notice, turned out of doors without a character" and, at the time of publication, were still without work, despite having been given assurances that they would be protected if they testified (14:209–10). The jury found for the plaintiff and Paget was fined one hundred pounds. The trial was widely known and covered extensively in both *The English Churchman* and the *Times,* and probably in many other papers. It is not surprising then that, despite the desire for verisimilitude, writers after Paget chose not to use personal testimony; even when using standard protective devices such as the initial followed by an extended dash, the risk was too great.

6. For a fuller definition see Robert Hodge and Gunther Kress, *Social Semiotics* (Ithaca: Cornell University Press, 1988), p. 3.

7. See also John Clubbe, *Victorian Forerunner: The Later Career of Thomas Hood* (Durham, N.C.: Duke University Press, 1968); John W. Dodds, *The Age of Paradox: A Biography of England 1841–1851* (New York: Victor Gollancz, 1952); and M. H. Spielman, *A History of Punch* (London: Cassell and Co., 1895).

8. For a further discussion see Alvin Whitley's "Thomas Hood and 'The Times,'" *TLS* (17 May 1957): 309.

9. Edwin Chadwick's 1842 report, *The Sanitary Conditions of the Labouring Population of Great Britain,* was well known, and the stories and articles of the day focused on the issue as well. For example the *Times,* in "The White Slaves of London," complained that "sometimes as many as five or six girls occupy one small room in which they work and sleep and take their meals in common, plying their needles from morn to night, without a ray of hope to cheer them" (4).

CHAPTER 3

1. *Jessie Phillips* originally appeared in monthly parts during 1842 and 1843, was reviewed in 1843, and was subsequently published in novel form in 1844. It was again serialized in *Reynolds's Miscellany* in 1857.

2. *Fanny, the Little Milliner* originally appeared in serial form in 1844 and was subsequently published in novel form in 1846.

3. When Jane Eyre has run away from Rochester and is hungry and homeless, she enters a shop and inquires "'if there were any dressmaker or plainwork-woman in the village?'" When told, "'Yes; two or three. Quite as many as there was employment for,'" she finds she has few alternatives. "I reflected. I was driven to the point now. I was brought face to face with necessity. I stood in the position of one without resource; without a friend; without a coin. I must do something. What? I must apply somewhere. Where?" It is soon after that she arrives on the Rivers' doorstep (321). Brontë's use reflects both the acceptability of the occupation for middle-class women and the limited employment opportunities away from London. To many reformers the overabundance of women trying to earn a living by sewing was the cause of low prices for needlework.

4. Redgrave originally executed the composition for the Etching Club. He painted at least one copy of the picture exhibited at the Royal Academy in 1844—but it is the version of 1846 that is now in the Forbes Magazine Collection. The differences between the 1844 and 1846 versions are minor: in the first version the clock shows 1:30 and a cup and a scrap of bread are on the table; in the second version the clock shows 2:30, there is a wilting plant in the window, a broken washbasin sits on a stand, and there is a bottle of medicine on the mantel-piece. The location of the 1844 painting is unknown.

5. In "They Sang 'The Song of the Shirt': The Visual Iconology of the Seamstress," T. J. Edelstein explains that the single figure "simplifies the composition and the implied narrative, thus making [them] more direct and effective" (188).

6. E. [Elias] Moses and Son, a cut-rate tailoring establishment, was frequently associated with the plight of slopworkers. The name appeared in versified copy in newspaper advertising columns and supplements to serialized novels, often correlating them with the seasons or news events—even, in the case of Dickens's *Bleak House,* with the novel itself. The association with the plight of needleworkers probably arose from the 27 April 1844 publication of the verse advertisement "The Song of the 'Suit'"—only four months after the appearance of Hood's poem. The questionable taste of the advertisement, and others like it, led to numerous satirical portraits linking the firm with the abuse of slopworkers, especially in *Punch,* where it was lampooned in the poem "Moses and Co." (1843), the satiric article "The Commercial Phenomenon: Moses and Son" (1844), and the drawing "'A Shroud as well as a Shirt'" (1848).

7. When it was published in *Reynolds's Miscellany* a third subtitle was used: *A Tale of the Union Workhouse.* But as do the other subtitles, this one focuses the reader's attention on the social issues surrounding the title character.

8. *Phiz* is the pseudonym for Habot Knight Browne, arguably the most eminent nineteenth-century British book illustrator. Best known for his work with Charles Dickens, Browne illustrated the works of a number of other writers, including Fielding, Smollett, and Mayhew. The pseudonym probably comes from "Phizzes," the third plate of Dickens's *The Pickwick Papers,* Browne's first major commision.

CHAPTER 4

1. As Deborah Epstein Nord explains in *Walking the Victorian Streets: Women, Representation, and the City* (Ithaca: Cornell University Press, 1995), "Women alone on the street in the mid-nineteenth-century city were considered to be . . . 'either endangered or dangerous'" (3).

2. During this period, *gay* was a colloquial epithet for *whore.* Further supporting this interpretation is the poster for *La Traviata* in the background. The opera, about the life and death of a prostitute, opened in London in 1857 to great controversy. The name became equivalent with prostitution, as shown in works such as William Acton's *Prostitution* (1857) and journals such as the *Lancet.*

3. Countering this association, however, is the fact that the couple is not going to Australia, the emigration site most frequently associated with criminality in the nineteenth century, but rather to Canada, a site associated with respectability and independence. Thus Gaskell underscores Jem's innocence while presenting emigration as a means of starting over.

4. When publishing the work in book form in 1853, Reynolds combined the two versions of the title, calling the novel *The Seamstress; or the White Slave of England.*

5. The publication of *Ellen Linn* in *Tait's* reflects both the public's and the magazine's continuing interest in the seamstress, since the magazine also published Galt's "The Seamstress"

in 1833 and *A London Dressmaker's Diary* in 1843. It is an interest that *Tait's* continued to demonstrate long after the literary interest had waned, with the publication of articles such as "Dress Makers and Dress Wearers" in 1858 and "The Employment of Females" in 1860.

CHAPTER 5

1. One of the best summations of Dickens's role remains that of Humphrey House: "He seemed topical to thousands: he was not too topical for them to see the point, nor too advanced to have the public conscience on his side. Detached now from his time he may seem more original and adventurous than he was; for then he was only giving wider publicity in 'inimitable' form to a number of social facts and social abuses which had already been recognized if not explored before him. He shared a great deal of common experience with his public, so that it could gratefully and proudly say, 'How true!'; he so exploited his knowledge that the public recognized its master in knowing; but he also shared with it an attitude to what they both knew, and caught exactly the tone which clarified and reinforced the public's sense of right and wrong, and flattered its moral feelings" (41–42).

2. Kathleen Tillotson uses *Fraser's* November 1850 review of *Alton Locke* (575) to note that "as early as 1850 reviewers were complaining of the growing practice of 'writing political pamphlets, ethical treatises, and social dissertations in the disguise of novels. . . . To open a book under the expectation of deriving from it a certain sort of pleasure, with a few wholesome truths scattered amongst the leaves, and to find ourselves entrapped into an essay upon labour and capital, is by no means agreeable'" (125).

3. Such background demonstrates both Mayhew's strength and weakness: the familiarity of the scene allowed Victorian readers to readily accept his information, but Mayhew's perceptions were shaped by what he expected to see.

4. Originally published in 1851, *The Unprotected* received little attention until its reissue in 1857, when it was reviewed in journals such as the *Athenaeum* (13 June 1857, 757).

5. When the serial publication of *Paved with Gold* began in 1857, both Henry and Augustus Mayhew were involved. However, Henry Mayhew only worked on the first five numbers, primarily those portraying the seamstress, and when the story was published in novel form in 1858, Augustus Mayhew received sole credit.

6. Mr. and Mrs. Isaacson, the owners of Madame Elise, denied any responsibility for Mary Walkley's death, pointing out that she had been in ill health when she began working for them two years earlier, and that she recently had been depressed because of an unhappy love affair. As questions arose in various publications, Isaacson wrote a letter to the *Times* defending his work practices. Long and often incoherent, the letter did little to improve public opinion. Ironically the resulting parliamentary investigation found Madame Elise to be one of the best-run dressmaking establishments and cleared the Isaacsons of responsibility for Walkley's death. For most publications and for the public, however, Isaacson remained a scapegoat. Walkley's story is detailed in Christina Walkley's *The Ghost in the Looking Glass* (London: Peter Owne, 1981).

7. Hughes exhibited a second version of this work with updated fashions in 1871, indicating that he viewed the problem as continuing.

8. The painting, also known as *The Song of the Shirt*, was used to illustrate the *Penny Illustrated Paper's* obituary for Hood in 1862, indicating that Victorians recognized the strong linking of the verbal and visual iconography.

9. Deborah Cherry, *Painting Women: Victorian Women Artists* (New York: Routledge, 1993), 55.

10. Redgrave was cognizant of the candle's semiotic coding. He once confided that when he was a young child, his mother, dying of consumption, prophesied that if all the candles at her bedside kept burning she would live. Of course, they eventually burned out, and she died (see F. M. Redgrave's *Richard Redgrave, R.A., A Memoir,* 1891), p. 10.

11. This painting was executed during Peele's visit to America. And it is probable that his later composition *The Song of the Shirt* (location unknown), exhibited at the British Institution in 1852 with the quotation from Hood—"Oh! But to breathe the breath / Of the cowslip and primrose sweet"—would have been of a similar composition.

12. In "Seduction, Prostitution, Suicide: *On the Brink* by Alfred Elmore," Lynda Nead admits that the dating and attribution of the painting are problematic (the canvas is signed "C. HUNT" and dated 1881, four years after Hunt's death), but argues for Charles Hunt and the 1860 date based on genre, style, types, costumes, and subject matter.

CHAPTER 6

1. Although the agricultural working class was not included until the Third Reform Act of 1844, the Second Reform Act was nevertheless seen as the pivotal movement. Although a propertied franchise, it included laborers who were: 1) householders, subject to a one-year residential qualification and payment of rates; and 2) lodgers in accommodation worth ten pounds per year, subject to a one-year residential qualification. It was also an occupation franchise for those with lands/tenements worth ten pounds per annum.

2. Although Sarah Grand did not coin the term *New Woman* until 1894, the social and literary type indicated emerged in the 1880s: a middle-class woman, working at a job newly opened to women. She insists on sexual freedom and eschews marriage as imprisoning, advocates dress reform, engages in physical exercise, and smokes and drinks openly. Thus the New Woman embodied many of the developing ideas about female independence and was often equated with feminism.

3. While working on *Autumn Leaves* (1856) Millais observed in a letter to Charles Collins, "Now this is evidently the game the Greeks played in Art, they avoided all expression, feeling that it was detrimental to beauty" (qtd. in Warner, 29).

4. The reproduction of the work as an engraving entitled "Home" increases the ambiguity, since it is unclear whether the title indicates that the work is part of the tradition of the young woman remembering and even yearning for home as she works, or whether it removes the work from the tradition through the signification of place rather than thought.

5. In *Home and Abroad* Sir Merton Russell-Cotes also calls the work *The Song of the Shirt.* A smaller version of the work was made around 1873 or 1874 for the Duke of Albany when he discovered the original had already been purchased by Russell-Cotes. In 1877 the *Art Journal* produced a full-page engraving of the work, presumably from the copy, since there are several notable differences: the bowl in the left foreground is no longer chipped, there are prints on the wall and noticeable cracks in the plaster, and "a black bottle, suggestive of something stronger and more pernicious," has been added.

6. Two other paintings illustrating Hood's poem probably incorporate the motif as well: Miss J. Sutherland's *The Lady's Dream* (1852), exhibited at the British Institute with the quotation "Death, death and nothing but death," and F. D. Hardy's *The Wedding Dress—The Lady's Dream—Hood* (1875), exhibited in the Royal Academy. Little is known of these works other than their titles; their locations are unknown.

CONCLUSION

1. See Catherine Gallagher's *The Industrial Reformation of English Fiction* (Chicago: University of Chicago Press, 1985) for a fuller discussion of pre-1840 usage of slave imagery in connection with industrial workers.

2. For an examination of Britain's attitudes toward slavery see Peter Fryer's *Staying Power: The History of Black People in Britain* (London: Pluto Press, 1984). Although Victorian essayists such as Thomas Carlyle, William Rathbone Greg, and John Stuart Mill continued to address the issue of slavery in occasional pieces well into the 1860s, it was to argue the issue in the abstract, from various philosophical stances, rather than as an issue immediately affecting their lives.

PRIMARY WORKS: FICTION

Alexander, Gabriel. *Lilias, the Milliner's Apprentice.* London: John Dicks, 1854.

"The Belgravian Venus Attired by the Graces." *Punch* 24 (1853): 151

Besant, Walter. *All Sorts and Conditions of Men: An Impossible Story.* 3 vols. London: Chatto and Windus, 1882.

Brontë, Charlotte. *Jane Eyre.* 1847. Reprint, New York: Bedford, 1996.

Carey, Rosa Nouchette. *Not Like Other Girls.* New York: F. M. Lupton, n.d.

Collins, Wilkie. "Brother Owen's Story of Anne Rodway." In *The Queen of Hearts. The Complete Works of Wilkie Collins.* Vol. 14. New York: Collier, n.d.

Confessions of a Needlewoman! London: W. M. Clark, n.d.

Dickens, Charles. *The Chimes.* In *The Christmas Books.* Vol. 1. New York: Penguin, 1982.

——. *The Life and Adventures of Nicholas Nickleby.* 1839. Reprint, New York: E. P. Dutton, 1930.

——. *Little Dorrit.* 1857. Reprint, New York: New American Library, 1980.

——. "The Mistaken Milliner. A Tale of Ambition." *Sketches by Boz.* 1836. Reprint, London: Oxford University Press, 1957.

——. *The Personal History, Adventures, Experience, & Observation of David Copperfield, the Younger.* 1850. Reprint, Oxford: Clarendon Press, 1982.

"A Digger's Diary." *Household Words* 8 (3 September 1853): 6–11.

"A Dream of Unfairly-Treated Women." *Punch* (2 August 1890): 50.

"The Dressmakers." *Good Words* 12 (1871): 62–71, 143–52.

Ellen Linn, the Needlewoman. In *Tait's Edinburgh Magazine* 17 (August 1850): 465–70.

"F. D." "The Dressmaker's Apprentices; A Tale of Woman's Oppression." *Lloyd's Penny Weekly Miscellany* 3.132 (1844): 433–34.

Galt, John. "The Seamstress." 1833. Reprinted in *Selected Short Stories,* ed. Ian Gordon. Edinburgh: Scottish Academic Press, 1978.

Gaskell, Elizabeth. *Libbie Marsh's Three Eras.* 1847. Reprinted in *The Works of Mrs. Gaskell.* Vol. 1. London: Smith, Elder, 1906.

——. "Lizzie Leigh." 1850. Reprinted in *The Works of Mrs. Gaskell.* Vol. 1. London: Smith, Elder, 1906.

———. *Mary Barton: A Tale of Manchester Life*. 1848. Reprint, New York: Penguin, 1977.

———. *Ruth*. 1853. Reprint, New York: Everyman's Library, 1974.

[Guigard, Mary]. *The Unprotected; or Facts in Dressmaking Life*. London: Sampson, Low, Son, & Co., 1857.

Harrison, A. Stewart. "The Iceberg." *Once a Week* (3 October 1850): 407–14, 431–37.

Hood, Thomas. "The Lady's Dream." In *The Works of Thomas Hood*. Vol. IX. London: 1869–73.

[Hood, Thomas]. "The Song of the Shirt." *Punch* 5 (16 December 1843): 260.

[Jebb, Henry G.]. *Out of the Depths: The Story of a Woman's Life*. New York: W. A. Townsend, 1860.

Jerrold, Douglas. *The Story of a Feather. Punch* 4 (1843).

Jones, Ernest. *Woman's Wrongs*. In *Notes to the People* 2 (1852).

J. P. H. "The Slave of the Needle." *London Journal* 10 (16 February 1850): 378; (23 February 1850): 395–96; (2 March 1850): 411–12; 11 (16 March 1850): 28.

Kavanagh, Julia. *Rachel Gray: A Tale Founded on Fact*. London: Hurst and Blackett, 1856.

Kingsley, Charles. *Alton Locke, Tailor and Poet*. 1850. Reprint, New York: Oxford University Press, 1983.

Law, John [Margaret Elise Harkness]. *A City Girl: A Realistic Story*. London: Vizetelly, 1887.

———. *A Manchester Shirtmaker: A Realistic Story of To-day*. London: Authors Cooperative Publishing, 1890.

Lemon, Mark. *The Sempstress: A Drama, in Two Acts*. In *Dicks's British Drama*. London: J. Dicks, 1844, 2–15.

A London Dressmaker's Diary. In *Tait's Edinburgh Magazine* 9 (November 1842): 709–18.

Marsh, Anne. *Lettice Arnold: A Tale*. London: Henry Colloum, 1850.

Martineau, Harriet. *Deerbrook*. 1839. Reprint, New York: Doubleday, 1984.

———. *The Rioters*. Wellington, Salop: Houlston, 1827.

May Coverley, The Young Dressmaker. London: Religious Tract Society, 1860.

Mayhew, Augustus. *Kitty Lamere; A Dark Page in London Life*. London: Blackwood, 1855.

———. *Paved with Gold; or, the Romance and Reality of London Streets: An Unfashionable Novel*. London: Chapman and Hall, 1858.

Mayhew, Augustus and Henry. *Whom to Marry*. London: Chapman and Hall, 1848.

"The Milliner." In "Young Lovers to Sell," *Punch* 4 (February 1842): 10.

Mills, Thomas. "The Seamstress." *Penny Illustrated News* 2 (February 1851): 34.

"The Needlewomen's Farewell." *Punch* 18 (12 January 1850): 14.

"The Oppressed Needlewoman: A Sketch from Life." *The Working Man's Friend and Family Instructor* 16 (5 April 1851): 14–15.

Paget, Francis E. *The Pageant; or, Pleasure and Its Price*. London: James Burns, 1843.

Patterson, Jeannie Graham. *Short Threads from a Milliner's Needle: A Collection of Poems*. Glasgow: Carter and Pratt, 1894.

Rathbone, H. M. "The Routine of Daily Life: The Sempstress." *The Working Man's Friend and Family Instructor* 1 (1850): 306–8.

Reynolds, George W. M. *The Mysteries of London.* London: John Dicks, 1845–1848.

——. *The Seamstress.* In *Reynolds's Miscellany* 4 (23 March 1850) to 5 (10 August 1850).

Roberts, Edwin F. *Bertha Gray, the Parish Apprentice-Girl; or, Six Illustrations of Cruelty.* In *Reynolds's Miscellany* 6 (1851).

——. "The Life of a Labourer or, Six Episodes of Emigration." In *Reynolds's Miscellany* 2 (1848).

Rowcroft, Charles. *Fanny, the Little Milliner; or, the Rich and the Poor.* London: Smith, Elder and Co., 1846.

Rymer, James Malcolm. *The White Slave: A Romance for the Nineteenth Century.* London: E. Lloyd, 1844.

"The Seamstress." *Eliza Cook's Journal* 3.54 (11 May 1850): 17–19.

"The Seamstress." *The Working Man's Friend and Family Instructor, New Series* 1 (20 March 1852): 397–99.

Shey, Timothy Arthur. *The Seamstress: A Tale of the Times.* Philadelphia: R. G. Bedford, 1843.

Silverpen [Eliza Meteyard]. *Lucy Dean; the Noble Needlewoman.* In *Eliza Cook's Journal* 2 (16 March to 20 April 1850).

"The Snowdrop." *The Home Circle* 5 (27 December 1851): 418.

"Song of the Cheap Customer." *Punch* 7 (December 1844): 255.

Song of the Shirt. D. W. Griffith, director, 1908.

Stone, Elizabeth. *The Young Milliner.* London: Cunningham and Mortimer, 1843.

Stowe, Harriet Beecher. "The Sempstress." *The Working Man's Friend and Family Instructor* (20 November 1852): 115–17.

Stratford, A. F. "A Word for the 'Song of the Shirt.'" *Lloyd's Penny Weekly Miscellany* 3 (1844): 379.

"A Tale of Cheap Trousers." *Punch* 34 (30 January 1858): 225.

Tonna, Charlotte Elizabeth. *The Wrongs of Woman.* 1844. Reprinted in *The Works of Charlotte Elizabeth.* Vol. 2. New York: Dodd, 1849.

Toulmin, Camilla. *The Orphan Milliners. A Story of the West End. Illuminated Magazine* 2 (April 1844): 279–85.

Trollope, Frances. *Jessie Phillips: A Story of the Present Day.* London: Colburn, 1844.

Viner, G. M. *Aunt Eliza's Garret; or, Scenes in the Life of a Needle-Woman.* London: H. Elliot, 1854.

White, Mrs. "The Struggles of a Needlewoman." *The Home Circle* 6 (3–17 January 1852).

"The Young Widow and the Gold Locket." *Reynolds's Miscellany* 3 (1848): 331–35.

OTHER SOURCES: NINETEENTH CENTURY

"Alfred" [Kydd, Samuel H. G.]. *The History of the Factory Movement.* London: Simpkin, Marshall, 1857.

Bibliography

Ashley, Lord Anthony (Seventh Earl of Shaftsbury). *In Prelude to Victory of the Ten Hours Movement: Two Speeches, One Letter and a Report, 1844.* New York: Arno Press, 1972.

———. "The Ten Hours' Factory Bill," Speech in the House of Commons (15 March 1844).

Bagehot, Walter. *The English Constitution.* 1867. London: Cambridge University Press, 2001.

Bennett, John. "Watchwork *verses* Slopwork." *English Woman's Journal* 1 (1858): 282–83.

Booth, Charles. *Life and Labour of the People in London.* Vol 1. London: Williams and Northgate, 1889.

Carlyle, Thomas. "Chartism." *Selected Writings.* New York: Penguin, 1980. 149–232.

———. "Signs of the Times." *Scottish Essays and Other Miscellanies.* New York: Dutton, 1946.

"The Case of Mary Furley." *Punch* 6 (1844): 223.

Chadwick, Edwin. *Report on the Sanitary Condition of the Labouring Population of Great Britain.* Ed. M. W. Flinn. Edinburgh: Edinburgh University Press, 1968.

"The Chartist Meeting—Miss Mary Anne Walker Again." *Times* (25 October 1842): 6.

Chisholm, Caroline. *The A.B.C. of Colonization.* As cited in A. James Hammerton's *Emigrant Gentlewomen.* Totowa, N.J.: Rowman and Littlefield, 1979.

Cobbett, William. "Slave Trade." *Cobbett's Weekly Political Register* 9 (1806): 845.

Cobden, John. *The White Slaves of England: Compiled from Official Documents.* Shannon: Irish University Press, 1971.

Crosswaithe, John. "Needlewomen." *Good Words* 4 (1863): 684–88.

"Death among the Dressmakers." *London Review* 6.156 (27 June 1863): 682–83

"Death and the Drawing Room or The Young Dressmakers of England." *The Illuminated Magazine* 1 (October 1844): 97–100.

Dickens, Charles. "A Bundle of Emigrant's Letters." *Household Words* 1 (3 March 1850): 19–24.

———. "Home for Homeless Women." *Household Words* 7 (23 April 1853): 169–75.

———. "The Iron Seamstress." *Household Words* 9 (11 February 1854): 575.

———. *The Letters of Charles Dickens.* Vol. 3. Ed. Madeline House, Graham Storey, and Kathleen Tillotson. London: Oxford University Press, 1974.

———. "A Rainy Day on 'The Euphrates.'" *Household Words* 4 (24 January 1852): 409–11.

———. "Threatening Letter to Thomas Hood, from an Ancient Gentleman, by Favor of Charles Dickens." *Hood's Magazine and Comic Miscellany* 1 (May 1843): 409–10.

"The Dressmaker's Life." *English Woman's Journal* 1 (1858): 319–25.

[Eagle, John]. "Royal Academy." *Blackwood's* 63 (1848): 185.

"The Early Closing Movement: Milliners and Dressmakers." *Eliza Cook's Journal* 1 (7 July 1849): 154–56.

Eliot, George. *The Essays of George Eliot*. Ed. Thomas Pinney. New York: Columbia University Press, 1963.

[Eliot, George]. "Rachel Gray." *Leader* 7 (5 January 1856): 19.

"Emigration of Distressed Needlewomen." *The Illustrated London News* 17 (17 August 1850): 156.

"The Employment of Young Women." *Eliza Cook's Journal* 2.36 (5 January 1850): 145–47.

Engels, Friedrich. Letter to Margaret Harkness. In *Art in Theory, 1815–1900: An Anthology of Changing Ideas*, ed. Charles Harrison, Paul Wood, and Jason Gaiger. Malden, Mass.: Blackwell, 1998. 763–65.

"Exhibition of the English in China." *Punch* 6 (1844): 219–23.

"Famine and Fashion!" *Punch* 5 (4 November 1843): 203.

"Fine Arts: The Royal Academy." *Athenaeum* (1844): 459–61.

Gardiner, A. G. Introduction to *Sweated Industry and Minimum Wage*, by Clementina Black. London: Duckworth, 1907.

Gaskell, Elizabeth. *The Letters of Elizabeth Gaskell*. Ed. J. A. V. Chapple and Arthur Pollard. Cambridge: Harvard University Press, 1967.

Gavin-Duffy, T. "Two May Day Exhibitions: Princess, Pampered Dogs and the Sweated Poor." *Labour Leader* (May 1906): 744.

"The Great Woman Market." *The Spectator* (15 December 1849): 1184.

Greg, William Rathbone. "Why Are Women Redundant?" In *Literary and Social Judgments*. London: N. Trübner, 1869.

Grindrod, Ralph Barnes. *The Slaves of the Needle; An Exposure of the Distressed Condition, Moral and Physical, of Dress-Makers, Milliners, Embroiderers, Slop-workers, etc.* London: Brittain and Gilpin, 1845.

Hood, Thomas. "Living and Dying by the Needle." *English Woman's Domestic Magazine* (August 1863): 180–86.

Hughes, T. A. *A Lecture on the Slop System.* 1852.

"Jessie Phillips," *Athenaeum* (28 October 1844): 956–57.

"Jessie Phillips," *John Bull* 23 (1844): 732.

L. N. [Ellen Barlee]. "Annals of the Needlewomen." *English Woman's Journal* 9 (April 1862): 73–80; (June 1862): 217–26.

———. "Institution for the Employment of Needlewomen." *English Woman's Journal* 5 (June 1860): 255–59.

"The Labour Question No. 1: The Needlewomen of London." *The Penny Illustrated News* (5 January 1850): 34.

"Law Proceedings: Smith and Wife v. F. E. Paget, Clerk." *The English Churchman* (20 June 1844): 387–88.

Le Plastrier, Jane. "A Season with the Dressmakers, or the Experience of a First Hand." *English Woman's Journal* 11–12 (August–December 1863): 407–9; 7–24; 104–12; 181–87; 267–76.

"The Little Candle." *The Leisure Hour* 296 (27 August 1857): 559.

"Little Dorrit," *Athenaeum* (1 December 1855).

Lord, H. W. *Report to the Children's Employment Commission. Parliamentary Papers* (1864). Vol. 22.

[Ludlow, J. M.]. "Ruth," *North British Review* 19 (1853): 151–74.

Macaulay, Thomas. Letter dated 14 October 1851. *The Life and Letters of Lord Macaulay*. Vol. 2. Ed. George Trevelyan. London, 1876.

"Market and Track Report." *Punch* 25 (1854): 42.

Martineau, Harriet. "The Needlewoman." *Once a Week* (24 November 1860): 595–99.

Mayhew, Henry. *London Labour and the London Poor*. 4 vols. New York: Dover, 1968.

——. *The Unknown Mayhew: Selections from the Morning Chronicle, 1849–1850*. Ed. E. P. Thompson and Eileen Yeo. New York: Schocken, 1971.

"Milliners' Apprentices." *Fraser's Magazine* 33 (March 1846): 308–9.

"The Milliners' Assistants." *The Town: A Journal of Original Essays* 2 (27 April 1839): 1.

Munby, A. J. *The Life and Diaries of Arthur J. Munby, 1828–1910*. Ed. D. Hudson. 1972.

"Music and Drama." *Athenaeum* (1844): 533–34.

"The Needles of London." *Punch* (9 March 1850): 97.

"The Needlewomen and Their Rescue." *The Spectator* (8 December 1849): 1158–59.

"Needlewomen's Rescue—Ministerial Hopes." *The Spectator* (29 December 1849): 1232.

Oastler, Richard. "Yorkshire Slavery." *Leeds Mercury* (16 October 1830).

"On the Best Means of Relieving the Needlewomen." *Eliza Cook's Journal* 5 (19 July 1851): 189–91.

"Our Legacy from Mary Ann Walkley." *Once a Week* (25 July 1863): 119–23.

"Our Suffocated Sempstresses." *Punch* 45 (4 July 1863): 4

Parkes, Bessie Rayner. "Needlewomen at New York." *English Woman's Journal* 12 (January 1864): 318–25.

[Parkes, Bessie Rayner]. "Outline of a Plan for the Formation of Industrial Associations Amongst Women." *English Woman's Journal* (1 October 1860): 73–76.

Parliamentary Papers (1833). Vol. XXI.

"The Point of the Needle." *All the Year Round* 10 (5 September 1863): 36–41.

"Political Economy and the Needlewomen." *The Spectator* (15 December 1849): 1183–84.

"Punch on the Silkworm." *Punch* (23 August 1845): 92.

"Punch's Review of Books: *The Pride of London: A Poem*." *Punch* (9 December 1843): 249.

Redgrave, F. M. *Richard Redgrave: A Memoir Compiled from His Diary*. London, 1891.

Report of the Institution for the Employment of Needlewomen, 1863–64. London: Victoria Press, 1864.

Reynolds, George W. M. "A Few More Words of Warning to the "Needlewomen and Slopworkers." *Reynolds's Political Instructor* 1 (1849–1850): 74.

——. "A Warning to the Needlewomen and Slopworkers." *Reynolds's Political Instructor* 1 (1849–1850): 66–67.

"Royal Academy." *The Art Journal* 7 (June 1861): 170.

"The Royal Academy." *The Art-Union* 6 (June 1844): 158.

"Royal Academy." *Athenaeum* 20 (22 May 1847): 552.
"Royal Academy." *Athenaeum* 34 (20 May 1854): 627.
"Royal Academy." *Times* (8 May 1844): 7c.
"Scissors." *Why Dressmaking Does Not Pay and the Dressmaker's Future.* London: E. Marlborough, 1895.
"A Seamstress that Won't Starve." *Punch* 25 (9 July 1853): 14.
The Second Report of the Children's Employment Commission (1843). *Parliamentary Papers.* Vol. 14.
"The Sempstress at Home: In the Union and the Gaol." *Punch* (30 September 1848): 140.
"'A Shroud as Well as a Shirt.'" *Punch* 15 (19 August 1848): 76.
Silverpen [Eliza Meteyard]. "The Early Closing Movement—Milliners and Dressmakers." *Eliza Cook's Journal* 1 (7 July 1849): 154–56.
"Slaves of the Needle." *Pictorial Times* 10 (20 May 1843): 145.
"The Society of British Artists." *The Art Journal* 4 (May 1852): 137.
[Stone, Elizabeth]. *Art of Needlework.* Ed. the Countess of Wilton [M. M. Egerton]. London: Henry Colburn, 1842.
Suthers, R. B. "The Cannibal Exhibition." *The Clarion* (18 May 1906): 5.
"The Sweating System." *Northern Star* (2 November 1850): 8.
"A Tired Dressmaker." "Death in the Workroom." *Times* (17 June 1863): 5.
Tonna, Charlotte Elizabeth, ed. *Christian Lady's Magazine* 1–25 (January 1834–June 1846).
[Tonna, Charlotte Elizabeth.] *The Perils of the Nation: An Appeal to the Legislature, the Clergy, and the Higher and Middle Classes.* London: Seeley, Burnside and Seeley, 1843.
van Gogh, Vincent. *The Complete Letters of Vincent van Gogh.* New York: New York Graphic Society, 1958.
Wakefield, Edward Gibbon. *A View of the Art of Colonization with Present Reference to the British Empire: In Letters between a Statesman and a Colonist.* London: J. W. Parker, 1849.
"Weary." *Art Journal* 11 (1873): 68.
Whistler, J. M. *The Gentle Art of Making Enemies.* New York: Putnam, 1953.
"The White Slaves of London." *Times* (27 October 1843): 4.
"The Workwomen of London." *The Ladies Newspaper* (10 February 1849).
X. "Quiet Thoughts on Emigration." *The Spectator* (15 December 1849): 1182.

SECONDARY SOURCES: MODERN

Alexander, Lynn. "Following the Thread: Dickens and the Seamstress." *The Victorian Newsletter* 80 (fall 1991): 1–7.
———. "Loss of the Domestic Idyll: Slop Workers in Victorian Fiction." In *Victorian Domesticity,* ed. Vanessa Dickerson. New York: Garland, 1994.
Altick, Richard D. *The Presence of the Present: Topics of the Day in the Victorian Novel.* Columbus: Ohio State University Press, 1991.
Anderson, Benedict. *Imaginied Communities.* London: Verso, 1983.

Beckett, Jane, and Deborah Cherry, eds. *The Edwardian Era.* Oxford: Phaidon, 1987.

Bodenheimer, Rosemarie. *The Politics of Story in Victorian Social Fiction.* Ithaca: Cornell University Press, 1988.

Born, Daniel. *The Birth of Liberal Guilt in the English Novel: Charles Dickens to H. G. Wells.* Chapel Hill: University of North Carolina Press, 1995.

Casteras, Susan P. *Images of Victorian Womanhood in English Art.* Rutherford, N.J.: Fairleigh Dickinson University Press, 1987.

———. *The Substance or the Shadow: Images of Victorian Womanhood.* New Haven: Yale Center for British Art, 1982.

Casteras, Susan P. and Ronald Parkinson, eds. *Richard Redgrave.* New Haven: Yale University Press, 1988.

Cherry, Deborah. *Painting Women: Victorian Women Artists.* New York: Routledge, 1993.

Christ, Carol T. and John O. Jordan. Introduction to *Victorian Literature and the Victorian Visual Imagination.* Berkeley: University of California Press, 1995.

Clubbe, John. *Victorian Forerunner: The Later Career of Thomas Hood.* Durham, N.C.: Duke University Press, 1968.

Dodds, John W. *The Age of Paradox: A Biography of England, 1841–1851.* New York: Victor Gollancz, 1952.

Edelstein, T. J. "'But who shall paint the griefs of those oppress'd?': The Social Theme in Victorian Painting." Ph.D. diss., University of Pennsylvania, 1979.

———. "They Sang 'The Song of the Shirt': Visual Iconology of the Seamstress," *Victorian Studies* 23 (winter 1980): 183–210.

Errington, Lindsay. *Social and Religious Themes in English Art, 1840–1860.* New York: Garland, 1984.

Flint, Kate, ed. *The Victorian Novelist: Social Problems and Social Change.* New York: Coom Helm, 1987.

Gallagher, Catherine. *The Industrial Reformation of English Fiction: Social Discourse and Narrative Form, 1832–1867.* Chicago: Chicago University Press, 1985.

Geertz, Clifford. *The Interpretation of Cultures: Selected Essays.* New York: Basic Books, 1973.

Gillett, Paula. *Worlds of Art: Painters in Victorian Society.* New Brunswick: Rutgers University Press, 1990.

Greenblatt, Stephen. *Shakespearean Negotiations.* Berkeley: University of California Press, 1988.

Hammerton, A. James. *Emigrant Gentlewomen: Genteel Poverty and Female Emigration, 1830–1914.* Totowa, N.J.: Rowman and Littlefield, 1979.

Heineman, Helen. "Frances Trollope's *Jessie Phillips:* Sexual Politics and the New Poor Law." *International Journal of Women's Studies* 1 (1978): 96–106.

Himmelfarb, Gertrude. *The Idea of Poverty: England in the Early Industrial Age.* Boston: Faber and Faber, 1984.

Hodge, Robert and Gunther Kress. *Social Semiotics.* Ithaca: Cornell University Press, 1988.

House, Humphrey. *The Dickens World.* London: Oxford University Press, 1969.

Huggett, Frank E. *Victorian England as Seen by Punch.* London: Sidgwick and Jackson, 1978.

Irigaray, Luce. *This Sex Which Is Not One.* Trans. Catherine Porter. Ithaca: Cornell University Press, 1985.

Jameson, Fredric. *The Political Unconscious: Narrative as a Socially Symbolic Act.* Ithaca: Cornell University Press, 1981.

Johansson, Sheila Ryan. "Sex and Death in Victorian England: An Examination of Age- and Sex-Specific Death Rates, 1840–1910." In *A Widening Sphere: Changing Roles of Victorian Women,* ed. Martha Vicinus. Bloomington: Indiana University Press, 1977.

Keating, P. J. *The Working Classes in Victorian Fiction.* London: Routledge and K. Paul, 1971.

Kestner, Joseph. *Protest and Reform: The British Social Narrative by Women, 1827–1867.* Madison: University of Wisconsin Press, 1985.

Kovacevic, Ivanka. *Fact into Fiction: English Literature and the Industrial Scene, 1750–1850.* Atlantic Highlands, N.J.: Humanities Press, 1975.

Maas, Jeremy. *Victorian Painters.* New York: Harrison House, 1969.

Marcus, Steven. *Engels, Manchester, and the Working Class.* New York: Norton, 1974.

Michie, Elsie B. *Outside the Pale: Cultural Exclusion, Gender Difference, and the Victorian Woman Writer.* Ithaca: Cornell University Press, 1993.

Mitchell, Sally. *The Fallen Angel: Chastity, Class, and Women's Reading, 1835–1880.* Bowling Green, Ohio: Bowling Green University Popular Press, 1981.

Mulvey, Laura. *Visual and Other Pleasures: Theories of Representation and Difference.* Bloomington: Indiana University Press, 1989.

Nead, Lynda. "Seduction, Prostitution, Suicide: *On the Brink* by Alfred Elmore." *Art History* 5.3 (September 1982): 308–22.

Neff, Wanda. *Victorian Working Women: An Historical and Literary Study of Women in British Industries and Professions, 1832–1850.* New York: Columbia University Press, 1929.

Pike, E. Royston. *Human Documents of the Victorian Golden Age (1850–1875).* London: George Allen & Unwin, 1974.

Pinchbeck, Ivy. *Women Workers and the Industrial Revolution, 1750–1850.* London: Routledge, 1930.

Poovey, Mary. *Uneven Developments: The Ideological Work of Gender in Mid-Victorian England.* Chicago: University of Chicago Press, 1988.

Price, Richard. *A History of* Punch. London: Collins, 1957.

Pykett, Lyn. "Reading the Periodical Press: Text and Context." In *Investigating Victorian Journalism,* ed. Laurel Brake, et al. New York: St. Martin's Press, 1990.

Rogers, Helen. "'The Good Are Not Always Powerful, Nor The Powerful Always Good': The Politics of Women's Needlework in Mid-Victorian London." *Victorian Studies* 40.4 (summer 1997): 589–623.

Scholes, Robert. *Semiotics and Interpretation.* New Haven: Yale University Press, 1982.

Shattock, Joanne, and Michael Woolf. Introduction to Shattock, ed., *The Victorian*

Periodical Press: Samplings and Soundings. Toronto: Toronto University Press, 1982.

Spielman, M. H. *A History of* Punch. London: Cassell and Co., 1895.

Tillotson, Kathleen. *Novels of the Eighteen-Forties.* New York: Oxford University Press, 1961.

Treuherz, Julian. *Hard Times: Social Realism in Victorian Art.* London: Lund Humphries, 1987.

Walkley, Christina. *The Ghost in the Looking Glass: The Victorian Seamstress.* London: Peter Owen, 1981.

Warhol, Robyn R. *Gendered Interventions: Narrative Discourse in the Victorian Novel.* New Brunswick: Rutgers University Press, 1989.

Warner, Malcolm. *The Victorians: Britsh Painting 1837–1901.* Washington, D.C.: National Gallery of Art, 1997.

Williams, Raymond. *Culture and Society, 1780–1950.* London: Penguin, 1961.

Winn, Sharon A., and Lynn M. Alexander, eds. *The Slaughter-House of Mammon: An Anthology of Victorian Social Protest Literature.* West Cornwall, Conn.: Locust Hill Press, 1992.

Wood, Christopher. *Victorian Panorama: Paintings of Victorian Life.* London: Faber, 1976.

Index